PORTRAIT OF A DESPOT

Charles Ochen Okwir

AuthorHouse™ UK Ltd.
500 Avebury Boulevard
Central Milton Keynes, MK9 2BE
www.authorhouse.co.uk
Phone: 08001974150

c 2011. Charles Ochen Okwir. All rights reserved

No part of this book may be reproduced, stored in a retrieval system, or transmitted by any means without the written permission of the author.

First published by Author House 03/26/2011

ISBN: 978-1-4567-7567-4 (sc)
ISBN: 978-1-4567-7567-1 (e)

Any people depicted in stock imagery provided by Thinkstock are models, and such images are being used for illustrative purposes only.
Certain stock imagery○c Thinkstock

This book is printed on acid-free paper.

Because of the dynamic nature of the Internet, any web addresses or links contained in this book may have changed since publication and may no longer be valid. The views expressed in this work are solely those of the author and do not necessarily reflect the views of the publisher, and the publisher hereby disclaims any responsibility for them.

"Nothing, Simply Nothing is More Important to Africa than Good Governance"

Mo Ibrahim

Dedication:

To General. Yoweri K. Museveni whose egregious rule inspired this book

Contents

Dedication..iv
Preface..vii

Contextual Background..ix
   The Beginning of the 1981-86 Guerrilla War.........................xi
   The "Fundamental Change" of 1986..xii

Chapter One: *From Institutionalism to Individualism*......................1

Chapter Two: *The Gospel According to "Saint" Kaguta*..................7
   The Illusion of Free Education for All 20
   The Great Fallacy that is "Bonna Bagagawale"........................24
   Professionalization of the National Army 29
   The Death of the Cooperative Movement 31

Chapter Three: *A Modern Despot's "Alfa" Tool of Oppression*..........35
   The Political Parties & Organisation Act 2002..........................58
   Selective Enforcement of the Law 79
   The Rise & Fall of Brig. Henry Tumukunde 86
   Despotic Assault on Civic Education 95
   The Epic Battle for Fundamental Human Rights.....................99
   Kayihura: Why we have banned rallies at the Square 102

Chapter Four: *Despotic Politics & the PRA Treason Case*...............112
   The Second Coming of the Devil...126
   PRA Suspect: "I am a Guest of the Head of State".................. 135
   PRA 22: All Ugandans be Afraid (Part One)............................139
   PRA 22: All Ugandans be Afraid (Part Two) 142

Chapter Five: *"The Return of the Hammer"* 154
   The Greatest Political Epoch of the Century 157

Chapter Six: *The Final Assault on State Institutions*......................164
   Uganda Vs General Yoweri T. K. Museveni 168
The Judiciary Vs a Modern Despot 170
The Directorate of Public Prosecutions 176
   Test Case No. 1 (The Trial of the Century).............................177

Test Case No. 2 (Uganda Vs the PRA Suspects)..................185
A Modern Despot's "Personal" Army *189*
The Civil Face of Political Oppression *203*
Uganda Prison Service: The Final Exposure *207*
Desecration of the National Legislature *209*
   The Role of a Typical Legislature.................................211
   The Uganda-Rwanda Invasion of Zaire........................215
   The American Project in Lawless Somalia....................217
   Disciplining "Rebel" NRM-O Party MPs.......................221
   Militarisation of the Legislature..................................225
   The Cold Blooded Massacre of Article 105 (2)............228
   "I Captured Parliament" 237
The Great Loot of the Central Bank..................................*241*
   The Bassajja-Gate Affair..242
The Schizophrenic Watch-Dog...*246*
   Clipping the IGG's Wings Legally (Part One)..............247
   Clipping the IGG's Wings Legally (Part Two).............249
   Clipping the IGG's Wings Verbally..............................250
The Trusted Accomplice in Despot Country 253
The Deconstruction of Civil Service Ethics 257
Local Government & Political Mobilisation 262
The Truth From The Woods 268
   The Ultimate Betrayal of British Instincts 273

Chapter Seven: ***Governance lessons from the Museveni years***.........**278**

Preface

"Charles, I have known you for quite a while now. What happened to the optimist who once dreamt of being Uganda's Foreign Affairs Minister? Something must be going wrong in your country".

That was the response an English friend gave me when I told him that I was writing a book about the traits of the 21st century despot with Ugandan President General Yoweri Kaguta Museveni being the main reference character.

Not just in my country; I shot back! My country, whilst playing host to a most vicious modern despot at the moment, is in fact only a premise for me to demonstrate to whoever cares to listen that wherever they may be, they too may be hosting a modern despot without even knowing it.

I asked my friend if he had ever asked himself why former British Prime Minister Margaret Thatcher was sometimes referred to as *"an elected dictator"*. No, he said. It was for her uncompromising stance on certain issues, I told my friend.

The difference, I reasoned, is that modern despots like Margaret Thatcher, Yoweri Museveni, Tony Blair, Meles Zenawi, Zine El Abidine Ben Ali, George Bush Jnr etc, are merely more sophisticated in the way they go about their quest to achieve exactly the same ends as their medieval predecessors. I would later, rather pleasantly I must say, discover that I wasn't the only one to think of the ways of modern despots in such terms.

Writing several years earlier, Vittorio Alfieri had already appreciated what many of us are only appreciating today. In his incisive article titled *"On Tyranny"* that discussed possible remedies available against tyrannical rule, Alfieri wrote:

"...From this it comes about that in this much milder century, the art of ruling despotically has become more subtle and is based on not only well concealed and varied but firm foundations that so long as the tyrant does not commit excesses, or very rarely, against the mass of the people and almost never against individuals except under the guise of some appearance of legality, tyranny seems assured of lasting forever".

Alfieri then anticipates a question from his yet unknown readers and decides to ask himself pre-emptively: "...*How is it, then, that if these tyrannies are moderate and possible to endure, [do] you expose and persecute them with such heat and rancour?*".

Because, Alfieri answered himself, "...*it is not always the cruellest of injuries that offend most cruelly...injuries should be measured by their greatness and their effects rather than their force*".

To explain what he meant by what he had just said philosophically, Alfieri decided to hit it right on the head. He said: "...*the man who takes from you a few ounces of blood every day kills you in the end no less inevitably than he whose sudden violence causes you at once to bleed to death; but makes you suffer much more*".

I am not Vittorio Alfieri. But like him, I too believe that to feel all one's spiritual qualities numbed, all man's rights reduced or taken away; and, when a man's true life is in the spirit and the intellect, is not living that life a form of continual dying in itself? Of what importance is it to a man who feels of himself as born to act and think nobly to be forced to preserve all that in trepidation?

So it was necessary, I thought, that if people around the world, no matter where they happen to be, got to appreciate *"the true traits"* of a modern despot as captured in this

Uganda-centric case study, then perhaps, just perhaps, they could begin to look around themselves to see if there is such a despot quietly flourishing within their midst.

Again, like Alfieri, the thrust of my argument in this book is that like all modern despots, Uganda's ruler General Yoweri Kaguta Museveni prefers to use subtle and less crude means to *dictate* his will if he can afford it. Only if he can't afford it does he then go *"native"* and uses what Alfieri called the *"sudden violence"* that causes you at once to bleed to death.

So as we go along this literally voyage, I implore you pay particular attention to how Uganda's Yoweri Museveni uses public relations, public disenfranchisement, deceit, patronage, tribalism, nepotism, and the law among many other soft power tools. And because most modern despots behave in much the same way, you may be surprised at your conclusions about the man or woman at the helm of political power in your own country.

Contextual Background

From a distance, safe from the coercive state machinery in Uganda, I am able do and say what many of my colleagues, by their own admissions, are simply too terrified to do while within Uganda's jurisdiction. But the tragedy of it all is that the things I am able to enjoy from a distance are no more than the very basic democratic freedoms, taken for granted in other parts of the world.

I am talking about things like the freedom to criticise the ruling political establishment without being labelled an *"enemy"* if you are lucky; imprisoned if you have no political god-father within the system to plead for your freedom; or even killed if you are unlucky enough to be considered a threat to the illegitimate longevity of the ruling political establishment under Gen. YK Museveni.

One such person is Dr. Kizza Besigye, President of Uganda's leading opposition party the Forum for Democratic Change [FDC]. As we shall see, Dr. Besigye has faced all manner of harassment at the hands of Museveni's oppressive state machinery; all for his principled opposition against the regime's repression, corruption, nepotism, human rights abuses, to name but just a few.

Dr. Besigye's persecution by Museveni's regime is an interesting case because not only did he fight in the 1981-86 bush war that brought Museveni to power he was also Museveni's personal doctor during that bush war. But as soon as he criticised Museveni, and indeed pointed out the deficit in Museveni's democratic credentials, it immediately triggered his persecution.

But there is another interesting twist to the story of Dr. Besigye's persecution.
Some uncharitable political commentators have linked Besigye's persecution to the fact that he had *"snatched"* and in fact married a woman with whom Museveni had been intimately involved as a lover; not wife! To these so-called political analysts, the struggle between the two erstwhile comrades amounts to nothing more than revenge and recrimination within a *"love triangle"*. Of course, I disagree most vehemently.

To accept that simplistic analysis would be a vile insult to the intelligence of millions of Ugandans who supported, and continue to support the causes Dr. Besigye stands for. It simply trivialises a whole nation's democratic struggles; a fact which, I think, should elevate the debate beyond matters of passion.

The other simple fact that clearly takes the shine off the latter theory is that Dr. Besigye was not the first person to come face to face with Museveni's persecution machinery. Scores of other opposition politicians who had the audacity to oppose Museveni long before Dr. Besigye had already faced the full wrath of Museveni's violent allergy to fair political competitions. Many of these men, unfortunately, never lived to tell their stories.

The Beginning of the 1981-86 Guerrilla War

The genesis of Museveni's rise to power is comprehensively documented and available in the public domain. Briefly however, he contested the 1980 general elections in Uganda as the presidential flag bearer for his party the *Uganda Patriotic Movement* [UPM]. He of course lost miserably; failing to win even in his own parliamentary constituency. The question of who actually won those elections is a matter that still attracts huge controversy in Ugandan political discourse today. However, the popular perception then, and to some extent today, is that Dr. Paul Ssemogerere [the *Democratic Party's* presidential flag bearer] won those elections. The *Uganda People's Congress* under the leadership of the then incumbent President Dr. Apollo Milton Obote on the other hand, of course still maintains that their election victory was legitimate. There was absolutely no debate then, and there is still absolutely no debate today, about whether Museveni featured anywhere near the possible victors in that elections. It was too far-fetched for any sane person to contemplate. His loss was comprehensive.

The irony however, was that it was Museveni who cried foul the most. But I suspect this was more to do with the fact that Museveni's sights had long been set, firmly in fact, on taking the Presidency of Uganda through hook or crook. Nothing would stop him; not even a resounding rejection by the electorate. So what does Museveni do? Well, he mobilises 27 young men, arms them, and off to the jungle they went to launch an armed guerrilla struggle to overthrow the government.

The "Fundamental Change" of 1986

Museveni's guerrilla campaign ended on the 26th of January 1986 when his *National Resistance Army* [NRA] rebels finally marched onto the capital city Kampala as victorious *"liberators"* having triumphed over a disorganised, demoralised, and largely undisciplined national army.

And with that, the *"fundamental change"*, not a *"mere change of guard"* as he put, was well and truly underway. A change that saw a complete change in Uganda's political system from a multi-party democracy to one where political parties were barred by law from engaging in any political activities that could *"interfere"* with the operation of the new *"Movement"* political system! From then on, Ugandans could only compete for political offices on their *"individual merit"*. Only General Museveni would remain as the unchallengeable leader of the *National Resistance Movement* [NRM] and President of the Republic of Uganda. An omnipotent leader indeed!

Periodic change of a system of political governance is a tradition that is almost as old as politics itself. We also know that the reasons for these changes are often as varied as they are noble. We know too that they can be inspired by deceit and other truly dastardly motives. In developed democracies, it is sometimes inspired by an attempt to correct the shortcomings of a previous political system. Such changes, in some cases, have indeed been shown to be in the national interest.

Others on the other hand, have been no more than an attempt to create a false impression among the governed that the new leaders have something new to offer; whereas not. In such cases, the truth, when it finally comes, often shows that it was all the work of some deranged power hungry megalomaniacs.

Now, looking back at the changes in Uganda's political system that Museveni introduced in 1986, the conclusion I come to is that Museveni and his close political associates merely had some dishonourable personal political objectives to achieve. In fact, the *"genetic make-up"* of the *"Movement"* political system that was eventually forced into place after victory in 1986 may suggest that perhaps, with memories of the apocalyptic 1980 election defeat still fresh in his mind, a very incredulous Museveni often sat through the secret treason meetings with a pensive mood.

One can also imagine him scratching his receding hair intermittently, as if to release the building stress! Pen and paper at hand; he would probably take note of any suggestion of a political system that would put him through the trauma he suffered during the 1980 elections.

When his turn to contribute to the discussion came, Museveni, as Chairman, would probably make it his business to carefully steer the meeting clear of any trajectory that might lend weight to any suggestions of installing a genuine multi-party political dispensation in Uganda. How could he allow such a thing? After the 1980 experience, for Museveni at least, a man who says he went through a *"furnace"* to get where he is, free and fair elections would henceforth be considered *"haraam"*; forbidden!

Museveni saw political power as a hard earned prize; one that he would later compare to a *"carcass"* brought from a hunting expedition. That anyone should compare political power to a trophy from a hunting expedition is quite revealing. In fact, it contradicts and makes a complete mockery of the original causes {like restoring democracy and the rule of law} that Museveni gave to the world to justify his bloody guerrilla campaign.

Chapter One

From Institutionalism to Individualism

To understand this new system of political governance better, one might have to ask oneself a question that appears to have already been answered. And it is: What exactly is Museveni's "individual merit" system of governance all about? To crack that question, some creativity may be required.

For a start, "individual merit" was an alien political concept that was hitherto unknown to Ugandan political theorists. It may therefore help to start the search for an answer by casting our minds back to the system of governance that individual merit replaced. I also think that for a proper comparison to be achieved, it would serve no useful purpose to look to the system of governance that was in place immediately before the onset of individual merit; for that was a fully blown military junta where no claim to democracy was ever attempted.

This therefore means that one must look to the system of governance that was uprooted by the military junta. And that was a multi-party political system, probably in operation in your country now, by which political parties, as duly registered legal entities, would lay out their programmes for government in a manifesto. That would be the centre piece for their plea for support from the electorate. The electorate would then be at liberty to decide which political party to vote for. Simple and straightforward, isn't it?

Well, not quite. The reason being that without sufficient political goodwill, multi-party politics can actually be a cover behind which modern despots hide. So it's not that straightforward; regardless of where it is practiced. Under Museveni's individual merit system of governance, political parties were [as we shall later see in our discussion about *law as a tool of political oppression*] effectively outlawed. Every Ugandan was legally compelled to belong to Museveni's "broad-based" *Movement* system.

If for example, Mr. John Jones Carpenter from Mucwini in northern Uganda were to be interested in running for political office in Chua constituency, the minimum legal requirement that he would need to fulfil would be to have an *A-Level* secondary school certificate or its equivalent. Once that was out of the way, as a *Movementist* by law, he would only have to mobilise sufficient resources to produce his own manifesto, market it to the electorate, and generally run his own campaign. Deceptively simple and attractive democratic politics!

But first! The untested *individual merit* system, as expected, created its own set of problems for Mr. J.J. Carpenter as an individual. In fact, it created the same problems for the entire political culture of the nation. For that reason, I think the transition from multi-party politics to Museveni's *individual merit* system actually amounted to a complete shift from *institutionalism* to *individualism.* It was no longer institutions competing for power but individuals; and that brought with it a new degree of *"do or die"* desperation, corruption, ruthlessness, and selfishness; all things that Ugandans had never known that much before.

It also meant that, without the financial and human resource backing from a political party under a multi-party political system, the pressure on Mr. J.J Carpenter to mobilise sufficient resources to run his campaign would be immense; almost unbearable for most people of integrity. Let's assume for a moment that Mr. J.J Carpenter is your ordinary, fairly impecunious Mucwininian who travels on the back of a Pick-up Truck to and from Mucwini. Would he resist the temptation to resort to primitive means of accumulating wealth to finance his campaign? Most certainly not!

And that, I submit, may be a very significant contributory factor that is partly fuelling the rampant and totally unprecedented culture of corruption that is haemorrhaging the country to a slow but sure death today. As you have indeed seen, the *individual merit* system also made commercialisation of politics unavoidable. That is of course not to say that modern politics in multi-party democracies has not been equally commercialised; it has.

What *individual merit* meant was that all those who are not *"well positioned"* to corruptly acquire wealth to run such commercialised political campaigns would be effectively shut out of the country's political processes. This then gives the unaccountable modern despots the opportunity to use public funds to facilitate only those sycophantic regime cronies who profess unquestioning allegiance to them as individuals.

The net result, no doubt, will be that the despot will always get his way with these heavily indebted cronies who feel that without the despot's *"kind"* intervention, they would have amounted to naught. Seen differently, *National Service*, which is what politics is, and indeed ought to be about, was deliberately turned into *Service to the Despot.* It didn't really matter anymore that such regime cronies may also be mere intellectual dwarfs whose only reason for venturing into politics was personal gain.

In the end, you then find that some of the best brains in such a country are left out of the political process. That in turn, of course, has a direct impact on the overall quality of the country's Legislature and other arms of the State; just the way the modern despot wants it. A situation where no individual, or indeed institution, is independent and brave enough to hold the despot to account for his decisions and actions! So think very carefully. Do you recognise such a situation prevailing in your country? If so, then you may have a modern despot within your midst.

Going back to the Ugandan case, I think with such a state of affairs, there can be no better way of describing the impact of Museveni's *individual merit* political experiment in Uganda other than that it was a *"catastrophic success"* in undermining, and in fact, reversing Uganda's match towards a genuine democratic dispensation.

By that of course, I mean one that is practiced freely and fairly within an institutional framework. In fact, I suspect that even for those [including leaders in Western democracies] who still stubbornly choose to be fair in their assessment of Museveni's legacy, the best possible argument in mitigation at their disposal may be that *individual merit* was really only meant to be a half-hearted democratic experiment.

But even with that lame excuse, it would still be an implied admission that as a system of "democratic" governance, *individual merit* was in fact conceptually flawed to the bone. Not much thought was ever given to its long term impact on the overall culture of institutionalism; a culture that we all agree is absolutely critical to the democratic evolution of a nation.

Now here is a simple question for you to grapple with. If you have a President, or indeed Prime Minister, who still stubbornly chooses to be unfairly fair in his or her assessment of Museveni's legacy, then what exactly does that say about his or her own appreciation of how democrats ought to think, behave, and act? The *conscience-less* notion of *Strategic National Interests* aside, I would say probably not very different from Museveni's own assessment.

Of course, it comes as no surprise at all that some of the arch defenders of *individual merit* have since offered some highly questionable defences. One of their defences is that the failures of *individual merit* were merely brought about by an inadvertent oversight on Museveni's part. That contrary to what the cynics may think, Museveni did not actually have a *pre-meditated plan* to kill off Uganda's nascent culture of institutionalism for selfish political reasons.

That is a good excuse; but not good enough for me I am afraid! And moreover, on the strength of the evidence that is about to be adduced hereunder, the temptation to conclude that that is exactly what modern despots around the world like Museveni intend achieve would be hard to resist.

Chapter Two

The Gospel According to "Saint" Kaguta

Portrait of a Despot

There are so many fascinating, and yet terribly sad things to talk about as we go through the subtle political tricks employed by modern despots around the globe. These tricks are often conceptualised and implemented with the sole aim of ensuring that they maintain their despotic status as the *"Alfa"* bull on the political stage. Their emphasis and focus in all cases is always firmly fixed on the *"individual"*; not the *"institutions"* of common good.

So what exactly are these political tricks that modern despots deploy at will to achieve this emphasis and focus on themselves as individuals? Well naturally, there is no universal template. They vary from country to country; depending on the *prevailing political dynamics* at play at any given time.

Still with the factors that influence the choice of political tricks, sometimes, it could even boil down to what the despot thinks would be the most appropriate way to portray himself in good light before the governed. For example, one of Museveni's most favoured tricks is to portray his predecessors in bad light among the people he rules over.

To do this, he uses some derogatory words like *"swine"* to describe his predecessors; a word that Muslims in particular, associate with pigs, their number one *"harraam"* or forbidden food.

On some occasions, he has even referred to his predecessors as *"night-dancers"* [meaning witches]; *"biological mistakes"*; *"savages"* and so forth; just to embellish their real and even perceived political failures. Very powerful words indeed! In the end, Museveni will have succeeded in thoroughly demonising his predecessors. He will also have drawn attention himself as *The Man* who can never be as bad as his predecessors. After all, he says, he brought *sanity* back to the country.

So I think ordinary people need to be very weary of politicians who devote a great deal of their time and energy attacking their predecessors. And the reason I sound that caution is quite simple. In genuine democracies, a politician in Museveni's position, unlike Museveni of course, would be focusing his attacks on the policy failures of his predecessor's *"administration"*.

You know, like the *Labour* government did this very poorly; the *Democrats* couldn't have done that at all; the *Republicans* cannot be trusted with this; the *Liberal Democrats* are too soft on this; and so forth. That in my view is a legitimate form of political attack in the battle for votes.

The other *true traits* of a modern despot that I think can be clearly discerned from Museveni's political *modus operandi* is how he leaves no stone unturned to ensure that the electorate are totally disenfranchised; both politically and economically. Deceit too is inherent in a modern despot's body politick.

The modern despot, a bit like the medieval one in fact, also divides and rules his people with a big *"stick"* in one hand, and a tiny collection of sweet and sour *"carrots"* in the other. Perhaps a short sweet little story will do better justice to this subject.

The year is 1996. Mohammed, or *"Mo"* as we used call him, was a good friend of mine from a very Islamic country that I will not identify here; just in case he is identified and flogged for his past "un-Islamic" behaviour. Mo and I had met at law school. During one of our Friday evening after- class conversations about girls {under the influence of booze of course} at the Student Union pub, Mo pulled out a fast one!

Without warning, he shot up to his now unsteady feet and, in typical wannabe Lawyer language, he shouted out loudly to the amazement of many in the pub. *"Order, Order"*, he commanded! With a half-full pint of beer in his hand, and feeling every bit the top Barrister that he was aspiring to be, he turned and faced us and said:

"My Lords, it is the defence's case that my father, who, I submit, should be the accused No.1 in this case, advised me as boy, that the best way to ensure that your wife never leaves you, is to keep her skint {penniless in other words} and pregnant at all times. That way, she will have no choice but to stay".

Mo's drunken submission achieved the desired objective. As soon as he shut his big mouth up, the entire pub erupted into a prolonged fit of laughter. It was obviously a sick and *"politically incorrect"* joke. But, as young men, that did not stop us from having a good old drunken laugh about it.

It is the sort of thing that men of all ages get up to now and again when, like the mighty River Nile, beer is flowing incessantly. After all, there was no sober girl or woman nearby anyway! So he got away with it. But what exactly is the analogical relevance of Mo's sick joke to a despot's political tricks? Disenfranchisement is the answer!

Either it was sheer coincidence, or Museveni, with his much coveted clairvoyance, had already been into Mo's mind and picked up his theory long before he had even stated it! Let's consider this non scientific, but politically appropriate way of applying Mo's theory to Museveni's disenfranchisement politics.

First of all, Museveni systematically disenfranchised and divided the electorate through his *no party-individual merit-Movement* system of governance. The reason being that by its very nature, and reverse implication, the *no party-individual merit-Movement* system discouraged cooperation and unity of purpose.

So it was simply a case of *"every man for himself and God for us all"*. This is precisely one of the things that I keep banging on about when I am talking about political disenfranchisement by modern despots around the world. Thereafter, Museveni then set about his quest to make the rural electorate totally *"skint"*. He did this by destroying the *Cooperative Movement;* a conceptually simple and yet fiercely effective institution through which Uganda's farmers were organised and helped to market their cash crops.

The *Cooperative Movement* had for a long time been the rock-solid back-borne of Uganda's agricultural economy; a great source of hope for its people's struggles against abject poverty too. Liberation from poverty would have meant liberation from Museveni's corrupt handouts too; and Museveni knew the political implications of that very well.

But Museveni didn't stop there. He had something *"very special"* for one particular group of Ugandans; his real, or in fact, perceived political *"enemies"*. These were the people from eastern and northern Uganda. They were of course the very communities whose sons and daughters had occupied high political offices in the military junta that Museveni overthrew. So, perhaps unsurprisingly, they were also the ones who rebelled against Museveni's unconstitutional ascent to power. So what does Museveni do?

He took full advantage of the rebellion in eastern and northern Uganda; a perfect *"prevailing political dynamic"* if you recall, to impoverish this particular group. Through a highly suspect security policy, he herded these people into what the disinterested parties, the media, and the NGO community called *"internally displaced people's camps"* {IDPs}.

To the victims, these were nothing short of Nazi style concentration camps. Almost one thousand people a week were dying from preventable diseases in these camps. From then on, these people were totally unproductive; economically at least!

At this stage, Museveni now had a bunch of past leaders living in exile who were increasingly viewed by the gullible electorate as *"a bunch evil demons"* who should never be trusted with the mantles of State power. Perception is everything in politics; we are told! If that is true, then these past leaders would never pose any real political threat to Museveni.

Most importantly however, by dividing, disenfranchising, and impoverishing the electorate, Museveni had also ensured that his *"enemies"* would have no capacity to effectively organise themselves against him. Incredibly however, even with all that political advantage, the invincible military General [full sarcasm intended] of the 1986 revolution still felt insecure.

So to solve that political insecurity, Museveni went for the *"kill"*. He quickly commercialised Ugandan politics in its entirety. And by that I mean the corrupt ancient practice of bribing voters to secure their votes became widespread. It's now fully entrenched. In fact, it has completely changed Uganda's political culture. Without deep pockets, you would definitely lose your *"deposit"*; aka *"nomination fees"* in political contests. That way, poor Ugandans were left trapped; exactly like the wife in *Mo's theory*.

The situation may not be as bad as this for people in other countries. But what is not in doubt is that politics around the world, for varied reasons, has become a lot more expensive than it was a few years ago. The net result therefore, in both Uganda and other countries, is that the majority have become disenfranchised. The difference is only in degree; not the fact of disenfranchisement. It is for this very reason that I think some cynics, even in settled democracies, are beginning to view their political elite very suspiciously.

Charles Ochen Okwir

Allow me a quick very personal word about the IDP camps in eastern and northern Uganda before we move on! Even if we ignore the political value of the IDP scheme to Museveni for a moment, I think it would still be the very height of un-altruistic behaviour for anyone, absolutely anyone on this planet, to do such things to fellow human beings. Surely, in this, the twenty first century, it must be beyond debate that human dignity and inherent self-respect are greatly undermined when men, women and children are condemned to more than 23yrs of idleness in filthy disease ridden IDP camps.

Their culture, way of life, and self-esteem has been shattered to the point that it now fully justifies a charge of genocide against General Museveni and his henchmen. That is, and continues to be, to this day as I write, the worst form of waste of Uganda's most precious resource. And that is of course, the talents, dexterity and energy of its people! For those reasons, I think the consistent claims by Museveni that Uganda is recording record economic growth year after year is a complete fallacy. It has to be! Especially when you consider the fact that both eastern and northern regions, huge and fertile chunks of agricultural land, have remained unproductive for the entire period of the supposed growth. In fact, instead of paying taxes, they feed off the treasury!

So to believe Museveni's heavily embellished growth figures would lend credibility to the suggestion that the budget speeches that are read with pomp and ceremony by Finance Ministers in the world's poorest countries are in fact written thousands of miles away by armchair technocrats at the World Bank and IMF. Technocrats who haven't got the slightest clue about the actual facts on the ground!

And that just goes to show that no country, absolutely no country in the world in my view, can, or should lay claim to full independence if it cannot pay its own way on the world stage. To do otherwise would simply be delusional; a trait that you will find in most modern despots! So watch those glittering Presidential Palaces very closely; you might be surprised at what you find lurking in there.

In Uganda's case however, once Museveni was sure that poverty had indeed set in; sure that the commercialisation of politics had taken shape; he quickly re-positioned himself as the philanthropist *Father of the Nation*. A man with answers to everyone's problems!

And to demonstrate that, he unashamedly started using taxpayers' money {sealed in brown envelopes} as handouts to the now impoverished Ugandan citizens. His handlers made sure that the infamous brown envelopes that have now come to symbolise an acceptable form of political corruption were handed out by Museveni in-front of cameras for maximum publicity. And for that, the totally downtrodden peasantry were supposed to be grateful. Delusional indeed!

Alongside all those insidious political manoeuvres, Museveni also worked hard [through empty Public Relations rhetoric] to keep Ugandans and the international community heavily *"pregnant"* with the *Hope* of a better and brighter future; just as Mo's theory prescribes.

And for that illusion of hope, and its inability to see through Museveni's political deceit, the Clinton Administration, itself having swept to power in the USA on the same platform of hope, was bursting with unrealistic optimism about Museveni's democratic credentials. So optimistic was the Clinton government that it *"baptised"* Museveni and a few other modern despots in the Great Lakes region of Africa as the *"New Breed"* of African leaders.

Museveni in particular succeeded in offering that false sense of hope in many forms. Being the skilful political demagogue that he is, Museveni had succeeded in embellishing his predecessors' shortcomings to appeal to the negative prejudices of both the local and international community.

In the process, he had also succeeded in *mis*-leading them into believing that he had come up with the most accurate diagnosis of the fundamental causes of Uganda's problems. For those reasons, Museveni claimed, he was therefore best placed to treat and cure Uganda's problems decisively. Sounds familiar? Well, let's move on. Part of Museveni's supposed diagnosis had earlier come in the form of a *cleverly* worded document called *"The 10 Point Programme"*; a contract of sorts with the people of Uganda. And I say cleverly in quotes for a good reason. We now know, almost beyond any reasonable doubt, that Museveni's so-called *10 Point Programme* had in fact been a work of plagiarism. It had been lifted almost 100% from Fidel Castro's own *10 Point Programme* written during the latter's own revolutionary armed struggle in the *Sierra Maestra* forests of Cuba decades earlier.

So in my view, Museveni deserves no credit whatsoever for the originality of *"his"* 10 Point Programme. It was a stolen one; pure and simple! Put differently, we now know that as a politician, Museveni had failed to demonstrate that he could come up with new ideas of his own. That said, the stolen 10 Point Programme managed to capture a lot of peasant imagination; especially from his Western Uganda enclave. It is for that reason that the same people ending up forming the nucleus of his ethno-centric political/military organisation.

In fact, when Museveni only sought out people from his region to form the nucleus of his organisation, alarm bells should have been ringing immediately about the underlying ideological basis of his political struggle. Nepotism is, and must indeed be, one of the clearest indications anywhere in the world that you may have a modern despot on your hands. For them, the imagination of people from other ethnic backgrounds is, and will never be as critical to the success of their political schemes as that of people from his own ethnic group.

To his original comrades to the bush, and to those from the wider Western part of Uganda, Museveni, in a most vile and sectarian way, decided and in fact wildly exaggerated the so-called *"north-south divide"*. This so-called *"north-south divide"* is said to have its origins in the legacy British colonialism. But that is not the important thing here. The important thing is that it's still a *prevailing political dynamic* in Uganda; one that Museveni, like the true modern despot that he is, took full advantage of.

One of the ways in which he exaggerated the *north-south divide* was through indoctrination. For example, we now know for a fact that Museveni's guerrilla fighters were routinely required to sing emotive *ethnic-hatred* songs like "*sina dola, sina dola, anyanya*".

It's very easy not to read too much into the mental poisoning capacity of a mere song. This one was however very different. It was a most derogatory battle song that was composed, God knows by who, to carry a powerful and provocative message to Museveni's guerrilla fighters that people from West Nile, Northern Uganda, and to some extent those from North Eastern Uganda, were unpatriotic *"Anyanya"* aliens who were responsible for all Uganda's political problems.

A young man who was one of Museveni's guerrilla fighters once told me that the most dangerous thing about that song was that it created a perception among them that the *"Anyanya"* were people who were hell bent on wiping out all *Bantu* speaking people from Uganda; and most of them were *Bantu* speaking people. The impact of such indoctrination cannot be over emphasised. It makes the threat of being ethnically cleansed a very real one. And for that, a man will fight bravely in the interest of self preservation; however false that may be.

he view held in this book therefore is that the cumulative effect of that pre-meditated and carefully orchestrated indoctrination exercise amounted to nothing less than Tincitement of genocide within the meaning of the *International Criminal Court Statute*. The key fact here is that the incitement was done "...*in the knowledge that it will cause incidental loss of innocent lives*".

That, my friends, would have brought General Museveni and his top guerrilla commanders to The Hague to face trial for inciting genocide had it not been for the simple fact of Jurisprudence that the ICC statute, like most laws, does not have retrospective effect. So they should thank their lucky stars.

That said however, I also think the majority of Museveni's bush war followers and sympathisers were actually innocent victims of a modern despot's deceit. And the reason is that for all their enthusiasm in helping to prosecute the so-called *liberation war* against the *"Anyanya"* northerners, most of them did not actually know that Museveni's mission in politics was very different. He was motivated by a more sinister objective. As he put it himself during the heat of the 2006 presidential campaigns, his mission in politics was, and I quote, "...*to liberate my tribesmen from their nomadic lifestyle*".

So there you have it; plain and simple! In fact, if you think about it now with the wonderful benefit of hindsight, you may find that what Museveni confirmed to the world in 2006 may actually have been the very thing his young son Muhoozi was talking about ten years earlier {in 1996}when he said *"...we shall never have lasting peace unless the state and government come under the control of those who have a bigger stake in it; that is, those who have accumulated a lot of property...".*

Now, by both definition and nature, Museveni's nomadic tribesmen lived a very mobile life that made it almost impossible for them to acquire and hold fixed assets like the "property" that Museveni's son was talking about. So by saying he wanted to liberate his tribesmen from their nomadic lifestyle, Museveni may in fact have intended to give his tribesmen the opportunity to accumulate *"a lot of property"* with the corrupt backing of the State. And boy, rise to the challenge they did! In under two decades, there is absolutely no dispute that some of the wealthiest people in Uganda today are from Museveni's ethnic group. And that was the last piece of the jigsaw that Museveni and his son needed to bring the State and government *"...under the control of those who have a bigger stake in it"*.

This is not something that is entirely unique to Uganda. Across Africa, Latin America, Asia, the Middle East, you name it, there are modern despots like Uganda's Yoweri Museveni building such political dynasties. The challenge, to which I hope I am making a humble contribution, is to empower people in those countries with the knowledge to immediately recognize it and demand that it be stopped forthwith.

But let's go back to our reference Uganda. Museveni's confession that he went into politics to liberate his tribesmen from their nomadic lifestyle still leaves one very big question unanswered; and it is: Where does that leave the official *"national liberation"* rhetoric that Ugandans and the international community bought en-mass and offered Museveni their support for? Absolutely nowhere!

The bitter truth is that it was all a deceitful fraud whose purpose was anything but the liberation of Uganda. That of course does not in any way negate the fact that at that time, Uganda probably needed a true liberator to deliver it from military rule and give it hope of a democratic future where egalitarianism would reign supreme. But it was never to be. It ended up with a cunning modern despot at the helm of power. As expected, Museveni's mission to *liberate his tribesmen from their nomadic lifestyle* only delivered cronyism, nepotism, sectarianism, and unrivalled hedonism for the materialistic members of the *"mafia clan"* who had been deprived of the pleasures of modern living for the entire duration of the 1981-1986 bush war. So when *"their time"* to indulge in these pleasures came, Ugandans were treated to a free spectacle of unprecedented flamboyance punctuated by nasty experiences of unrivalled arrogance. That is perhaps as much as we should say for now lest we lose track of the more serious issues in this political rollercoaster.

Anyway still with the *"Mo doctrine"* {as I sometimes like to call it} and the subject of the false hope that Museveni sold to all who cared to listen, as I said, it came in different forms. One of the very first ones was what Museveni's political strategists exotically called *"Entandikwa"*. Loosely translated from the local *Luganda* language, *Entandikwa* meant *small interest-free loans from the State* which Ugandans could access to start income generating activities for themselves. That as I said, gave Ugandans the false hope that they would finally have a fighting chance in their war against poverty; and they swallowed it.

The Illusion of Free Education for All

The second and third false hopes were the promises of *Universal Primary Education* [UPE] and *Universal Secondary Education* [USE] for all. With these, Ugandans dared to hope that their children would be educated free of charge. The State, in the form of Gen. Museveni, would pick up the bills. But let's examine both UPE and USE in greater detail and see what we come up with.

It is 2006; the year of a general election in Uganda. The recycling, re-packaging, and fraudulent marketing of old and failed political gimmicks by Museveni's NRM government continues. USE was one of those *"big new ideas"* in Museveni's 2006 election manifesto. USE was essentially a re-packaged version of the old, ill conceived and poorly implemented *Universal Primary Education* [UPE] idea. As any Ugandan will tell you, UPE only succeeded in delivering half baked primary school graduates. And yet, as an electoral political gimmick, it had successfully delivered peasant votes to Museveni.

Evidence of the UPE disaster is there for all to see. Very few [if any at all] UPE graduates could construct a sensible sentence in English. And yet, very tragically, these were the same pupils who were now supposed to join secondary school education under the new USE programme. If any credit should be due to the UPE programme, then it is that it produced the desired quantity that the regime was looking for. The focus on *quantity* as opposed to *quality* was not for nothing; how could it be?
With the help of modern computer software, these quantities could be easily converted into impressive statistics that the regime could then use to showcase its *"achievements"* to the electorate. Beyond local politics, the same impressive statistics could also be fraudulently fronted as evidence of Uganda's progress in the pursuit of the *UN Millennium Development Goals* [MDG's].

That would then ensure that donor aid and debt relief from developed countries continued to flow towards Museveni. But Museveni wasn't the only beneficiary of the great free education illusion. The Western donor countries that had hailed Uganda as the *"success story of Africa"* would also be saved the embarrassment that would have come their way from a honest appraisal of the real impact UPE. So in the end, as Museveni and his financiers benefited from the UPE/USE hoax, innocent young children from poor families ended up being the net losers.

But don't take my word for it. Hear this: Of the many expressions of disappointment with UPE and USE by Ugandan parents, I feel this particular letter to the Editor by a certain Ben Musoke Kizza captures the sentiments of the majority very well. It was published in the *Daily Monitor* newspaper of July 17th 2007 under the title *"Is it Right to Charge Fees in UPE Schools"?*

Like a tale being told around a typical evening African fireplace, the author, obviously disappointed, opens his historical testimony with the standard of sophistication that you would expect from the very UPE graduates that he is talking about. *"Once upon a time, I felt*

very pleased when I heard President Yoweri Museveni was introducing Universal Primary Education. This was during the 1996 presidential elections campaigns but after more than a decade, I am becoming disturbed when I see our primary school Head Teacher sending away pupils just for the sake of going back home to collect the so called "school dues", he said.

The first significance, in case you missed it, is in the author's reference to *school fees* by its new UPE name of *"school dues"*. In other words, the very *school fees* that the UPE programme had purportedly consigned to history had in fact been re-introduced through the back door and baptised *school dues*. The second significance is in

Kizza's reference to the timing of the introduction of UPE. When he identified the 1996 presidential election campaigns in his letter, he was merely putting the UPE promise into its proper political context. In fact, it may well suggest that our poor old Ben Musoke Kizza may have voted for Museveni in 1996 on the strength of that bogus UPE promise.

Kizza then goes on to capture the feeling of hopelessness that is experienced by many others like him. "...*Why then is it that the Head Teacher* [is] *chasing away our children from school? Is it under the laws and ethics which govern UPE policy?*", he wondered.

As parents like Ben Musoke Kizza cried about the UPE mess, Museveni decided to pull another logic defying move. Using billions of taxpayers' money from the *"Donations Account"* of President's Office, he decided to build schools for children in neighbouring Tanzania; a sovereign nation that ironically has the highest literacy rate in Africa. Absolutely incredible stuff! How I wish I could get into the minds of despots like Museveni to see what drives them to do the ghastly things they do.

The sense of injustice is further compounded by the fact that the same Museveni clique who have condemned millions of children to intellectual decay through UPE and USE are themselves sending their children and relatives abroad to get top quality education using a most sectarian *State House Scholarship* scheme. It is despicable!

Then on July 19th, a mere two days after Ben Musoke Kizza's letter, Hosborn Ogwang's letter was alsoublished in the same newspaper. While condemning the dangerous condition of UPE classrooms, Ogwang posed a pertinent question to the powers that be: "...*Is the Ministry of Education aware of the predicaments facing these pupils? They need to know that these children's lives are more important than the poor peducation they give to our children. I feel pain whenever I hear the resident praising the UPE programme. The implementers of this programme are letting him down.*

Charles Ochen Okwir

Someone must Ptake action", Ogwang charged.

Just consider this for a moment: While Ben Musoke Kizza expressed *"sadness"* about the mess that is UPE, Hosborn Ogwang expressed *"pain"*. Two totally different people who have probably never met cannot be expressing similar sentiments out of politically inspired malice. There is obviously a very serious problem with the entire UPE programme. And the greatest betrayal is that Museveni himself is aware of it but still praises it to milk whatever political capital is left in it.

As far as USE is concerned, in 2008, it finally emerged that the half baked UPE graduates may not even be able to enrol for secondary school education after all. The reason being that the *Ministry of Education* had failed to find 120billion Shillings [approx $58million] to fund the programme that year. And to seal the fate of these poor kids even further, it also emerged that students who were already in their first year of secondary school may not be able to proceed to the second year unless the *Ministry of Education* finds an additional 18.2billion Shillings for the academic year that was due to end in July, 2007.

As expected, the verdict from Parliament's *Budget Committee* couldn't have been any clearer. *"...the entire USE programme may not continue in the new financial year because the Government has earmarked just Uganda Shillings 30billion out of the required Shillings 150billion"*; the Committee said. Secondly, market forces in the education sector also had something to say about USE. For a start, private schools were overtaking government aided schools in both numbers and quality of performance. There is also evidence to suggest that even the few government schools that were still clinging on to dear life were now reluctant to take on students on the USE programme.

The reason was that the same government had placed a cap on the tuition fees it was willing to pay in government schools at no more than a miserable 29,000 Shillings per academic term. For private schools, the cap was put at a pathetic 47,000 Shillings per academic term and yet ordinarily, these schools would have charged hundreds of thousands more.

In the end, I think many Ugandan parents who voted to return Museveni to power on the strength of his free education promise will have kicked themselves hard upon discovering that it was all a big fat political fraud. For the poverty stricken parents, that reality literally meant *the end of the road of hope* for their children. All Museveni wanted from them was their votes. No more, no less!

The Great Fallacy that is Bonna Bagagawale

If there is a modern despot who has mastered the art of recycling, re-packaging and fraudulently selling old, failed, and totally un-costed political gimmicks, then it must be Uganda's Yoweri Museveni. And the 2006 Ugandan general elections again provided us with a perfect demonstration of that.

The *"great"* and *"new"* economic development initiative that flew out of the immaculate confines of State House was something that Museveni's political wordsmiths called *Bonna Bagagawale* [BB]. BB was, and still is, no more than an empty political slogan plucked out of the local *Luganda* language to excite uncritical minds. The best English translation of BB that a man from a different tribe like me can manage here will simply be *"may all be wealthy"*.

You can immediately see that by definition, BB was effectively a mere wish. And as realists would say, *"if wishes were horses, all beggars would ride"*; wouldn't they? The truth of the matter is that, just like Museveni's defunct *Entandikwa* programme, BB was also designed with the sole aim of keeping peasants *"heavily pregnant"* with hope. Yes, hope; that invisible but mighty commodity that keeps the world's political stock markets ticking like Usain Bolt's athletic heart.

Today, a spanking new *Ministry of Micro Finance* has been created to manage the BB programme. And who was the *"most qualified economist"* in the land chosen to manage this flagship economic programme? Well, if you are not a Ugandan, then I suspect you are thinking of some well schooled Professor of economics like Jeffrey Sachs; or at least some economics graduate. You would be wrong. It was of course, General Museveni's young brother General Salim Saleh; the hedonistic mature High School graduate who joined secondary school as a decorated army General.

Salim Saleh also happens to be one who, having been implicated in some of the biggest corruption scandals Uganda has ever seen, still owes his freedom to his big brother's dubious exercise of the prerogative of mercy vested in him as President. Now, how about that for a CV? Impressive isn't it?

But strange things do happen in Uganda. Even some of the very best brains in Museveni's political camp seized upon the BB nonsense with dogmatic zeal and went about selling it to the electorate as aggressively as they could. Never mind that the salesmen themselves didn't have a clue about how this magic wand would suddenly make every Ugandan wealthy.

The evidence of course suggests that BB was never meant for all Ugandans. Only those who *actually* supported Museveni's candidature would benefit. The second tier of possible beneficiaries would be those who didn't support Museveni but had now *"seen the light"* and demonstrated a verifiable willingness to support Museveni's NRM-O party. Others can simply go to hell. If you are still in doubt, then here this.

When Hon. Beti Kamya was still the opposition FDC party MP for Rubaga North Constituency, she organised her constituents into small *Savings and Credit Cooperative Organizations* {SACCOs} to enable them apply for the BB funds. At this stage, everything appeared to be going according to plan for Hon. Kamya and her constituents. But they were terribly mistaken in thinking that BB was a *national* programme.

As soon as news broke that the regime's *Micro Finance* Minister Gen. Salim Saleh was about to launch the programme in Kamya's *"opposition"* constituency, all hell broke loose. Museveni's NRM-O party faithful went up in arms. They demanded an explanation from their party leaders as to why their BB cake was going to be served in an *"opposition"* constituency.

These NRM diehards of course had every reason to expect that they would be given preferential treatment to stuff themselves silly before opposition supporters are invited to the BB dinner table. After all, that was exactly how the so-called *"1986 Millionaires"* were created by the regime; all for what Museveni has since called their *"sacrifices"* to the *"liberation struggle"*.

As for Rubaga North, the NRM-O party diehards won the day. The *Micro Finance* Minister succumbed to their pressure and pulled the plug on Hon. Kamya's BB launch party. And for the excuse, Hon. Beti Kamya was finally told that her constituents could not access the funds because, and I quote, the "...*policies and guidelines for the disbursement of the funds had not yet been formulated".* Nice!

And there is further evidence to prove that BB was never a *bona fide* economic policy. It was simply a modern despot's patronage vehicle; and here is why. In its wit and wisdom, Museveni's regime decided that *Sub-County Chiefs* would be best placed to oversee the mplementation of the BB programme. ⁞ And for that, they needed to undergo some training to prepare them for the task they were about to embark on. Nothing wrong with that!

And not only that, I also happen to think that if BB had not been a vote winning fraud but a genuine economic programme, then involving *Sub-County Chiefs* in its implementation wouldn't have been such a bad thing. After all, *Sub-County Chiefs* have historically provided good and fairly impartial leadership at the bottom of Uganda's socio-political superstructure.

The problem with the training that Museveni's regime was proposing for *Sub-County Chiefs* this time round was that it had absolutely nothing to do with the implementation of an economic programme. According to the regime, the training would involve what it called mandatory "*...basic military training and politicisation with special emphasis on the NRM-O ideology and economic programme for Uganda*". You really have to ask yourself whether the pressing need to combat abject poverty in Uganda has anything to do with the NRM's ideology. Of course not! By its emphasis on the NRM-O ideology, the regime was sending a message to the country's *Sub-County Chiefs*. That message was that BB was essentially an NRM-O political patronage initiative designed and intended to be for the exclusive benefit of NRM-O party supporters.

But here is the most disturbing implication of it all. By requiring *Sub-County Chiefs* to first undergo mandatory "*...politicisation with special emphasis on the NRM-O ideology*", all of them had effectively been turned into local NRM-O party agents by covert conscription. And guess what? These new NRM-O party agents would now be paid by the State!
If you were to look at it more broadly, what this also means is that in that simple act covert political conscription, the *Civil Service* that employs the *Chiefs* was now working "*for and on*

behalf of" Museveni's NRM-O party. That is a vintage modern despot at work. It simply can't get any better than that.

And to show its determination, the regime raised the stakes for the *Sub-County Chiefs*. It issued a threat that should any *Sub-County Chief* dare miss the training, then losing his or her job would be a very real possibility. And reason for that was simple. Refusal to attend such training would be the clearest indication to NRM-O leaders that such a *Chief* may be harbouring sympathy for opposition parties.

If you now cast your mind back to the discussion we had about the *Civil Service*, then you will find that the regime's insistence on politicising *Sub-County Chiefs* actually lends great weight to the conclusion that the colonial policy of stopping *Civil Servants* from joining political parties was in reality a covert means of restraining them from joining opposition parties.

With such a state of affairs, the opposition would clearly be no match for the incumbent modern despot in grassroots political mobilisation. Because from then on, if any Ugandan wanted some kind of recommendation from the *Chiefs* to enable them access the BB funds, then they would have to behave and act in a manner that conforms to the NRM's political ideology. It is really as simple as that.

But let me leave you to ponder over this editorial opinion published in the *Daily Monitor* newspaper of August 20th 2007. The title simply read: "*Cash for NRM poll losers is a big shame*". This was in response to the news that Museveni's government was planning give 2billion shillings to a BB *Savings and Credit Cooperative Organizations* [SACCO] formed by Ex-NRM-O party MPs who had lost their seats in the 2006 elections. In perhaps one of the greatest contradictions of the political decade, the Chairperson of this disgraceful group of losersdenied that their SACCO was specifically targeting BB funds.

And then, in the same breath, he immediately contradicted himself and said they were only "...*responding to the call of national policy that everyone should get rich*".

Reading this excerpt [below] from the *Daily Monitor* editorial, you would be forgiven for thinking the editorial team had somehow eavesdropped into my mind as I wrote the last few paragraphs. It said, "...*ultimately all the Bonna bagaggawale money will be shared out among NRM loyalists while the rest of Ugandans will go home empty handed. These developments are coming in the wake of the NRM's warning that it will start recruiting its cadres into Public Service. It's a big national shame*". I have absolutely nothing to add to that!

Professionalization of the National Army

Other than the *Bonna Bagaggawale* programme that is now ridiculed as *"Bonna Bakonne"* {meaning *"Stagnation for All"*}, the other *"big idea"* that was crafted and sold to Ugandans to justify Museveni's quest to remain in power was the need to *"professionalize"* the army.

Indiscipline and luck of professionalism in the previous armies, they said, were the major causes of Uganda's political problems. Admittedly, if you were to ask Ugandans today, many would probably accept that it was indeed an accurate diagnosis. So all credit to Museveni then; you might think! Well, not quite.

And reason is this: If you were to ask the same respondents whether after 23years of uninterrupted stay in power they thought Museveni had actually professionalised the army, probably an astonishing 85% would give you a resounding *No*. Museveni's insatiable appetite for power would never be tolerated by any professional army whose primary allegiance is to the constitution as opposed to the individual ruler.

So why would Museveni decide to put a noose around his own neck by professionalizing the army? He simply can't. To survive, Museveni has had to call his informal bush war methods of unilateral governance back into active service. That again is the other *true trait* of a modern despot. There are no two ways about it. Without it, they are history. All this will become clearer in my discussion about how Museveni has managed the *Uganda Peoples Defence Forces* {UPDF}.

For now, we shall only ask ourselves whether *"informal bush war methods of unilateral governance"* are indeed what a young State like Uganda needs at such a defining moment in its history. The consensus, I hope, will be that it is the last thing Uganda needs as it embarks on a journey towards a community of civilised nations. As a *Nation State* that has been "independent" for more than 48yrs, Uganda shouldn't be struggling to merely avoid being declared a *"Failed State"*.

In fact, that alone lends weight to the criticism that as a people, Ugandans have by their own lukewarm push for high standards, allowed their leaders to set their democratic benchmarks too low. Therefore if there is any global lesson to be learnt from this regrettable Ugandan state of affairs, then it must be that everyone in any given jurisdiction must play an active civic role in ensuring their democratic aspirations are not thwarted by modern despots and their cohorts.

The reason being that when a few people within any State system become too powerful to the extent of not recognising the difference between themselves and the State, then the majority will feel that they count for less and less. An individual's feeling of relevance in shaping the destiny of the country is in my view the true hallmark of any democratic dispensation. So the question is this: Do you feel that you count for something in the daily business of shaping the political destiny of your country? If your answer is no, then be afraid; very afraid indeed because you may have a canning modern despot presiding over the affairs of State in your country without you knowing it.

And the most regrettable thing is that if such a situation is left unchecked, the State will end up draining society of its wealth, initiative, energy, and above all, the will to improve as well as to preserve what is best. It is therefore your fundamental civic duty, you the citizen, to ensure that the State, at all times, remains accountable to you. It is only through that that you will know and feel that you count for more and more.

A great nation must be the creation of its own people. Anything short of that will simply not suffice. It will be a mirage; an illusion of greatness perpetuated by the despot and his henchmen. If people feel that they contributed to the making of a great nation, then so it shall remain; great! It will remain great because they will be ready and willing to make sacrifices to keep it great.

Coercion, disenfranchisement, political deceit, intimidation, and oppressive laws have been, and will continue to be the timeless hallmarks of modern despots around the world. It is also true that these same ghastly things cannot and will never make a nation any greater that than great armies can. In the end, it all ends in failure! Of that my friends, there can be little doubt.

The Death of the Cooperative Movement

Even the most ardent defendants of the Museveni *"revolution"* will and have indeed privately conceded that President Milton Obote's old *Cooperative Movement* had been a resounding success. As most Ugandans recall with pride and nostalgia these days, through it, the rural farmer, typically a middle aged man with a wife or two and several children, would mobilise the local community to help his family cultivate, harvest, and transport his cash crops to his home in return for a feast of traditional beer and food. Such a feast would on occasions go on into the *"young"* hours of the morning. Everyone one involved would leave happy. It was as simple as that and yet in the end, collectively, such successful small scale community initiatives made a huge difference to the overall health of the national economy.

Once the harvest was safely at home, the family would set upon the task of preparing it meticulously to improve its quality and by necessary implication, its market value too. And again, in most cases, such preparation for the market would be done communally with the help of local boys. For these young men, a reward of thinly sliced strips of car tyre tubes for them to make hunting catapults would be all they ask.

The beauty of it all for these young village boys was that they never considered helping out with such chores to be an economic activity from which proper remuneration should accrue. It was merely a good excuse to meet their peers for a good old chat. That alone transformed the whole gathering into one big happy social event.

It was also at such events that they would plot their more naughty evening plans and agree on a rendezvous. An absolutely wonderful display of the beautiful African spirit; a spirit that is now threatened with extinction as capitalism goes global! What a shame.

In the case of cotton for example, it would be many such days of careful sorting in the cool breeze of the homestead's tree shades that provide shelter from the scorching heat of tropical Africa. Once the sorting was done, our typical farmer, probably bare-chested and wearing a ten year old trouser that exposes him indecently now and again, would only have to carry his cash crops on the back of his equally buttered but faithful bicycle to what were called *"Societies"* then.

The *Societies* themselves were spectacularly simple warehouses made from corrugated iron sheets. But they were not just spectacular in-the-face large shiny warehouses. They also had an all together different functional purpose that was in all likelihood never envisaged by those who came up with the *Cooperative Movement* idea.

Their overall character, as described above, also meant that they served as important local navigational landmarks for strangers. So if I was to give directions to a friend visiting my village, I would only ask him to get to Mucwini trading centre, ask for directions to *Akara Society,* and he would be home and dry because everybody knew everybody from there on.

Anyway at the *Societies*, our farmer would sell off his crops and set off *"laughing all the way to the bank"* that in most cases would be an old clay pot safely tucked away in the darkest corner of the favourite wife's hut. That wife, probably the latest addition to the polygamous man's family, was literally the family's bank manager with keys to the clay pot vault.

Thereafter, the huge chocolate brown *Cooperative Movement* trucks would pick up the accumulated cash crops and ferry them further along what contemporary logisticians like my friend Patrice Namisano would probably call the *"supply chain"*. That process was the norm across the country and with it, Uganda's exports boomed and the economy grew strongly. That, in a nutshell, is the elegance of simplicity.

But if it was that elegant, simple and effective, then what on earth inspired Museveni's regime to dismantle the *Cooperative Movement*? That should be a question that is opened and shut immediately. There is no doubt that one of the things that inspired Museveni's regime to dismantle the *Cooperative Movement* was that its success was inextricably linked to Milton Obote's economic policies. That naked fact could never sit comfortably alongside Museveni's crusade to demonise Obote and every good thing he ever did for Uganda.

Secondly, the efficiency and effectiveness of the *Cooperative Movement* actually posed a serious political threat to Museveni *"the political strategist"*. First of all, the *Cooperative Movement* had a huge commercial interest in ensuring that all rural feeder roads used by its trucks are kept in a good state. It made good economic sense to them if their trucks were able to move swiftly on those roads without breaking any expensive parts.

Thirdly, the *Cooperative Movement* also provided *free* properly treated seeds for Uganda's farmers. That ensured that the farmers got a good yield, and the *Cooperative Movement* would in return, get near uniformity in the quality of the cash crops they were interested in.

Finally, when the *Cooperative Movement* sent word down to the grassroots that it would do something in a specific area on a specific date, it would be done. In summary, it provided farmers with packaging sacks. It kept their roads in good repair. It kept its promises to the farmers. It paid them in cash on delivery. And it relieved farmers of their logistical burdens.

When you consider all those facts, then it's not difficult to see that in the eyes of Uganda's farmers, the *Cooperative Movement* would be a more relevant development partner than the government of the day. So clearly, there was a very real risk that the *Cooperative Movement,* with its elaborate network of trusted rural leaders, could have easily become a more powerful political entity than Museveni's NRM machinery. Museveni saw that coming and decided that the *Cooperative Movement* had to be dismantled. I see no other plausible reasons.

Chapter Three

A Modern Despot's "Alfa" Tool of Oppression

Portrait of a Despot

The use of law, the most unlikely tool of political oppression, is for me one of the things that most ably define the character of the modern despot. And Uganda's Yoweri Museveni has proved to be a master of that art. An art which any Lawyer, even one of average worth, would and should be passionately against. And because of that, I find great difficulty in merely coming up with a fitting way of introducing the subject. That is just how much the mere thought it chuns my stomach; but try I must!

It is exactly 12:39:08pm on the 24th of February 2007. Two hours and 39minutes earlier, I had just boarded a British Airways flight from London to Nairobi-Kenya. Unbeknown to me, my good political friend Sam Akaki had just sent me an email.

I later discovered that the subject of Akaki's email was the use of *law as a tool of political oppression*. Like me, I suspect this was one of the many *True Traits* of a modern despot that have bothered him since I first delivered a paper on the subject at a London conference organised by the *The Reform Agenda*; a political pressure group that we both subscribed to. That was in mid 2002; or thereabouts. Since then, Akaki has never stopped making reference to the indictment in my paper and its significance to Uganda's politics under Museveni. On this particular occassion, Akaki wrote:

Dear Charles

"Former American Attorney General John David Ashcroft yesterday cautioned Ugandan legislators and other leaders against using the law to veto the will of the people. In other words, he told them not to use the law as tool of oppression"."The last piece is one of the most enduring comments that I will take to my grave! Being clever is not just about how many books you have read, or how many degrees you have collected. It is all these together with the ability to summarise what you have read, and applying them

in the context of the everyday life of the man, or woman in the street in a way that will make them stand up and think. Mr Ashcroft should apologise for plagiarising from the document you presented at a meeting of Ugandan MPs in 2002"!

Best wishes

Sam

For the uneasy access to email services where I was, it would be several days before I got the opportunity to read Sam's email; something that I often did several times a day from the comfort of my living room back in the UK.

In the end, when I finally got the opportunity, I wrote back to Sam acknowledging receipt of his email and of course went through the mandatory pleasantries of civility that even the world's greatest hypocrites find hard to avoid these days; not that I am one of them of course!

This time round, it didn't just stop at that; I couldn't have left it at that. Something, however humble, had to be done. And so I promised Sam that an appropriate time, I would expand, update and explore the possibilities of publishing that 2002 paper that I presented that so stuck to his mind.

Traditionally, the popular perception has always been that law is a civilised tool through which justice, a common good to mankind, is dispensed without fear or favour. The task of dispensing justice then falls to the Judiciary, an organised, structured, and logic driven institution of righteousness, civility, reason, and equity. So how does the word *"oppression"*, one that means everything that law is not supposed to represent, sworn enemies if you like, come to be used in the same sentence? Very good question indeed!

If I were to take a shot at addressing it, which I am, chances are that I would probably give you the same answer I gave you earlier; namely, that it is the very oxymoron that perfectly describes what is required to sustain a modern depot's quest for power, power, and more political power. Within the Ugandan context, it could also represent the sort of steps and actions required to sustain the logic defying contradiction that is the *"individual merit Movement system"* of governance that Museveni introduced to the world of political theory.

We shall delve a bit deeper into that later and hopefully confirm the hypothesis in this book that the *Movement* system of governance was in fact nothing but a disguised *one party state system* in all but name. What that would mean therefore would be that actually, Museveni never introduced anything new at all because one party States existed long before the onset of Museveni's own brand of the same.

In this part however, my sole intention is to simply demonstrate as well as I reasonably can, how modern despots like Museveni have used the law, the most unlikely tool of oppression, to oppress the people they rule. I do hope too that I will be able to demonstrate how the same despots use retrogressive laws to manipulate the political landscape to the detriment of their country's democratic development. My working assumption would therefore be that anyone with even the slightest interest in the political affairs of their country will have at some point thought about the possibility of their country's laws being taken advantage of and unjustly used as tools of political oppression.

The only people who refuse to even think about it are those who benefit from the practice of using the law as a tool of political oppression. I am most definitely not one of those people. At the beginning of this book, I promised to be critical; even harsh if need be, in my assessment of how modern despots like Museveni have undermined the democratic evolution of the countries they rule over. That intention remains undiminished in this Chapter.

But first! I think it would be serious intellectual dishonesty, {a crime that I am often quick to despise} if I didn't expressly admit here and now that being away from *"the scene of crime"* has also meant that some of the issues {not all} discussed herein, are based on media reports from Uganda's and other international media houses.

You should however be reassured that all reasonable steps have been taken to ensure that most, if not all of the issues and reports discussed herein are also ones whose factual contents have not been openly contested in any public forum by the parties concerned. I do hope too that at the end of this conversation, a case for fundamental legal and administrative reforms in some key sectors that affect the development of democracy in many countries will have become apparent from a review of some Uganda-centric cases that I shall randomly tackle hereunder.

But before we get to that, allow me, if you will, share one more little story with you before we get to the crux of the matter under this Chapter. Its relevance to this Chapter will be revealed at the end of the story. Sometime back in 2003, news broke of the discovery of the body of the late Shabhan Nkutu {RIP}. Mr. Nkutu, a key figure in Ugandan politics, had disappeared under mysterious circumstances in the 1970's during Idi Amin's reign of terror.

At the time of his disappearance, and the aftermath thereof, there appeared to be little doubt within Mr. Nkutu's inner family circle that he had indeed fallen victim to Idi Amin's notorious murder squad. But of course, none of them could dare come out openly to point the finger of blame at Idi Amin or anyone close to him at the time.

Portrait of a Despot

In those days, that would probably have amounted to an outright invitation to Amin's murder squad to come and silence you; probably forever! When Nkutu's remains were finally found, thanks to someone who *"was in the know"* at the time of his disappearance, it made news in Uganda and to some extent around the world.

In the United Kingdom for example, a country that received the bulk of Asians Idi Amin had expelled in the early 1970's, anything to do with Idi Amin makes news.

So when news of the discovery of Mr. Nkutu's body broke, media houses in the UK went on the lookout for anyone who could comment on Ugandan political issues.

And that is how I, in my capacity as Secretary General of the UK branch of the *Reform Agenda* at the time got a call from *Black Entertainment Network* {BEN} asking for an interview on the subject of Mr. Nkutu's death; the discovery of his remains; and the Amin years in general. I obliged. The reason I have brought you through this little story is simply to bring your attention to what I thought then, and now, about modern despots like Uganda's Yoweri Museveni. Towards the end of the interview at BEN TV's studio near Great Portland Street in London, my interviewer Charles asked me if, as popular perception has it, Museveni was indeed fundamentally different from Idi Amin. My answer was, without a blink of an eye, an emphatic yes! Of course he was, I said. But my interviewer could never have been prepared for the reason I was about to give.

Museveni is merely *"...a more sophisticated version of Idi Amin"*, I said. The only difference, I submitted, was that Museveni is fundamentally more insidious and by necessary implication, therefore more dangerous to Uganda's future stability than Idi Amin ever was. In that split second, I had also remembered one of Martin Luther's famous statements in which he said, *"...the most dangerous object one can meet* on earth is not a python, lion or leopard but an educated man with no character". Bless him!

I think Martin Luther's words are the most fitting description of the modern despots who roam our planet today. Uganda's Yoweri Kaguta Museveni inclusive of course! *"I am like a Chameleon",* Museveni proudly describes himself. A man with no permanent character! He is scientific and meticulous in choosing illusionary *"costumes"* to suit every political gimmick or deceit that he deploys!

Not bad at all if you are in theatrical entertainment as opposed to the serious business of leading a country!

On a more serious note though, when Uganda's Museveni said he was like a chameleon, I think he had also acknowledged, be it inadvertently, that modern despots like him share certain illusionary abilities with the chameleon. So politically speaking, it was nothing short of a total confession. A confession to the world that as a politician, he too was a master at dishing out political illusions dressed in democratic colours. He had confessed too, that like his fellow modern despots, he also lacks that crucial *"must-have"* commodity that any good leader must to have. A set of values and principles that guide his actions!

In fact, he had also effectively declared that when it suits him, he can be anything and everything to absolutely anyone. That, if need be, he can shamelessly lie through his teeth and make promises that he has absolutely no intention of keeping; if by so doing, it will help enhance his stranglehold on to power. A *true trait* of a modern despot indeed!

And true to his lack of character, despite the fact that he had made a firm manifesto commitment to Ugandans during the 2001 presidential election campaigns that the 2001–2006 term of office would be his last, he surprised many when he turned around and masterminded the amendment of the constitution to allow himself indefinite eligibility to contest for the presidency of Uganda.

While that was an abominable act of political dishonesty in itself, the manner in which it was done easily surpasses that abomination by a *"country mile"* as the English would say. It was also one of the most shameful events in the history of Uganda's Legislature; a subject to which we shall return later as we look at the demise of institutions of State.

So where Idi Amin did his dirty political bidding crudely without a care in the world, contemporary global despots like Museveni are more insidious; worried about the impact of their actions on public opinion. And they have to worry about public opinion because more often than not, they will have come to power through illegitimate and unconstitutional means. Therefore winning both local and international support becomes a must for them.

What that also says to me is that while modern despots cannot afford to ignore public opinion in this enlightened world that they find themselves in, they also, at the same time, seem to be *ambilically* bonded to their ancient despotic calling to unilateralism. That may in fact explain their often unpredictable behavioural patterns.

Going back to the comparison between Idi Amin {the ancient despot} and Museveni {the modern despot} for example, where Idi Amin had no trouble issuing *"illegal orders"*, {as retired Ugandan Civil Servant Mzee Charles Abola once told me} Museveni will always try to cover all his ill intentions and actions in legality.

Like the great predatory Cheetah in Kenya's *Masai Mara* National Park, modern despots stealthily use the law to suffocate life out of their political opponents. You only have to look at the avalanche of criminal charges {to be discussed later} that Uganda's main opposition leader Dr. Kizza Besigye faced and you will know what I am talking about.

Charles Ochen Okwir

Now let's move on to a more detailed examination of how modern despots use the *law as a tool of political oppression.* For your contextual understanding, it might help to cast your mind back to the discussion we had earlier about the circumstances that led Museveni to pick up arms to fight the government of the day after the controversial 1980 general elections.

After seizing State power, Museveni's usurping force invariably abolished the constitution and the Legislature. It then fused the powers of the Executive and the Legislative into one. The net effect of Museveni's military conquest was then that the powers of the *"elected"* Executive were taken over by force of arms and vested in the new military leadership. The rule of law, as recognised by all civilised nations, was set aside and replaced by rule by decree or edict.

In Uganda's case, it was totally irrelevant that the formal restriction of political party activities by Museveni's new *National Resistance Council* {NRC} came much later; around 1989. The actual beginning of the regime's legal oppression of political dissent can and should be traced back to *Legal Notice No. 1 of 1986;* a *Presidential Decree* which came into force immediately Museveni overthrew the government of the day.

For the regime's fanatic apologists at the time, the justification for legally restricting political party activities was that they promoted tribalism and sectarianism. Both of which, they argued, were responsible for Uganda's past spells of political instability.

So publically, they reasoned that political parties needed to be *"tamed"* or forced by law into a period of involuntary hibernation to give *"national stability"* priority. What that also meant was that the full enjoyment of democratic rights would be put on hold; a very slippery and dangerous development in my view. Because once a leader gets used to doing things without being held accountable for his actions, then it would be very difficult for him to do otherwise at a later stage.

What we also know for sure is that modern despots are very good at coming up with noble excuses under which they pursue their ignoble political intentions. So I think the restriction of political party activities should be judged with that in mind. The other thing of course is that their inherent political insecurity always gives one the feeling that they may not be telling the truth. And it's that insecurity that forces them to secure themselves behind the mighty force of law.

But as soon as the law is passed, everything changes. There will be no more *noble* talk that political party activities were banned "*...to give national stability priority over the full enjoyment of democratic rights*". Now, the new justification for legally oppressing their political opponents will simply be: It is *"against the law"*, it is *"illegal"*, it is *"unconstitutional"*, and so forth. It's as if they had absolutely nothing to do with the Bill that gave birth to the law that created the illegalities they are now citing and yet we all know that the Bill was essentially the regime's own policy position.

In the case of Museveni's *Legal Notice No. 1 of 1986*, a key defector from the regime later spilt the beans to me and confessed that the forcing of political parties into involuntary hibernation was really never about giving priority to national political stability. There was a more sinister reason for it. It was meant to give sufficient time to Museveni's regime to disenfranchise, dismantle, and ultimately wrestle all political power from the *"regions"* of Uganda that the regime felt had *"dominated power for too long"*.

Such ill intentioned political manoeuvres are not new to despotic politics. From Tunisia to Zimbabwe; from the Baltic states, to Latin America; and from Sri Lanka to Iraq and

Nigeria, they are all over. Perhaps even in your own country, wherever that may be.

In Uganda, those who worship the enjoyment of full democratic rights of course maintained with commensurate passion that there can be no justification whatsoever, even momentarily, for legally curbing the enjoyment of democratic rights and freedoms.

On the whole however, it has to be conceded that the mood of the nation at the time seemed to suggest that the *"dodgy"* justification for restricting political party activities had found favour in most parts of the country. That said, I also think that to get a fair appreciation of the mood of the nation at the time, one must take into account the aggressive propaganda campaign that Museveni had launched against political parties.

In the end, painfully perhaps, some political parties concluded that they had no option but to give the regime the benefit of the doubt. No more than. What did not change however, and could never be factually changed, was that *Legal Notice No. 1 of 1986* had effectively outlawed all multi-party political activities in Uganda.

The oldest political parties that existed before 1986 were however spared total annihilation and allowed to exist. Their *"existence"* was only in name though; as they were totally confined to their party headquarters. Like wet birds, they were trapped in their nests without a single dry feather to spread and fly across the country to deliver their messages. The politically induced torrential legal downpour called *Legal Notice No. 1 of 1986*, a downpour of almost *tsunamic* proportions, just wouldn't let them.

Political parties were therefore left with only their party flags flying over their headquarters in what, for me, amounted to no more than a symbolic gesture of defiance. They were also faced with clear and stark choices. To either remain principled, stay put and ride out the storm; or, as some of their activists did, jump ship and join the devil himself in order to earn a buck and put food on the family's dinner table. Eating became the name of the game.

And that *"eating"* culture, for many elites and politicians in Uganda, has sadly come to define what life and politics means to them. Eating, eating and eating; until, as former British High Commissioner to Kenya Sir Edward Clay once put it, *"...they vomit on their shoes"*. How pathetic! Twenty four gruesome years down the road, the effects of *Legal Notice No. 1 of 1986*, plus a host of other draconian laws, have left the old traditional political parties like UPC {which my father still worships to-date} and DP struggling to remain relevant to both the people and politics of Uganda.

To modern despots, being men who have a pathological fear of multi-party democracy, the *"death"* of political parties was music to their ears. For Museveni in particular, it was simply too good to be true. And frankly, it was probably more than he had bargained for.

But being the political *Chameleon* and unconscionable political opportunist that he is, he has happily taken the *"gift of death"* without a grimace of remorse on his face. And that my friends, is yet another typical characteristic that you are likely to find in both old and modern despots; you stand duly warned!

And one of the strangest things, a political reality perhaps, is that it's not only incumbent modern despots who admire their own despotic *traits* and accomplishments. Some in the opposition do too; so they shouldn't escape your watchful eye, because they may be in control of state power tomorrow.

The reason I say that is because in Uganda, as late as September 2007, a prominent opposition politician {whom I shall spare the embarrassment of being identified} appeared to bestow political mastery on modern despots like Museveni. In this chap's view, would you believe it, Museveni should be given credit "*...for managing to keep opposition political parties at bay for over twenty years*". Prior to all this, it will be recalled that the victorious guerrilla war leader Y.K. Museveni had famously assured the country and the world on the steps of the Ugandan Parliament that theirs {meaning the so-called *"revolution"* of 1986 of course} was not "*...a mere change of guard*" but "*...a fundamental change*".

A fundamental change that would lead to comprehensive processes of reform {led by Museveni the more educated leader} designed to nurse the politically traumatised country towards full democratic governance, constitutionalism, and observance of human rights and the rule of law.

There is no doubt in my mind that that simple statement, coming when it did, at that defining moment, must have stimulated enthusiasm, optimism, and hope in large parts of Uganda and the world. And who could blame them? After all, it's no secret that most of Museveni's predecessors, or their close associates at least, were not exactly *angels*.

But the *fundamental* reform processes that had been promised were only symbolic in the end. In fact, some analysts have since argued that both Ugandans and the international community should have known better. That history should have taught then that men of Museveni's demeanour often degenerate into vicious despots.

So the first attempt at these reforms really only came with the institution of a *Constitutional Review Commission* that was chaired by the then High Court Judge {now Chief Justice of Uganda} His Lordship Benjamin Odoki. That process resulted in the promulgation of the 1995 constitution of the Republic

Uganda. The 1995 constitution was supposed to be, and is still supposed to be the supreme law of the land.

And I use the phrase *"supposed to be"* very advisedly in that context because the reality tells its own story; a very different story in fact. But if it is accepted that the 1995 constitution is the supreme law of the land, then its impact on the politics of Uganda must be a subject of great interest to anyone attempting to discuss the use of *law as a tool of political oppression*. In this book, I therefore find that I have no option but to pay particular heed to the 1995 constitution.

Under article 263 of that constitution, Museveni's *Movement* system of governance was supposed to be a *"Transitional"*. Transitional in the sense that it was supposed to be temporary arrangement; not a permanent feature of Ugandan politics! Its purpose, on paper, was to govern temporarily while preparing the country for an eventual return to multi-party politics. But don't they all start like that?

In the end, the so-called *"transitional arrangement"* turned out to be a deceitful fallacy that had been glorified in the legal draftsman's language. The final exposure of that deceit then came when opposition parties challenged the constitutionality of Museveni's *"individual merit"* brand of democracy in the *Constitutional Court*. In a sentence, the *Constitutional Court* found that Museveni's *"individual merit"* system was in fact a *"One Party"* State system in all but name. For that reason, it was declared unconstitutional.

In fact, I can now see why some people thought that history should have taught Ugandans and the international community better. Just look at what happened in Guinea several years after Museveni's *Transitional Arrangement* promise. When Capt. Moussa Dadis Camara seized power in December 2008 after the death of long serving despot Lasana Conte, he promised the people of Guinea that his job was *"merely to run the transition to democracy"*. That word *"transition"* again! The rest as they say is now history.

Capt. Camara not only abandoned his promise, he also refused to rule himself out of any future presidential election. Not only that. He went even further and clamped down hard on political dissent; a trend that sadly climaxed with the September 2009 cold blooded massacre of nearly 100 protesters. That massacre opened the eyes of the world and drew attention to Guinea.

In Uganda's case, while the *Constitutional Court's* ruling may not have had the same impact as the killing of 100 protesters in Guinea, it certainly proved to the unrealistic optimists that there was a different, hidden, and in fact sinister agenda behind Museveni's move to use the law to restrict political party activities.

It was an agenda that was completely different from the one officially stated by Museveni's regime. In fact, it may even vindicate the suggestion that the real reason for the regime's legal restriction of political party activities was to buy enough time to *"...wrestle all political power from the regions of Uganda that the regime felt had dominated power for far too long"*.

What happened subsequently may actually lend considerable weight to that conspiracy theory. The same *Movement* system that was supposed to be a *transitional arrangement* under article 263 was by operation of article 269 of the same Constitution entrenched as a permanent feature of Ugandan politics.

A feature that would not be changed until the *"people of Uganda"* {a euphemism for Western donors}emphatically said so in a referendum. And therein lay the first contradiction that comes almost *"as standard"* in cases where the law is used to do what is not in form with its *"genetic make-up"*. In other words, when it's used by modern despots to deliver *injustice* in place of *justice*!

In this great Ugandan legal quagmire, the supreme law of the land became effectively inconsistent with itself. For me, that perfectly captures the great injustice that was Museveni's *Movement* system of governance. Put simply, political parties could not exist and function in any manner that interfered with the operation of the *Movement* system. Only this time, the restriction was not imposed by *Legal Notice No. 1 of 1986* but by the constitution; the supreme law of the land itself.

So clearly, this was *not* a system that was designed to allow for even the remotest semblance of multi-party politics. And the reason is quite simple. In any multi-party democracy, a conducive and enabling environment will have been created [deliberately] and given the full backing of the law. That would then enable democratic principles to fully entrench themselves into the psyche of the nation through what political theorists might describe as an evolutionary process.

No armed revolution, or any other type of revolution for that matter, however well intentioned, can in my view be *"the"* perfect substitute for such an evolutionary process. That is of course, not the same thing as saying a popular people's revolution against a despot can never be justified; it can. It's just that it should and must be the very last resort when everything else has failed.

Going back to the so-called *"evolutionary process"*, it's clear that for it to be enabled, all political protagonists must have the legal right and opportunity to establish effective mechanisms and structures that enable them to freely get their messages across the country without undue hindrance from an incumbent's security operatives.

The trouble however is that in most countries that are ruled by modern despots, this most important characteristic of modern democracy is also one that is severely compromised by legal and bureaucratic obstacles. In the end, opposition activists will have been denied the opportunity to freely express themselves on the viability of their alternative programmes for government.

It amounts to nothing less than an overt affront to freedom of expression; the very thing that lies at the heart of, and in fact defines a free and democratic society. *"...I totally detest what you say, but I will defend to death your inherent right to say it"*. That is the immortal proclamation of liberty from times gone by. Several freedom fighters have sacrificed their lives in defence of this principle. To them, and I hope to you too, the freedom to speak one's mind is not only a vital aspect of individual liberty but it also sits at the helm of the common quest for truth and vitality in any society. For the libertarians of the contemporary political world, freedom of expression also entails the right of society to hear and to be heard. These are a rare breed of people. They are unlike your typical modern despot. They are noble and courageous people who have great faith in their intellect. And because of that, they also despise censorship in all its forms.

In fact to them, the other reason for the existence of the principle of freedom of expression in democratic societies is to emphatically discourage the State and its coercive apparatus from *"assuming total custodianship of the public mind"*; mark those words carefully! And the reason I say that is because I firmly believe that not many leaders around the world, let alone the modern despots we are talking about here, are capable of resisting that temptation to assume total custodianship of the public mind. It is simply too sumptuous a prospect.

A close *"Learned Friend"* once offered me some wise counsel as I researched this book. In his view, any discourse that attempts to discuss the laws that seek to protect freedom of expression must look no further than India. Why, I asked? The reason, he said, was that India, by virtue of its one billion plus population, and its entrenched system of multi-party politics, is officially the biggest democracy in the world. So it's bound to have some great lessons, he said.

In my friend's view, the key conflict zone that must never be ignored by analysis is the perception that different people have about the relationship between law and democracy. That while some political analysts and scientists might see *law and democracy* as being mutually exclusive of each other, the more rational stance, he said, must be to view them as being mutually inclusive of each other. Quite philosophical, I thought! But I later found out that his audacious conclusion actually derived its authority from one of the most significant [pro-democracy] judicial pronouncements ever to emanate from the Indian sub-continent.

In that case *{Romesh Thapper Vs The State of Madrus Air [1950] 2 SCC 121 at 126}*, court held that: *"...freedom of speech and of the press lay at the foundation of all democratic organisations, for without free political discussion, no public education so essential for the proper functioning of the process of popular government is possible".*

I am not so naïve as to think that countries that are ruled by modern despots, with great Lawyers among them, may not have known this. They probably did. But despite their knowledge of this significant pro-democracy piece of Asian jurisprudence, the reality is that freedom to express and hear politically divergent views in some of these countries is still virtually unheard of.

For example, the poor Ugandan electorate were by law only allowed to consume *Movement Views* espoused by *Movement Leaders*. At the time, infraction of this most despotic law would have certainly earned the perpetrator an audience with the regime's nocturnal merchants of torture and death. The difference, as I said, is that while such a *"crime"* would in the eyes of an ancient despot warrant summary execution for the accused, to the modern despot, a *"James Bond"* of sorts, it would be the perfect legal *"Licence to Kill"* off the political parties that posed the most threat to his stranglehold on power.

And it's that sort of political cowardice that forced Museveni's *Movement* regime to enact *The Movement Act 1997*. By both its theoretical and practical operation, this law effectively conscripted all Ugandans to belong to Museveni's *Movement;* a *Movement* which, as the *Constitutional Court* found, was actually a *One Party State* system and therefore unconstitutional!

But the *Movement* leaders didn't seem to see, or at least pretended not to have seen the legal mess they had created. A classic case of the proverbial Ostrich burying its head in the sand! In their minds, I suspect, they must have been wallowing in the delusional comfort that because they avoided calling the *Movement* a *"party"*, they had somehow found a loophole in the constitution to exploit.

Even Members of Parliament from opposition parties were considered [by law] to be subscribers to Museveni's *Movement* party. How then, one might ask, will a Legislature with no official opposition be able to perform its function of checking Executive excesses? It's simply a no-brainer! The *Movement* was never meant to be a democratic system of governance. It was a pseudo-democratic vehicle through which modern despots like Museveni secure their desire to rule indefinitely.

The other question that I would like to raise here about Museveni's *legal conscription business* is this: If it is accepted, as it ought to be, that a successful and democratic State is supposed to have a vibrant civil society, then can

Uganda be said to be *"a successful democratic State"* when the *Movement Act* actually conscripted all Ugandans to belong to Museveni's *Movement*? The propensity to cripple the effectiveness of civil society organisations is one of the enduring traits of the modern despot that democrats should constantly look out for.

But the goodwill of the world was withering fast. Pressure, especially from Western donor countries, played a great role in bringing about this change. Very soon, Museveni's regime realised that both local and international goodwill towards his autocratic *Movement* system was on the verge of collapse. So he was forced to change. That is how multi-party politics was painfully re-introduced to Uganda.

In the end, Museveni had to transform his beloved *no party Movement* in order to fit into the new political dispensation. With that, a new party called the *National Resistance Movement "Organisation"* {NRM-O} was born. Shamelessly however, the *brand new* NRM-O inherited all the structures of the defunct State funded *Movement* system of governance.

I am sure you can already see where this is heading. If you can't, then let me tell you. Even under the new multi-party dispensation, Museveni's propensity to treat his opponents unfairly continued. As an unconscionable modern despot, it really didn't matter to Museveni that the opposition parties were already struggling to survive in Uganda's turbulent political waters. So while the opposition parties were still struggling to find their feet in the new dispensation, Museveni's *"new"* NRM-O already had structures across the entire country.

Again, for many democrats, this would of course be seen for what it really is; an astonishing display of political cowardice. But political cowardice is not a phrase that modern despots recognise. As far as they are concerned, in the *"life and death"* business that is the pursuit of and maintenance of State power, cowardice, even for most of them as serving

Military Generals, is a crime that has become a tolerated evil. why, in their view perhaps, should "mere" civilians find political cowardice so utterly objectionable considering all the great rewards that can potentially and do often accrue from tolerating it? And, before you ask, my use of the word "mere" in the last sentence was not because of some freak accident or editorial negligence on my part. Far from it!

Rather, it is because these modern despots, wherever they may be, often have a unique degree of contempt for civilians; never mind that some of them are civilians themselves. Not even Judges survive their contempt; in fact, if anything, they even get the lion's share of it.

In Uganda for example, during one of the most heated sessions of the Judicial Inquiry into the plunder of the *"Global Fund"* money for Aids and TB, one of the prime suspects called to testify was Brigadier Jim Muhwezi. He was the Minister of Health at the time of the alleged plunder. So even if he had nothing to do with the theft of those funds, {and that is very debatable} as the political head, he should have had the dignity to take political responsibility for the mess in his Ministry; and that usually means resigning. But it wasn't to be.

On the contrary, in one of the most grotesque displays of the sort of arrogance I alluded to at the beginning of this book, Brigadier Muhwezi asked the presiding Judge His Lordship Justice James Ogola, Uganda's Principal Judge no less, where he was when they, the *"patriotic"* sons of Uganda were fighting to *"liberate"* Uganda from tyranny.

But Brigadier Muhwezi's antics were not new to Ugandans. They were the usual taunts that Ugandans had become accustomed to as Museveni's bush war *heroes* took turns to accuse Ugandan civilians of *hiding under the bed* as they fought in the jungles of *Luwero Triangle* to liberate the country. Somehow, like so many so-called *liberators* turned despots around the world, they feel that for their sacrifices, they should have a *carte blanche* to do as they please. The brutal impunity of ZANU-PF operatives in Zimbabwe; and the widespread cases of corruption in Angola and within South Africa's ruling ANC government for example, may all be partly attributable to this type of attitude.

In fact, just to give you a clear indication of the magnitude of the problem {of detachment from morality and reality}we are talking about here, Uganda's Museveni once shocked the world when he came out, for the first time, and publicly expressed *"surprise"* that there was corruption in his NRM government. To put it into its proper context, perhaps I should add that Museveni's reaction in this case was prompted by just one out of hundreds of corruption scandals that his government had been accused of or involved in over a twenty year period. Amazing isn't it?

Anyway, let's get back to a more detailed discussion about the legal anomaly that *The Movement Act 1997* represented in real terms. One classic example of how Museveni's despotic NRM regime used the *law as a tool of political oppression* and manipulation was captured in *Section 32* of *The Movement Act 1997*.

This Section enabled the *Movement* dominated Parliament to legally misappropriate funds from the treasury for use in its partisan political activities. The *"structures of political injustice"*, in particular the *Movement Secretariat* that had been set up by regime, acted as the lead agency in the disbursement of these ill-gotten public funds.

And when I say *"Movement dominated Parliament"*, it's not because I think the *Movement* democratically won more seats in Parliament; not at all! As I said earlier, it's because *The Movement Act 1997* legally conscripted all Ugandans to belong to Museveni's *Movement*. So technically, it had a 100% majority in Parliament.

But there was also a very sad irony in all this. The regime's deceit was often laid bare for all to see by the *Movement* leaders themselves. On many occasions, they inadvertently let their dishonesty guards loose and referred to all MPs who disagreed with the *Movement* system as members of the *opposition*. *"Crime is in the end smarter than the criminal"*.

Those were the most instructive words that ever graced the English lips of Professor Malcom Davis who taught me Criminal Justice at law school. In other words, what the good old Professor was saying was that crime in the end always has the last laugh! I think there can be no better illustration of that principle than the inadvertent confession of the *Movement* leaders that I just referred to above.

It tells us that deep down the architects of the *Movement Act* actually knew that it would be practically impossible to legislate against a principled man's deep conscience. So their decision to use the law was merely a recruitment tactic that they hoped would coerce as many faint hearted people as possible to join Museveni's *Movement*.

If you thought that was the absolute limit of political hypocrisy and manipulation, then think again. The modern despot leaves very little to chance. There is a lot more to come as legal oppression of a slightly different kind takes shape; one that is wrought with gross unfairness against the opposing political parties! As I said, the *Movement Act* already allowed Museveni's partisan *Movement* to dip its dirty hands into the national coffers at will. Secondly, the *Act* also allowed the same *Movement* to receive grants and donations from within and outside the country.

On the other hand, not only were the other political parties denied access to public funds, their capacity to privately raise funds had also been severely restricted; partly because they were barred by law from organising themselves and mobilising beyond their symbolic headquarters in the Capital

City Kampala; trapped like *"wet birds"* in a torrential legal downpour as you recall me saying. It is therefore easy to see that when it came to political mobilisation in a heavily commercialised political environment like the Ugandan one, there would be no contest between Museveni's ruling *Movement* party and the penniless opposition parties. There surely can't be any arguments there; I hope. So let's move on and see what else we can find in the contemporary despot's legal arsenal of political oppression.

The Political Parties & Organisations Act 2002

It's the turn of another law from your typical modern despot's legal arsenal of political oppression. *The Political Parties & Organisations Act 2002 {PPOA 2002}* was enacted by the Museveni regime ostensibly to deal with and regulate the operation of political parties and organisations.

Under *Section 14* of the *"new" Political Parties and Organisations Act,* neither the old political parties {like DP, UPC and CP} nor the new political pressure groups like *The Reform Agenda* that had germinated from the carcass of the *Elect Kizza Besigye Task Force* of 2001 were allowed to freely solicit for grants and donations to fund their political activities. So, as far as the funding of opposition political parties was concerned, there was really nothing new introduced by the *PPOA 2002*. It was simply *"business as usual".* Their growth stifled; and their very survival hanging precariously in the balance.

So the question still remains: How can any other political party, or political pressure group for that matter, seek to influence public opinion and favourably compete against the well funded NRM political machine? A ruthless politico-military machine that operates unhindered in one of the most corrupt countries in the world; a country where money {not ideas} not only plays a significant role, but it is the ultimate factor that determines whether an election is lost or won.

All the while, the incumbent's party will of course be enjoying unfettered access to public funds to fund its partisan political activities. This is precisely the sort of scenario that your typical modern despot, always masquerading as a democrat, worships and fights to maintain. Besides the mere fact of survival, in Uganda, something even more basic was at stake for opposition parties.

In a strict legal sense, even their right to legally exist was at best, extremely uncertain. And the simple reason for that uncertainty was that although the *Constitutional Court* had declared in its ruling in *Constitutional Petition No. 5 of 2002* that *Sections* 18 and 19 of the *PPOA 2002* were unconstitutional and therefore null and void, it also made no specific pronouncement about the legal requirement under the same *PPOA 2002* for all political parties to register afresh in order to enjoy the political freedoms ushered in by the nullification of *Sections* 18 and 19 of the *PPOA 2002*.

I am sure you can see the dilemma for political parties here. But first, I think it is absolutely imperative that you get a good contextual understanding of this whole mess. And to do that may call for a brief journey back in time to enable us see what the nullified *Sections* 18 and 19 of the *PPOA 2002* had originally provided for. So put your legal lenses on, concentrate, and you will see how modern despots use the law to shamelessly manipulate the political landscape in their favour. The nullified *Section* 18{1} provided thus:

"...Notwithstanding anything in this Act, during the period when the Movement political system is in force, political activities may continue except that no political party or organisation shall:- {a}sponsor or offer a platform to or in any way campaign for or against a candidate in any Presidential or Parliamentary election or any other election organised by the Electoral Commission; {b}use a symbol, slogan, colour or name identifying any political party or organisation for the purpose of campaigning for or against

any candidate in any election referred to in paragraph {a}; {c}open offices below the national level; {d}hold public meetings, except for national conferences, executive committee meetings, seminars and conferences held at national level and the meetings referred to in sub-sections {7}and {8} of Section 10 of this Act".

Of course, it goes without saying that to properly understand this legal minefield, one would also have to look at *Sub-Sections* {7}and {8}of *Section* 10 in order to see the sort of meetings that General Museveni was comfortable with. But let's get *Section* 19 of the *PPOA 2002* out of the way first. It provided that:

"...Subject to clause {2} of article 73 of the Constitution, during the period when the Movement political system is in force and until another political system is adopted in accordance with the Constitution, no organisation subscribing to any other political system shall carry on any activity that may interfere with the operation of the Movement political system".

Now, before we go any further, and perhaps just to drive home the absurdity of this law, as promised, let us see the sort of meetings that the all powerful *"revolutionary"* General Yoweri Kaguta Museveni allowed under *Sub-Sections* {7}and {8} of *Section* 10 of the *PPOA 2002*. It would however be helpful to bear in mind that these sub-sections are themselves still subject to other provisions of this entire Act which may have further restrictions of their own. So here we go then!

Under *Sub-Section* {7}, *"...the founding members of a political party or organisation may hold meetings at national level for the purpose of forming a political party or organisation"*. Remember the term *"national level"* that we made reference to at the beginning? Well, if like me, you think you have already smelt a rat, then wait and see what the more *interesting* but utterly pathetic *Sub-Section* {8} has to say. It provides that:

"...After the issue of the certificate of registration to a political party or organisation under section 7 of this Act, the political party or organisation may, within one month after the issue to it of the certificate of registration, hold only one meeting in each district to elect members to the national conference for the purpose of electing its first members of the executive committee; and after the election of the members at the district, any structures established for the purpose of that election shall cease to exist".

Bingo! Clearly, under *Sub-Section* {7}, meetings were only allowed at *"national level"* which as I said, means within the symbolic party headquarters in the Capital City Kampala. Anything beyond that would contravene the law.

Secondly, under *Sub-Section* {8}, one couldn't have failed to notice that whereas Museveni's *Movement* government [by using the word *"may"*] gave political parties and organisations registered under *Section* 7 the discretion to hold one meeting in each district to elect members to their *National Delegates Conference*, it also made it mandatory that any such structures formed for those purposes would cease to exist immediately upon the conclusion of those elections.

In other words, the conclusion of such district elections were in fact, rather absurdly, the *self-destruct* trigger for the party's district structures; structures that are crucially important for any political party to get its *"messages across"* the country. Exactly as the Judges in the Indian case that we saw earlier *{Romesh Vs Thapper}* counselled.

I am sure you can now see how laws that are enacted with ill intentions can severely cripple the entrenchment of democracy in countries ruled by modern despots. Now let's go back and do a further {but brief} analysis of Section 18{1} of the PPOA 2002 before we move on to Section 19 of the same Act to see even more evidence of political oppression using the law.

And to do *justice* to the *injustice* contained in Section 18{1}, I think it would be crucial for us to trace its origins as far back as possible. As far as I can reasonably discern, Section 18{1} of the PPOA 2002 was a direct consequence of an age-old principle of law that requires a government to enact a Municipal Act of Parliament to bring some provisions of the country's constitution into force. The same applies to international treaties and conventions too. In the case of Section 18{1} of the PPOA 2002 for example, the provisions of Article 269 of the Constitution of Uganda 1995 that dealt with the regulation of political parties at the time are quite instructive. It provided that:

"...on the commencement of this Constitution and until Parliament makes laws regulating the activities of political organisations in accordance with article 73 of this Constitution, political activities may continue except; {a} opening and operating branch offices; {b} holding delegates conferences; {c} holding public rallies; {d} sponsoring or offering a platform to or in any way campaigning for or against a candidate for any public elections; {e} carrying on any activities that may interfere with the Movement political system for the time being in force".

ust for emphasis, and perhaps to simplify the legal draftsman's language a bit, I think it is important to understand that if the all important word *"except"* in Article 269 is read, as it must, together with everything contained in clauses {a} to {e} of the same article, then you will find that Jeverything contained in clauses {a} to {e} above were in fact expressly forbidden by law. So to appreciate the full impact of that law, I suggest you take a quick glance at clauses [a] to [c] of Article 269 again.

Secondly, I am pretty sure you noticed the striking similarities between wording of *Sections* 18 & 19 of the *PPOA 2002* and the wording of the old *Article 269* of the Constitution. If you didn't, then look at them again.

You will find that the net effect of both *Section* 18{1} and *Section* 19 of the *PPOA 2002* was merely to bring into effect the restrictions on political party activities that had been prescribed by *Article 269* of the Constitution.

Indeed, ever since *Sections* 18 and 19 of the *PPOA 2002* came into force, a good number of eagle-eyed political analysts have argued that the two *Sections* actually re-introduced the crippling effects of *Article 269 "through the back door"*. I am not sure I can argue with that. The stakes were clearly high enough to justify such emotive political clichés as re-introduction *through the back door.*

In fact, before the eventual nullification of *Sections* 18 & 19 of the *PPOA 2002* by the *Constitutional Court*, a dangerous consensus was steadily building within opposition circles that if everything constitutional failed, then a different level of political activism that would boarder on outright militancy would be required to effectively challenge the crippling effects of those laws.

Unfortunately, more than two decades of constant threats of a possible return to the bush by Museveni also ensured that not even the most aggrieved individuals and political entities in Uganda could gather the courage to take to the streets to protest against the use of *law as a tool of political oppression.*

So clearly, the threat of violence, chaos and or doom from modern despots often delivers the desired result for them. The objective of such threats is to force you to consider your personal safety and self preservation first.

Portrait of a Despot

The modern despot knows that self preservation is an instinctive human reaction. So to take full advantage of it, he will issue threats even when he actually intends no harm. And to maintain the advantage, he will never let you know whether he means business or not.

So it may be unfair to blame people who choose the path of self preservation. Their tragic history will have taught them that the consequences of disregarding a despot's threats could be loss of innocent lives at the hands of trigger happy security operatives. If they are lucky enough to survive the State's bullets, then they would certainly get a free and unforgettable *"blind-date"* with the regime's ghastly creatures of torture; crocodiles and snakes among them!

The very lucky ones might *only* end up in unlawful custody for days on end. In Uganda, that would mean being locked up in dark, dingy, and un-gazetted torture chambers that are, with sadistic irony, often referred to as *"Safe Houses"* by Museveni's regime. On the whole, trial in accordance with the law in a modern despot's country is sometimes a very cruel lottery.

In most cases, the decision to charge or release a political suspect will be left to the regime's overzealous cadres who will have been deployed by the modern despot within State institutions like the *Directorate of Public Prosecutions*. And that is precisely why modern despots across the globe can never really do away with nepotism; how can they? To do otherwise would leave them perilously exposed to the due process of law; and yet that is something they inherently distrust.

And the overzealous cadres often make no attempt to disassociate their despotic boss from their illegal individual actions. In fact, whenever they are challenged about their illegal actions, their standard response will always be that they acted on *"orders from above"*. Well, who can blame them? After all, it is a well established fact that the service of a modern despot's overbearing ultra ego naturally eats away at the servant's own self esteem.

So when they shout *"orders from above"*, it may actually be the only time they feel truly connected to the *"high and mighty"* in the land. What that also suggests to me is that the other good way of determining whether or not you have a modern despot on your hands may be to study the self esteem of those who serve at the pleasure of the Head of State. Just a wild thought!

But if that is what could happen to individual political suspects, then how about the fate of offending political institutions or parties? How would they come off under such laws and despotic practices? Naturally, the answer cannot be significantly different. Not if we are talking about the ways of a typical modern despot; wherever he may be on God's earth!

In Uganda, if a *stubborn* political party tries to challenge the status quo through civil disobedience for example, then *Section* 20{1} of the *PPOA 2002* gives General Museveni a very *"big stick"* with which to smash such a party off the political landscape. And I am not dramatising anything here; far from it! It is pretty serious.

The law {as in *Section* 20{1} of the *PPOA 2002*}says the Registrar General *"...may apply to the High Court for an order winding up the political party or organisation"* if it commits any offence under the *PPOA 2002.* It's literally as simple as that; and that party would be history. As I said, that entire process could be over in the blink of an eye if the Registrar General, like many others strategically positioned within the state system, also happens to be a *Movement* cadre acting on *"orders from above"*.

But even without the intervention of the Registrar General, *Section* 20{2}{b} of the *PPOA 2002* still provides that conviction for *"...any offence under this Act more than three times"* means that such a political organisation shall automatically *"...cease to exist and the High Court shall, on application by the Official Receiver, make such orders as may be just for the disposition of the property, assets, rights and liabilities of the political party or organisation".* End of story!

The other point to note about this *Sub-Section* is this: By saying the High Court *"shall"* on application by the *Official Receiver* make such orders as may be just for the disposition of the property, assets, rights and liabilities of the political party or organisation, the regime actually managed to deprive the Judiciary of any discretion to determine the extent of the punishment to be suffered by the *"offending"* party. It simply left the Judiciary with the discretion to do it in a *"just"* manner. In other words, *kill them, but do so in a manner that will not cause widespread public alarm.*

This is exactly what I meant when I said earlier that modern despots have both the killer instincts of their medieval predecessors and the obligatory regard for public opinion that you find in true democrats. So in a canny way, they somehow manage to position themselves within the precincts of that *"grey area"* beyond which you either become a democrat or a modern despot. In other words, they deceitfully keep themselves *"half in and half out"* of full democratic conduct.

Anyway having tied both the hands and legs of the existing Judges using the law, the regime then set off on a final mission to take full control of the Judiciary by flooding it with its own *"Cadre Judges"*. With that, any independent minded and pro-democracy Judges who might still be left on the Bench will quickly find that they are in the minority with very little room to manoeuvre the wheels of justice through the treacherous terrain established by the despot.

And before I forget, let me tell you something that has just popped into my mind. I think this elaborate and well orchestrated process of legally suppressing peaceful political dissent also brings out one of the most important political lessons that modern despots have failed to learn.

If as President, or Prime Minister, you decide to close all avenues for peaceful political dissent, then by default, you will also have opened alternative avenues for expressing that same political dissent. And these will usually be more dangerous means like civil disobedience, a coup d'état, or even a fully blown armed rebellion. The irony of it is that not only does that threaten national stability but it also threatens [very seriously in fact] the very power that the despot was desperately trying to preserve in the first place.

The other thing that I think is worthy of mention here is this. The very fact that political activists can, and do often find the courage to take difficult decisions to resort to dangerous means of expressing their dissent should be the perfect measure of how dearly they hold their *inherent* democratic rights.

The trouble is that modern despots seem to be inherently incapable of *living in peace* with the enjoyment of those fundamental human rights. It is completely irrelevant to them that these same rights, in most cases, are always enshrined in the constitutions of the same countries they rule. So to tamper with those rights would in my view amount to nothing short of overthrowing the established constitutional order. And that in itself aggravates the despot's crime to such an extent that recourse to any of the dangerous means of expressing political dissent becomes fully justified.

But let's stay with Uganda's *PPOA 2002* for a little longer; if we may. As we saw earlier, *Section* 6{4} thereof introduced a requirement for all political parties to register afresh in order to legally exist. Their *freedom to operate freely* in Uganda was, and still is today as I write, a totally different matter.

In fact, in most countries ruled by modern despots, the right of political parties to operate freely must be the actual battleground in the struggle for democracy. For the record, Section 6{4} of Uganda's *PPOA 2002* simply stated that, *"...subject to Sub-Section 3 of this Section, any existing political party or organisation which fails to file the necessary documents for registration shall legally cease to exist and operate".*

That requirement for registration was not only meant for the newly formed political parties and pressure groups. Even the *"grey-haired"* and almost senile parties like the *Democratic Party* {DP}, the *Uganda People's Congress* {UPC}, and the *Conservative Party* {CP} were required to apply for re-registration. In that respect therefore, if ever there were any *"fundamental changes"* ushered into Uganda by Museveni & Co, then this was certainly one of them. And we all know that *change*, especially among the elderly, {read DP, UPC, CP etc} causes considerable anxiety.

So not surprisingly, there was resistance; be it half heartedly! With perfectly understandable rage, the greying men and women in these old parties must have asked: *"How can these young pretenders even dare ask us to register again"?*

And it's not difficult to imagine that to these old folks, it must have felt like being ordered by a disrespectful political toddler to go and wash your hands when the toddler himself has mud and blood all over his fingers. After all, the offending political toddler in the form of the NRM government had acquired his right to exist through the barrel of the gun and not through legal registration.

Charles Ochen Okwir

When the time finally came, and as testimony to their deeply held values, the resistance put up by the old parties against the legal requirement to re-register was a civilised affair by any standards. In fact, you may even say it was as dignified as the political grandpas and grandmas themselves; men and women who, unlike Museveni, decided to take their grievances to the courts of law.

Unfortunately, the court's judgement in *Miscellaneous Application No. 6 of 2003* created even more confusion among politicians on either side. It wasn't at all clear whether the *Constitutional Court* had simply suspended the six months statutory deadline for registration or whether it had actually suspended the requirement for registration itself.

So predictably, the belligerents on either side interpreted the judgement in ways that they thought would best serve their respective political interests. That meant that while Museveni's regime argued that the *Constitutional Court* only suspended the six months statutory deadline for registration, the opposition parties {perhaps sensing some freedom in the distance} maintained that the actual requirement for registration had been suspended.

There was now a fresh political and legal standoff between the opposing protagonists. A standoff which I think was totally unnecessary. Unnecessary because if any of them had had the composure to expunge their respective political interests from their minds, they would have found that in fact, the *Constitutional Court* had reserved judgement on that matter because the Petitioners had not specifically moved it to pronounce itself on the constitutionality of the actual requirement for registration. But politics being what it is, sometimes does not accord those in the heat of it the luxury of rational thinking that disinterested analysts take for granted. So the debate raged on.

But I think the correct interpretation should have been that the requirement for re-registration under Section 6{4} still stood. After all, the court's suspension of the six months statutory deadline *per se* couldn't have caused the demise of the actual requirement for re-registration at the same time. In addition, a close look at the preamble of the *PPOA 2002* {being a law that was passed to regulate the existence and operation of political parties} would also suggest that it indeed caused the natural demise of article 270 of the Constitution which had previously provided for the continued existence of the old political parties.

But in a modern despot's country, complying with the requirement for fresh registration is one thing. Enjoying the freedom to operate freely thereafter is a completely different matter. That may require more than just a decision of a court presided over by men who, in Museveni's own words, "*...do not understand the ideals of the bush war revolution*". That in my view is a Museveni euphemism for suggesting that some Ugandan Judges do not take his regime's revolutionary *modus operandi* into account when deciding politically significant cases.

All said and done, I still think Section 6{4} of the *PPOA 2002* produced fresh legal complications; complications that its architects had probably never anticipated. On close scrutiny, it becomes apparent that it enabled what I think is a logically unsustainable interpretation of the concept of legal "*existence*" on the one hand, and that of legal "*operation*" on the other. In other words, it made it possible for one to wrongly view the twin concepts as being mutually exclusive of each other.

If such an interpretation were to be allowed to stand, then we all know that neither the concept of "*legal existence*" nor that of "*legal operation*" would be of any use without the other. In other words, it would be absolutely useless for any political party to be allowed to "*exist*" while at the same time being denied the freedom to conduct countrywide political activities. After all, isn't that what *"operation"* is, or at least should be about?

Indeed, in giving their reasons for annulling Sections 18 and 19 of the *PPOA 2002*, the *Constitutional Court* had noted that all the State witnesses *"...could not satisfactorily explain how a legislation which puts 98% stop on political activities, except within the Movement only, could be justified that it was...needed to protect the operation of the Movement"*.

And in my view, the *"...98% stop on political activities"* that court talked about there was essentially the *"legal operation"* that *Section* 6{4} absurdly says is supposed to be mutually exclusive of *"legal existence"*. It simply doesn't make sense.

And the icing on the cake for democracy lovers came when the court added that *"...the restrictions were no doubt too draconian and make a mockery of guaranteed freedoms and rights of association and assembly"*. A mockery indeed; and that is exactly why I argued a few moments ago that it would be absolutely useless to be allowed to *"exist"* while at the same time being denied the freedom to conduct countrywide political activities.

Therefore, by trying to retain those draconian legal restrictions on the enjoyment of political freedoms, Museveni, like the typical modern despot that is the cause of my rage here, was in effect using the law to send a clear message to everyone in the land that he intends to retain his party's unfair dominance of Uganda's political landscape.

And it's not just Uganda's Museveni who enjoys of that despotic propensity. All modern despots, white or black, youthful or senile, feel no qualms whatsoever about using the law to appropriate such unfair political advantages to themselves. It is entirely consistent with their *modus operandi*.

In the United Kingdom for example, a major broadsheet newspaper once suggested that Prime Minister Tony Blair's *'New Labour'* government had taken a firm policy decision [that was later given the force of law] to *"go soft"* on immigration into the UK. In other words, the alleged strategy was to take in as many foreigners as possible and deport a minimal amount of illegal immigrants.

On the face of it, not many people would have serious problems welcoming such a policy. After all, it looks like nothing more than a benign act of contemporary global citizenship; a refreshing act of liberal enlightenment, tolerance; you name it. Well, not quite. We may all have to think again.

Apparently, the paper argued, *'New Labour'* had done its homework fair well. Its research had allegedly found that on the whole, immigrants tend to be quite *'suspicious'* of the *Conservative Party* and its conservative values. Values that, according to some, place great emphasis on guarding the capitalist privileges of the indigenous British middle class families! *"The true Brits"* if you like; whatever that might mean these days.

Crucially however, the paper also alleged that New Labour's research had found that because of the *'suspicion'* that most immigrants had towards the *Conservative Party,* they also, quite naturally in fact, tended to identify more with the ordinary working class families. And it is the working class families that have for generations formed the bedrock of *Labour's* core vote. So there was a real chance that the new immigrants might themselves [through social influence] choose to vote *New Labour*. Wild allegations, you might think. Well, perhaps. We may never know for sure.

However, if the allegations were to be true, then I think it wouldn't be too difficult to see exactly how modern despots use the law to softly manipulate the political landscape in their favour. The difference, as I said, may simply boil down to the individual despot's judgement and degree of perversion. These are the things that ultimately determine how far he goes to avoid the more crude forms of abusing the law to tilt the political landscape in his favour.

So whereas Museveni's overt acts of using the law to frustrate the operation of political parties in Uganda may be said to be a crude form of political manipulation, *New Labour's* legalised *"social engineering"* approach [if true] was more subtle and less obvious. But the law remained the tool of choice in both cases.

In Uganda however, the despot whose legal architects drafted the law that required all political parties to re-register also never got what he had hoped for. The reason being that by simply suspending the six months statutory deadline for registration under the *PPOA 2002*, the *Constitutional Court* had given opposition political parties that would have been time barred a new lease of life.

There is absolutely no doubt in my mind that without this simple but timely intervention, the Museveni regime, being in firm control of the Registrar General's office, could have easily retained the liberty to determine which political party succeeded in beating the six months deadline, and which one did not.

With that of course, they could then have denied registration to the parties that they, in their cowardice, thought posed the biggest threat to their continued stay in power. But a political coward never gives up his quest for unfair political advantages that easily. Even after their defeat in court over the infamous re-registration saga, the regime still wanted to flex its muscles by demonstrating its huge political and financial influence over the Registrar General's office. And how did they do that?

Well, to no one's great surprise, when the newly formed *Forum for Democratic Change* {FDC} sought registration prior to the 2006 general elections, General Museveni's regime tried out all the tricks in the book in a desperate but ultimately futile attempt to frustrate it. The most absurd thing in the regime's futile attempt was the excuse it gave for dragging its feet over FDC's registration. It claimed, rather foolishly, that the Registrar General's office did not have a mere 100,000/= *Shillings* {approx $60} to facilitate FDC's registration. How ridiculous can it get?

In fact, even though many Ugandans knew exactly what General Museveni's regime was capable of doing and was in fact trying to do, they were still shocked by the silly and sheer audacity of it all. The FDC too, as the primary victim of the regime's cowardly political manoeuvres, knew exactly what the government was trying to do.
So they decided that they were having none of it; not without a good old dogged political fight anyway! In the end, a good old dogged political fight was what FDC put up. It issued threats of legal action, embarked on symbolic street protests, and a host of other political protest activities.

But one particular FDC protest action impressed me the most. As a party fighting against a modern depot's oppression, FDC, with nothing more than its brains, decided to embarrass the regime. And they did it by publicly offering the *Ministry of Finance* the 100,000/= *Shillings* that the regime said it didn't have to cover FDC's registration fees.

And for the icing on the cake, scores of FDC activists decided to physically take a little back bag containing 100,000/= *Shillings* worth of coins directly to the *Ministry of Finance* headquarters. The media of course loved the stunt and gave it full coverage. Embarrassed by it all, the regime finally succumbed and facilitated the issuance of a certificate of registration to FDC. A classic political victory secured through psychological warfare if you ask me!

But as I said, the real reason for regime's dilly darling antics was that in their calculation, they had come to the conclusion that FDC, with its formidable arsenal of leaders, including a host who had broken away from the ruling NRM itself, was the party that posed the greatest threat to the regime.

In fact, a not-so-close friend of mine who works for one of the regime's intelligence agencies came very close to confirming exactly that to me. And he went even further and came clean about something that was totally unrelated to the FDC registration saga that we were talking about in a restaurant at *Adam's Arcade* in Nairobi-Kenya. On this fine July afternoon, my friend said: *"Charles, I am with these crooks for nothing but the money. When the time comes, don't judge me harshly my brother"*.

I can still see the look of shame on this guy's face. It was a sad sight. And I think it summed it up beautifully for me. Not only was this poor chap utterly disgusted by what the Museveni regime was trying to do to FDC, but he actually, deep down, didn't even subscribe an inch to the system he was forced into serving by the sheer need for economic survival. That is some sumptuous food for thought for all the oppressive modern despots out there.

The lesson from my friend's confession is simple: Intimidation, coercion, legal oppression, economic disenfranchisement, and even military might, can never procure genuine loyalty to an ideology. Skilful persuasion does! There are quite simply, no two ways about it. The sooner these contemporary depots get it into their heads, the better for everyone; including themselves for that matter.

Anyway going back our Uganda reference point, it will be recalled that the *PPOA 2002* itself had a rather chequered and dishonourable history. Like most laws introduced to the Legislature by modern despots, the *PPOA 2002* too started life as a very controversial *Political*

Organisations Bill. It was inevitable. The Bill had malice, deceit, cowardice, and fraud written all over it.

Most interestingly however, when the Bill was put to a vote on the floor of Parliament, the same *"learned"* Francis Ayume, as the Speaker of Parliament then, decided to pull a disgraceful and unprecedented political master stroke; one that Uganda had never seen before. This is how he did it.

As soon the announcement came that the government side had *"won"*, a vigilant opposition MP immediately smelt a rat and raised an objection which seriously questioned the validity of the vote. His contention was that the Bill had been passed without sufficient quorum in the House. Then straight into the ensuing fray came Speaker Francis Ayume!

In a most flagrant and grotesque abuse of Parliamentary Rules of procedure, Ayume, having been caught unaware by the opposition MP's objection, in desperation, decided to look at the attendance register of MPs for a solution to the impasse. To his great relief, I imagine, Ayume found that the attendance register had sufficient signatures.

And on the strength of that *"paper"* fact, and with a straight face devoid of shame, Ayume ruled that the Bill had been passed with sufficient *signature* quorum. A physical head count of MPs who were *actually* present in the House at the relevant time of course told its own story; a very different story; one which revealed that there was indeed *no quorum.* So the Bill couldn't have been validly passed.

The independent media of course picked up on this absurdity and made a real meal of it. Not surprisingly, a huge section of the population loved what the media had served on the front pages. So they voiced their displeasure consistently in different forums for days on end. Because of that, I think it soon became apparent to the offending regime that the general public, and the opposition parties, were not going to allow such injustice to go unchallenged. And it was indeed challenged in court. But a modern despot is a sly character.

Sensing the humiliating defeat that awaited it in the courts of law, Museveni's regime, in characteristic style, shot down the court's decision by tabling a fresh Bill in Parliament pre-emptively. This time round, the *Political Organisations Bill* that was being challenged in court had been re-baptised and re-presented in Parliament as the *Political Parties and Organisations Bill*.

With that, many Ugandans, and observers of Ugandan politics alike, thought the stage had been well and truly set for *"Round Two"* of the gigantic political contest between the Museveni dictatorship and the opposition parties acting on behalf of, and for the greater good of the nation.

But it wasn't to be. It couldn't be; not if Museveni's legal architects and political advisors had anything to do with it. And they had. In perhaps one of the most disgraceful political acts in Uganda's history, the "new" *Political Parties and Organisations Bill* was rushed through Parliament in a record 24hours. Impressive; isn't it? So how did they do it; these clever chaps!

Well, a ruling NRM MP [of course] moved a motion urging the House to suspend virtually all the relevant Parliamentary Rules of procedure. When the motion was put to a vote, Museveni's ruling NRM, with its fraudulent majority, of course carried the day. The motion was adopted and the rules were suspended. For the ruling NRM MPs, this was a sweet political *"victory"*!

But I think the immoral euphoria of that political *"victory"* should in itself tell us something frightening about people who choose to identify with and subscribe to a modern despot's political philosophy. These are feral creatures in my view; creatures with a conscience that has a *"For Sale"* sign written on it, creatures with no principles of their own, unpatriotic creatures, creatures with only two things on their minds: Power and their stomachs!

For that they will do absolutely anything to anyone; anything, including that which puts the future of their own country in serious jeopardy; all in the name of pleasing the modern despot that gives them the two things they most want in life: Power and food!.

Anyway that aside, this *"new"* Bill was then fast-tracked through Parliament; even avoiding the most crucial committee stages. Not even the rule that provided for voting by secret ballot in such matters of constitutional significance was spared. This meant that all MPs whose patriotic conscience could have prevailed upon them in a secret ballot would be put on the spot and required to publicly declare their loyalty or disloyalty to the despot by a show of hands. It all sounds like trivial political theatrics now doesn't it?

Well, it isn't. In fact, to keep tabs on the significance of what we are talking about, we must remind ourselves here that we are talking about the use of *"law as a tool of political oppression"* by modern despots. So I think you will agree that the processes by which such laws are passed in the first place must be of interest to us.

Now, as voting commenced in Uganda's parliament, to make sure nothing was left to chance, Gen. Museveni's regime conspicuously positioned ten *"no-nonsense"* mean-looking army Generals on the government side of the House. Clad in full combat gear, they sat there with their full inherent might; menacingly looking on, as if about to pounce on dissenting MPs; and yet, only taking note of how each MP was voting. Remember the voting was now being done by show of hands. These, the world was told, were the army's representatives in Parliament.

The rest is history! A modern despot's regime proclaimed "*victory*" once again. An ecstatic Museveni, as *President*, wasted no time in accenting to the Bill. That, my friends, is how the most oppressive provisions of the *PPOA 2002* that we have been discussing came into force. When you finish pondering over that, then come and join me and we look at how modern despots enforce the law selectively.

Selective Enforcement of the Law

If we now agree that the law can and has been used as *a tool of political oppression,* then I am sure we can also agree that that legal oppression by modern despots comes in different forms. Sometimes, as this subtitle indeed suggests, all modern despots have to do is pretend to be deaf and blind to political lawlessness and still achieve the same objective. In other words, they could simply choose to condone impunity. History has shown that this usually happens when their own henchmen are the prime suspects. Take this hypothetical situation in a modern despot's country; a country that could in fact be your very own.

An enabling law may allow peaceful assemblies and demonstrations. An overzealous regime operative then learns that a particular opposition party is due to assemble at a specific place for a political rally or some other event. He then takes it upon himself to disrupt or even disperse the opposition rally; all in direct contravention of the law.

With all the executive powers vested in him as Head of State, the modern despot then steps in and protects his operative from prosecution. The net effect will be the same. The opposition party will have been denied the opportunity to build its support base; much in the same way as a direct ban on their political activities would have done. Just consider this Ugandan scenario [below] and you will see how selective enforcement of the law can do political miracles for a modern despot.

Section 16{1} of the *PPOA 2002* for example states that *"...a member of the Uganda People's Defence Forces {UPDF}, the Uganda Police Force {UPF}, the Uganda Prisons Service {UPS} or a public officer or a traditional or cultural leader shall not": {a}be a founding or other member of a political party or organisation; or {b}hold office in a political party or organisation; or {c} speak in public or publish anything involving matters of political party or organisation controversy; or {d}engage in canvassing support for a political party or organisation or for a candidate standing for public election sponsored by a political party or organisation"*.

Now that is the law. Simple and clear in all its glory! For their close association with political turbulence, many Ugandans welcomed the fact that the army in particular had now been legally divorced from national politics. In fact, General Museveni himself, as *Commander-in-Chief* of the army, personally went on record in support of the move.

I suspect that deep down, he knew very well that the implications of that move would also require him as a serving military officer to first resign from the army before he can legally do any political work for his party. But the million dollar question is: Did *Section 16* of the *PPOA 2002* actually succeed in stopping the named category of individuals from engaging in active politics? Well, let's see then shall we?

Before Museveni was *"promoted"* to the rank of full General and then immediately *"allowed"* to retire from the army, {an absurdity in its own right} the then Lt. General Y.K. Museveni, and many others like him, were openly engaging in partisan political activities on behalf of their ruling NRM party. That is a fact that is not up for debate. The best the regime's ardent defenders can do is to argue that as *President,* there is no way Museveni can avoid being politically active. Granted!

But that is still a political defence; not a legal one. Even then, the more witty political thinkers on the other side of the same argument could quickly counter that convenient regime excuse with two very pedestrian questions: Why, for example, did Museveni as *Head of State* assent to the *Political Parties and Organisations Bill* {to make it law} without internalising its full implications; even for himself! Secondly, would Museveni, or any other despot for that matter, have quickly assented to such a *Bill* if it was going to be a truly *bona fide* law from which he would enjoy no political advantage? I think your guess is as good as mine on that one; but I will tell you mine anyway.

I think the answer lies in what we already know about the mindset of the typical modern despot. In fact, this is especially the case among those who like to call themselves *"Freedom Fighters"* or *"Revolutionaries"*. These creatures have a tendency to think that they should be routinely exempted from compliance with the laws that they bring to life with the mighty stroke of their despotic pens.

That like true Monarchs, {Museveni calls himself *"The Ssabbagabe"* or *"King of Kings"*} they should be above the law. And for that same reason, you will also find that these *wannabe* Monarchs often have nothing but contempt for institutions of State that are constitutionally charged with enforcing the rule of law and the administration of justice.

The Judiciary, for example, will often be rubbished; its relevance contemptuously questioned; and its capacity to deliver justice deliberately frustrated. It will be blamed for virtually everything that goes wrong in the country; including political failures that ought, as they must, fall squarely within the modern despot's heavily fortified courtyard.

Failure to fight corruption in government and society, failure to entrench the rule of law and democracy, failure to observe, respect and protect human rights, failure to improve the country's infrastructure and socio-economic welfare of the population *inter alia* are all political failures that modern despots are quick to blame on other State institutions.

But if Uganda's *"King of Kings"* Yoweri Museveni feels that he is above the laws of the land, then how about his juniors? Did they, for example, feel bound by the provisions of the *PPOA 2002* at all? Quite simply, No! And to prove it, you need look no further than the title and activities of one of Museveni's closest political *"assassins"*.

I think I should mention this here too. The modern despot, whilst always careful to make sure he remains in the *Back Seat* from where he issues his illegal orders, cannot afford to do without frontline political *"assassins"* who have little or nothing to lose. During the 2001 elections in Uganda, this particular *"hit-man"* held the very fitting title of *Presidential Adviser on Political Affairs*. He was then, and probably still is as I write now, a serving officer in Uganda's national army. He is of course the ex-Journalist and self-styled *"Kingmaker"* Major Ronald Kakooza Mutale.

So the drill is clear and simple. If Museveni had appointed Kakooza Mutale as his adviser on political affairs before the *PPOA 2002* came into force, then to remain within the law, he should have relieved Mutale of his duties immediately the *PPOA 2002* came into force. He did not, and he couldn't possibly have; because every modern despot needs such hit-men to do their dirty work.

In fact, Kakooza Mutale personified and indeed became the real face of Museveni's regime during the 2001 elections. The regime simply turned a blind eye to him when he commandeered the yellow NRM election battle bus. Then, perhaps feeling re-assured and energised by that implied nod from the top, Mutale decided to fill the infamous NRM election battle bus with blood thirsty, gun and stick welding paramilitary men from his illegal *Kalangala Action Plan* {KAP}.

KAP then went on the rampage. In the capital city Kampala for example, they went from suburb to suburb menacingly looking out for opportunities to beat the life out of opposition leader Dr. Kizza Besigye's supporters. On and on the yellow NRM bus went, working up a cloud of dust in its wake as city folks scampered for dear life. From Ntinda to Bulange; from Makerere to Bwaise; from Makindye to Bugolobi; and from Katwe to Ndeeba; the savagery went on unabated in these dusty but bustling city suburbs.

Along the Kampala-Jinja highway, another senior military officer was also at it. It was as if they had drawn up a political violence action plan in advance. Obviously incensed by Dr. Besigye's growing popularity, popularity that had already motivated hundreds of Besigye's supporters to sweep the Kampala-Jinja highway ahead of their hero's campaign visit to Jinja, this military officer, another Major in fact, decided that he was having none of that *"nonsense"*. And what does he do?

He decided to drive straight through Dr. Besigye's supporters; killing some and injuring scores. Still not contented with what he had already *"achieved"*, he reversed his monstrous military truck over the dead and wounded again; just to make sure the job is done properly. Absolutely astonishing brutality; all in the name of helping their *Commander-in-Chief* General Museveni retain power!

The media of course dutifully covered this and most of Kakooza Mutale's violent political activities. The general public too raised their strong concerns about the brutality of Mutale's group; they simply had to. But there was one very senior Ugandan citizen, out of millions, who failed to see anything wrong with what Kakooza Mutale *et al* were doing. Yes, you guessed it right!

Portrait of a Despot

That man was called Lt. General Yoweri T.K Museveni, *"President"* of the Republic of Uganda. Not only did he fail to see anything wrong with Mutale's activities, but he went further, on record in fact, and defended him. He challenged anyone with evidence of Kakooza Mutale's brutality to report it directly to him; well knowing that for most ordinary Ugandans, getting access to him would be next to impossible.

That was the 2001 general elections. As the next elections scheduled for February 2006 approached, the good old Major Kakooza Mutale resurfaced again. In a chilling warning to the nation, Mutale said they [as KAP] had *"...long anticipated and prepared"* for the 2006 elections. The year of our Lord 2006 came. The February elections of that year came too. But Kakooza Mutale was nowhere to be seen.

What on earth is going on; one or two people surely must have wondered...quietly of course! Strange as that may sound, Kakooza Mutale's absence on the political scene after his chilling warning caused a bit of a stir across the board. The media was no exception. Many newspapers were awash with speculation; some very wild of course!

Personally, one thing struck me the most about Kakooza Mutale'a absence. The mere fact that Ugandans expected Kakooza Mutale and his KAP gang to come and *"persuade"* them with whips and guns to vote *"wisely"* for candidate Museveni speaks volumes. In fact, it perfectly summed up what the state of democracy was in Museveni's Uganda.

But let's re-focus on the 2006 general elections a little longer. In so far as the prevalence of state orchestrated violence was concerned, I would certainly say that even with Kakooza Mutale's absence, the 2006 general elections didn't *"disappoint"*. In Mutale's place were several overzealous regime operatives; all falling over themselves like grasshoppers for the opportunity to impress the *Emperor*.

Most notable among them was a one Lt. Ramathan Magara! Like his comrades in arms during the 2001 elections, in 2006, Magara decided, in broad day light, to open fire on Dr. Besigye's supporters who had thronged the precincts of Buganda Kingdom's symbolic seat of power; a neat white-washed colonial looking structure located at Bulange–Mengo.

These innocent victims of Magara's violence had in the eyes of the State committed the cardinal sin of gathering audaciously around the Palace to catch a glimpse of their leader Dr. Besigye who had paid a courtesy call to the *"Kabaka"* [or King] of Buganda Ronald Muwenda Mutebi II. And for that, Lt. Magara's orgy of violence left three of them dead; including one who had wrapped his entire body in Dr. Besigye's campaign posters! One of the survivors was seriously injured and is now confined to a wheelchair.

Today, several years after Magara's killings, I still can't find the most appropriate words to describe my feelings about that incident. But my emotions of raw bitterness are still only those of a mere supporter. How about Dr. Besigye's own emotions? I have never found the courage to ask him how he felt; several hours of conversations notwithstanding. So I still wonder what he must have felt upon seeing his staunch supporter who had his campaign posters all over his body lying dead in a pool of blood. It's too painful to even imagine.

But what must never be in doubt is that that image will forever remain in the minds of Ugandans as a permanent reminder of their *"glorious years of political freedom"* under Museveni's *Fundamental Change* politics. Yes, *glorious years* when, as my Mucwini village-mate Archbishop Janani Luwum {RIP}once said in his courageous letter to Idi Amin, *"...the guns of the army were being used not to protect but to terrorise the people of Uganda"*!

Portrait of a Despot

The reality is that such proxy criminal acts are irresistible to modern despots. In their perversion, they may even consider such things to be a *macho* way of showing the governed *"Who is the Daddy"*. In fact, not only do modern despots turn a blind eye in cases where their loyal officers are prime suspects, they also, quite hypocritically, often enforce the law with vigour against army officers whose loyalty is deemed inadequate. Let's discuss one such case.

The Rise & Fall of Brig. Henry Tumukunde

The arrest and detention of Brigadier Henry Tumukunde was a great example, a classic one even, of how modern despots selectively enforce the law. Classic because it demonstrated, almost to perfection, how easily and dramatically one can *rise and fall* from grace in the service of a despot.

So before I even delve into the facts of Tumukunde's case, I think the moral lesson for those who aspire to serve or are already serving in rogue regimes is crystal clear: *Avoid trampling on people's heads during your ascendancy to what is no more than an illusion of power.* You might need those very people when the time comes, as it sure does, for a dramatic and undignified descent. In the service of a despot, an unwritten *code of service* exists. And it is that *"real power"* to act with impunity against absolutely anyone can only be exercised at the pleasure of the despot himself. That code is not negotiable to the despot; not an inch!

Poor old Tumukunde! During the violence ridden elections of 2001 when Kakooza Mutale *et al* featured with vicious prominence against Dr. Besigye's unarmed supporters, Tumukunde was still perceived to be one of Museveni's ultra loyal *"Blue Eyed Boys"*. Of course, that perception couldn't have come about without justification; valid or not. But my firm belief in the existence of *an unwritten code of service* in any dictatorship also leads me to believe that it is very unlikely that Museveni's own perception of Tumukunde's power was as unrealistic as that of the general public.

The other thing that was beyond mere speculation was that as the 2006 general elections approached, Brigadier Tumukunde's public utterances had somehow, for some strange reason, become more civilised. He began sounding tolerant and liberal. And if I were to be even more generous to him, I would say Tumukunde's arguments were beginning to sound as though they were democratically premised.

That was something very unusual for most of the *"heroes"* of the 1986 revolution that brought Museveni to power. But here is the most crucial observation about Tumukunde's sudden *"reform"*. If Tumukunde's public utterances were now beginning to sound democratic to ordinary members of the public like me, then I think they must have sounded like hostile enemy gunfire to General Museveni and his political advisors.

Clearly, something in Tumukunde's relationship with the regime had gone seriously wrong. Whatever it was, one thing cannot, and must never be ruled out. For his usual political insecurities, the modern despot is chronically suspicious; even of his close Aides. So it is more than likely that by the time Museveni struck, he had already detected an *"unhealthy"* appetite for greater political power in Tumukunde.

After all, Tumukunde was known to be a very ambitious chap. Big mistake when you are serving a despot! And his big mistake, if you can call it that, was that he had failed to keep his political ambitions under tight wraps. That, plus his now half-hearted and almost lukewarm defence of the dictatorship, ensured that Tumukunde's fate would be sealed.

His fate was sealed because in the eyes of the modern despot, such a combination will always be construed as final proof of an intention to start opposing the ruling political dynasty. And that can only lead to one thing; persecution! Accordingly, Tumukunde was arrested after he made some controversial statements on a Radio Talk Show in the capital city Kampala.

As expected, the regime stood its ground and insisted that Tumukunde's *"crime"* was straightforward: That as a serving officer in the national army, Brigadier Henry Tumukunde had made *"...politically controversial statements"* in the *"wrong forum"*. The Prosecution's case was therefore that by so doing, Tumukunde had contravened the provisions of the *Political Parties & Organisations Act 2002* that barred soldiers like him from active engagement in partisan political matters.

The rest as they say is now history. Tumukunde was arraigned before the General Military Court Martial, charged, and detained under house arrest. As I said earlier, a classic example of how modern despots selectively enforce the law to achieve a desired political end. So that is that.

But wasn't Major Kakooza Mutale [the *Presidential Advisor on Political Affairs* no less] also a serving army officer like Brigadier Tumukunde? Hadn't Kakooza Mutale made partisan and controversial political statements in the wrong forum? As leader of KAP, shouldn't Kakooza Mutale have been held accountable for his militia's vicious attacks on Dr. Besigye's supporters? Didn't Mutale's political activities contravene the same provisions of the *PPOA 2002*?

Of course they did. So why wasn't he arrested, charged, and detained like Brigadier Tumukunde? There is no doubt in my mind that the inequality seen in the regime's schizophrenic handling of the Tumukunde-Mutale cases represents a very dangerous development for a young State like Uganda. It is dangerous because it is inequality before the laws of the land.

In fact, to appreciate the gravity of such inequality even better, one must look no further than the fact that it was one of the top most grievances that Museveni himself had cited in the 1980s before he decided to pick up arms to fight Milton Obote's government. And like most modern despots, as soon as he captured power, Museveni pledged to restore *"equality before the laws of the land"* among many other things.

So it is particularly sad to see that far from restoring and jealously guarding the beautiful principle of *"equality before the law"*, the law itself is now one of the most lethal weapons of choice that modern despots like Museveni selectively unleash as they go about handling the *small matter* of oppressing their political opponents. *A week is a very long time in politics* indeed!

But let's look at one or two more provisions of the *PPOA 2002* before we leave the subject of *selective use of law* as a weapon of political oppression. Of all the politically oppressive provisions of the *PPOA 2002* that we have considered so far, this particular one, it seems to me, is the most audacious, ill thought out, and probably most blatant of all. And, as expected, it didn't take too long for Ugandans to work out who it had been designed for. The verdict was near-unanimous.

It had been designed to target and neutralise Museveni's exiled political opponents. Forget the official rationale that the regime propagated for including this nasty *Section* in the *PPOA 2002*. The real reason was, as I said earlier, typical political cowardice by a modern despot. Through this *Section of the PPOA 2002*, Museveni's legal draftsmen, like those in many other pseudo-democracies, thought they would finally succeed in deterring formidable opposition leaders living in exile from making a *"Rambo"* style come back.

And I have to tell you, the creativity of oppressed people has never ceased to amaze me. I am sure those of you who are old enough still remember the explosion of politically loaded songs of freedom sang by the oppressed Black population in apartheid South Africa.

Northern Uganda also experienced a similar explosion of songs of freedom. *"Kuc dong kyok dwogo"* [peace is about to return], *"Chaa wa pe ya"* [we don't have much time], Bosmic Otim sings; respectively praising peace advocates and pleading with war mongers to stop fighting and return home! Others sang painful songs about how the indignity of life in the IDP camps had caused a *"cultural genocide"*. This is the sort of creativity that I said never ceases to amaze me; powerful messages delivered in very simple ways. Wonderful!

In the case of this obnoxious *Section* of the *PPOA 2002* too, Ugandans who were suffering political oppression, in their close knit socio-political circles, quickly baptised the offensive *Section "The Besigye Clause"*. The reason, a very fitting one in my view, was that these politically oppressed Ugandans thought this particular *Section* of the *PPOA 2002* was conceived by the Museveni regime with one man and only one man in mind; and that man was Dr. Kizza Besigye; Museveni's most formidable political challenger who was exiled in South Africa at the time.

How else would anyone explain the frantic attempts by the regime's Attorney General to block Dr. Besigye's nomination to contest for the presidency of Uganda in the 2006 elections? In fact, to put it all into its proper context, I think it is crucial for all and sundry to know that the regime's attempts to block Dr. Besigye's nomination happened after this most offensive *Section* of the *PPOA 2002* had been declared unconstitutional and therefore null and void by the *Constitutional Court* of Uganda. But before its nullification, *"The Besigye Clause"*, which was in fact *Section 13{b}of the PPOA 2002*, had, with these most chilling words from the regime's legal draftsman, declared that *"...no person shall be appointed nor accept any political office in a political party or organisation in Uganda if he or she has immediately before he or she is to be appointed, lived outside Uganda continuously for more than three years"*.

In their devious political calculations, they had probably worked out that it would be at least three years before Dr. Besigye could even think of returning to Uganda for the next elections. That was how far Museveni's regime was prepared to go to ensure that it never faced any formidable opposition politician in any political contest; just in case they got overwhelmed. In fact, even the standard *default settings* {like rigging, harassment, bribery and intimidation}of a modern despot's *"democracy"* were not enough to give them sufficient confidence to leave Dr. Besigye alone.

To wrap up this debate on the selective use or abuse of the law by modern despots like Uganda's Yoweri Museveni, let us take a brief look at *Section 17{1}* of the beleaguered *PPOA 2002*. This section provided that *"...no person shall use government or public resources in the activities of any political party or organisation"*.

Even before we get into the actual facts, I can confidently predict that anyone who knows the political *modus operandi* favoured by most modern despots will immediately know that this would be the most difficult provision for the Museveni regime to observe. And why, you may rightly ask, is Charles Okwir this confident? Well, Okwir thinks that to observe the provisions of *Section 17{1} of the PPOA* would have meant that the Museveni regime would have had to surrender the massive financial and other resource advantages that it had hitherto enjoyed at the expense of its other political competitors.

And yes, you guessed it right again. This unfair political advantage had been made possible by another law in the form of the *Movement Act 1997*. This Act literally fused most institutions of State with Museveni's partisan *Movement*. This meant that the *Movement* could legally [more like fraudulently to me] use whatever facilities were meant for Uganda's State institutions for its own partisan political activities.

One such institution through which the Museveni regime committed some of its most abominable acts of political fraud was the gigantic bureaucracy that went by the names the *Movement Secretariat*. The *Secretariat* had been established by the *Movement Act* and it enjoyed full funding from the public purse. Its real purpose however was to coordinate the ruling *Movement's* partisan political activities; thus consolidating its political support base across the country.

But let's stay with *Section 17 [1]* of the *PPOA 2002* which barred anyone from using government or public resources for partisan political activities. As expected, the *Movement* was caught red handed *"in the act"* with its *"pants"* down; thanks to the vigilance of a Journalist. This is how it all unfolded.

During the 2006 general election campaigns, a very senior *Movement* leader [on paper] who says he is as tough as the *Mahogany* tree was photographed using a government vehicle for partisan political activities. This government vehicle, a Pick-Up Truck if my memory serves me right, had been poorly disguised as an ordinary vehicle.

But the villains had overlooked one incriminating piece of evidence: Probably acting in a hurry to avoid being caught, these political thugs had switched the vehicles registration plates but failed to notice that the suspect vehicle had in fact retained its unique government registration numbers inscribed on its windscreen and windows.

Talk of crime being smarter than the criminal eh! So as fate would have it, a *Daily Monitor* newspaper photo Journalist spotted the inscription on the windscreen and windows; took a picture of the vehicle; and ran off into the sunset with an exclusive and politically explosive story. But the regime's hardened political criminals didn't lose much sleep over that story. For them, there was something much bigger at stake. And for that, they were prepared to do anything and everything possible; legal or not, to ensure that Museveni returned to State House. And he did.

The evidence reviewed so far in this Ugandan-centric case clearly shows that laws in countries ruled by modern despots need comprehensive reforms to bring them into line with the democratic aspirations of the people. What I think is also beyond debate is that a modern despot's political survival needs will as a matter of routine, always bring his country's justice system into serious disrepute. Confusion will often reign.

Secondly, in most countries ruled by modern despots, even the police force that is charged with keeping law and order never seems to do any better than the lay men and women on the proverbial omnibus. Hardly the ideal situation for democratic evolution; surely! In fact in the case of Uganda, I think it this may explain why several attempts by opposition parties to address public rallies have been brutally dispersed by the police. And this is several years down the road after a *Constitutional Court* ruling gave political parties freedom to operate freely!

There have been attempts by opposition Members of Parliament to put the Executive to task over police brutality. But Museveni's personal and partisan interventions in times of controversy have always let the entire Legislature down. In frustration, opposition MPs simply opt for symbolic protest walkouts; walkouts which catch the headlines for a few days but in the end achieve nothing of great political significance.

On the other hand, Museveni, like any other modern despot, often has many options at his disposal. Using the laws passed by his fraudulently acquired majority in the Legislature, the modern despot gets most if not everything he pushes for or stands against.

In my view therefore, the most logical, and perhaps even *only* conclusion to be drawn from this debate about modern despots using the *law as a tool of political oppression* is this: The modern despot is not significantly different from his colonial role model. He is politically insecure; hence the resort to harsh and unfair laws. Laws that draw inspiration from the colonial ones that had been designed to implement the will of a foreign sovereign; a sovereign whose interests were far removed from the aspirations of the indigenous people!

In Uganda for example, I could not find a legitimate reason why the regime's then Attorney General Francis Ayume {RIP} once found it necessary to seek leave of court to appeal against the democracy-leaning judgement of the *Constitutional Court*; a judgement that had given duly registered political parties freedom to operate throughout the country.

In this case my friends, it is absolutely irrelevant that Ayume never saw his appeal through. As far as Ugandans were concerned, the fact that he and his boss even saw merit in seeking leave of court to appeal against a ruling that was meant to usher political freedom for Ugandans was sufficient evidence to convict him and the regime he served {as agents of colonial oppression} in the court of public opinion.

The Museveni regime that Francis Ayume served preferred, and still prefers the old legal regime that provided for a one party {NRM} state in all but name; much like the British colonial administration. In fact, Museveni's fundamental political philosophy is that *Uganda is still a pre-industrial society that is not fit for multi-party politics*. That is why his first choice is a *One Party* political system. As a modern despot, that is the only way he can guarantee his political survival without having to beat up or imprison his political opponents.

For Uganda's opposition parties, the struggle against Museveni's legal oppression was in fact a battle for their very survival. And because their survival was at stake, they buried their political differences for a while. And
they will be glad they did; because that bought them some valuable time within which to pull their thoughts and resources together before heading straight back to battle in the courts of law.

But there was something more important whose survival depended on the outcome of the legal battles the opposition was fighting. And it was, to my mind at least, the very viability of Uganda as a democratic State. For that, nothing less than the spirited fight that the opposition parties put up would have sufficed. So if for nothing else, then surely, I think they deserve more than just a round of applause. But a lot more still needs to be done to rescue Uganda from the powerful jaws of its home-grown tyrannosauruses; vicious feral beasts from times gone by.

Despotic Assault on Civic Education

The modern despot chooses his targets very well. Anything that is *not* of great significance to his continued stay in power will *not* be targeted for assault. These *less significant* things, like the *limited* press and media freedom that he allows, are the things that he will be more than happy to showcase; all in a deceitful bid to cover up his *undemocratic* credentials. If he is feeling generous, he might even invite independent scrutiny of how it's being handled; after he has skilfully managed the stage of course!

Sadly however, political civic education is not, and can never be one of these things. It is a factor that is probably more critical than any other in any democratic process. It literally *"opens the eyes"* of the electorate. So the modern despot will make it his primary business to closely control the conduct of civic education; that is if he doesn't outlaw it all together.

But if he doesn't, then you can be sure the law will be his favourite tool of control. And where legislation is deemed inappropriate, you can also be sure he will find alternative means of achieving exactly the same objective. He will, for example, never willingly allow an independent organisation over which he has no significant influence to conduct political civic education. That is simply out of the question.

For a long time in Uganda, the conduct of political civic education was an exclusive preserve of *"Saint"* Yoweri Kaguta Museveni and his political *"Disciples"*. You know, those ultra loyal ideologues who manned the political superstructure called the *Movement Secretariat* that I talked about earlier.

Together, they had the legal monopoly to define what political civic education was, how it should be imparted, to whom, by whom, and for the sole purpose of retaining state power. Even the country's *Electoral Commission* that should ordinarily have been the *Lead Agency* {with support from civil society organisations} in conducting political civic education was disenfranchised. The result then was, and it still is, that it would fall upon one or two independent commercial media houses to step in and try to compliment the political civic education effort. The results were of course, very predictable.

By their very nature, commercial media houses have to strike a fine balance between their public service role and the primary purpose of their existence; which is of course, the relentless pursuit of handsome financial returns for their shareholders. In the end, their need for economic survival often means that they would give priority to the pursuit of profits and leave the political civic education role lagging behind in the distance as a mere *by the way.*

If a situation such as the one described above were to arise in a well governed democratic state, its citizens would still have a legitimate expectation that other pro-democracy civil society organisations would step in and take up the mantle. *Non Governmental Organisations* {NGOs} would probably be the most suited for this monumental role; a role that is of critical importance to democracy.

Sadly for Uganda's citizens, this is also something that Museveni's regime has not allowed NGOs to do. And the finger of blame, yet again, points directly at the doors of the rigid and ridiculous laws that govern the formation and operation of NGOs. No surprises there for me! After all, I recall arguing earlier that a modern despot, especially the more politically insecure one, will never willingly allow an independent organisation over which he has no significant influence to undertake the conduct of political civic education. This is it. Uganda's Museveni is that politically insecure modern despot.

The purpose of these ridiculous laws that govern the operation of NGOs is basically to stop them from doing anything other than their old fashioned charitable work. You know, giving out food, cloths, and things like that to the needy. Liberating the minds of these same needy people, which is what civic education does, is considered *political* and therefore out of bounds for NGOs. It doesn't help in the least that the NGO Board that regulates the work of NGOs in Uganda is manned by people who are handpicked, almost exclusively, by regime loyalists.

That means that like Parliament, the NGO Board also has within its midst some military officers from the regime's intelligence agencies. These are men and women whose primary loyalty is to their *Commander-in-Chief* General Museveni. And they don't sit on the NGO Board as mere observers. Far from it! They are empowered to veto any decision taken by the other civilian members of the Board to issue operating licences to any NGOs over whom the intelligence community may still have *un-answered questions.*

And if the practice in other State departments is anything to go by, then the *"un-answered questions"* can only be interpreted to mean some sort of doubt over an NGO's loyalty to the regime. Put differently, it is the same thing as saying the regime's intelligence community still feels uncomfortable with that particular NGO's professionalism and impartiality.

The final nail in the coffin of political civic education is then that although a right of appeal exists against the decision of the NGO Board to turn down an NGO's application for registration, it only goes as far as the *Minister of Internal Affairs;* who as it happens, is a member of the cabinet appointed by the same modern despot.

It is therefore a no win situation whichever way you look at it. And that my friend, is the end of my brief journey through a modern despot's legal system. It is a journey that has showed us the devastating effectiveness that the law can have on democracy if left in wrong hands; a modern despot's hands.

As far as the modern despot is concerned, if the demands of real politick call for it, then the law is transformed from being a honourable vehicle through which justice, fairness and equity is delivered to one through which injustice, suffering, and political oppression is served out selectively in near toxic dozes. So if that was the law's relationship with the demands of a modern despot's politics, then how about its relationship with fundamental human rights? Let's take a quick peep into that.

The Epic Battle For Fundamental Human Rights

Here, I am assuming that it's now safe to say that one of the most fundamental benchmarks by which democratic practices are judged in civilised societies is the observance of, and protection of human rights. In this context, we are talking about common human rights like freedom of association, freedom of assembly, freedom of expression, freedom of movement, and of conscience *inter alia.*

We also know that in civilised nations, these fundamental rights have always been of a constitutional nature. As a result, they enjoy commensurate legal protection. Well, that is the theory. But theory, as we all know, can sometimes be notoriously difficult to reconcile with actual practice. So you can be sure of an epic battle between theory and practice. A draw, however desirable, is very unlikely; especially if we have a remorselessly crafty modern despot acting as *Referee*.

It is precisely for this reason that I think a country like Uganda, and many like it, are yet to demonstrate their fitness for inclusion into the community of civilised nations. The constitution of Uganda has of course made great strides in that direction. In fact, it is almost there. But by nature, a constitution still falls within the definition of theory; and we must not forget that a bitter *civil war* exists between practice and theory where modern despots are concerned.

In the case of Uganda, these great sounding human rights theories, or aspirations for that matter, are captured under *Chapter IV* of the Constitution of Uganda 1995. That

Chapter concerns itself with the *"Protection and Promotion of Fundamental and Other Human Rights and Freedoms"*. A *Bill of Rights,* if you like! In fact, *Article 20*[1] thereof goes even further and declares that *"fundamental rights and freedoms of individuals are inherent and not granted by the state".*

Put differently, it tells Ugandans that those rights are their *"God given"* rights and that the State has no power to grant or deprive anyone of them except as ordered by a competent court of law. For its part, clause [2] of the same *Article 20* declares that: *"...the rights and freedoms of the individual and groups enshrined in this Chapter shall be respected, upheld, and promoted by all organs and agencies of government and by all persons".*

Of course, like most legal instruments of that nature that we have come across around the world, the Ugandan constitution too appears at face value to be patriotic in aspiration. It also appears to conform to internationally accepted standards. But the reality is a different matter. History has shown us time and again that the similarities often end with great sounding theories and aspirations.

In the case of Uganda, its turbulent political history, almost from day one of its *independence,* has taught Ugandans that one of the most common deficiencies in written laws which are meant to protect and guarantee human rights is that they are notoriously inconsistent with and almost at variance with the actual practice of implementation.

In the pseudo democracies that modern despots preside over, these inconsistencies have been brought to the fore in cases where the State's security agencies are involved. That is not in dispute. In fact, in the case of Uganda, the brutality of the regime's security agencies makes a total mockery of the word *Shall* in clause [2] above which makes it mandatory for *"...all organs and agencies of government"* to respect, uphold, and promote those rights.

For nothing other than the fact that it places some limitations on the enjoyment of the rights and freedoms we are talking about here, I think *Article* 43[1] has been the biggest victim of misinterpretation by State security agents. It's too important an article in this debate not to be re-stated here. It provides that: *"...in the enjoyment of the rights and freedoms prescribed in this Chapter, no person shall prejudice the fundamental and other human rights and freedoms of others or the public interest"*.

Plain and simple! And of course, it makes perfect sense to any *bona fide* citizen because there can be no such thing as an absolute right. The enjoyment of any right must, as it should, carry some degree of responsibility for the person claiming it. The trouble however is that a modern despot's security agent is hardly your typical, rational minded or *bona fide* citizen. They are a different breed; a breed that is prepared to stretch the boundaries of legal interpretation into the illogical sphere.

In fact, any human rights activist worth his salt knows that denials and or violations of human rights by the State are often justified, invariably, by reference to constitutional limitations to the enjoyment of those very rights. And more often than not, you will find that those limitations are invoked arbitrarily by the frontline security agencies with an implied wink and nod of approval *from above*.

It's a very dangerous wink and nod; dangerous because it breeds impunity. As we shall soon see, it has enabled Uganda's security agencies to *milk* these constitutional limitations to the point of actually violating *Article* 43{2}{c}; another constitutional provision that counter imposes its own safeguards on *Article* 43[1] that places limitations on the enjoyment of fundamental human rights.

For the record, *Article* 43{2}{c} states that: *"...Public interest under this article shall not permit any limitation of the enjoyment of the rights and freedoms prescribed under* this chapter beyond what is acceptable and demonstrably justifiable in a free and democratic society, or what is provided in this constitution".

A very sensible *"watchdog clause"* in my view! But as I said earlier, even the police who are supposed to be the customary enforcers of law and order have [for lack of professionalism] been party to the execution of illegal orders emanating from modern despots. As always, don't take my word for it. Have a look [below] at the arguments advanced by Uganda's *Inspector General of Police* [IGP] Major General Kale Kayihura to justify police heavy handedness.

Kayihura: *"Why we have banned rallies at the Square"*

The Uganda Police Force continues to receive requests for convening public assemblies, processions and other functions at the constitutional square and the surrounding areas in the Central Business District of Kampala. In fact, Article 20 paragraph [1] of the Constitution of the Republic of Uganda, 1995 provides that the fundamental rights and freedoms of the individual are inherent, and not granted by the State.

Furthermore, Article 20 paragraph [1] also provides that the freedoms of the individual, and groups enshrined in the constitution shall be respected, upheld, and promoted by all organs and agencies of government and by all persons. Specifically, Article 29 of the Constitution grants every person, among others, the right of freedom to assemble, and to demonstrate, together with others, peacefully and unarmed.

However these rights and freedoms are not absolute. Indeed, article 43 paragraph [1] provides that in the enjoyment of the rights and freedoms prescribed, no person shall prejudice the rights and freedoms of others, or the public interest.

In fact, recent events in the central Business District have exemplified situations where convening of public assemblies, rallies, and other functions, resulted in incidents prejudicial to the rights and freedoms of others, public interest. Indeed, the City has recently suffered acts of vandalism, looting, malicious damage to property, and general disorder on account of such functions.

Accordingly, in conformity with the legal position abovementioned, and in pursuance of the powers coffered upon the Inspector General of Police under the provision of sections 32 sub section [2] of the Police Act Cap 303 notice is hereby given that the convening of assemblies, processions, and other functions, at the Constitutional Square, and the surrounding areas of the Central Business District of Kampala, is here by prohibited. This is in pursuance of our duty entrusted to us by article 212 of the Constitution to protect life and property in Uganda. **End.**

So there you have it. Clear, simple, and unedited; just as it appeared in a daily newspaper in Uganda! So the question then has to be: Didn't Kayihura know about *Article 43{2}{c}* that sets out the conditions under which the *Article 43{1}* limitations may not apply? Of course he did.

In fact, unlike some of his lay constables, Kayihura's case is made worse by the fact that he is actually a fully qualified Lawyer. So the assumption must be that he knew that his men were violating both people's human rights and the provisions of the constitution that protect those rights. He however, still decided to invoke the *Article 43{1}*limitations as a defence to his men's brutality.

To a well meaning government, *Article 43{2}{c}* would have been the perfect legal guide for democratic conduct. But by failing to be strict in its prescription, *Article 43{2}{c}*effectively gave the discretion back to the oppressive regime to subjectively decide what limitations are

"...acceptable and demonstrably justifiable" in a free and democratic society.

In fact, IGP Kayihura's subjective view that *"...recent events in the central business district"* resulted in *"...incidents prejudicial to the rights and freedoms of others and the public interest"* is the perfect example of how the law, by failing to be strict in its prescription, handed unfettered discretion back into the hands of the regime's frontline operatives.

So if General Museveni decides that a peaceful demonstration by an opposition party is *not "acceptable"*, then that is exactly how it will be treated by the police and other law enforcement agencies. Only a successful legal challenge can overturn his decision; by which time of course, serious harm may already have been done to innocent lives.

Secondly, if he decides that it is *"demonstrably justifiable in a free and democratic society"* for opposition parties to be banned from addressing political rallies, then they will be banned; full stop. Again, only a successful legal challenge can overturn his decision; but the damage to an opposition party's mobilisation efforts will of course already have been done.

And the saddest fact about this whole mess is that it is not just high ranking government officials like Museveni and Kayihura who have that obnoxious attitude engrained in their minds. In fact, other than corruption, cronyism and nepotism, that obnoxious *"Museveni-Kayihura"* attitude is probably the only other thing that has been fully institutionalised in Museveni's Uganda; from the very top to the grassroots level of the State. Indeed, in a *Daily Monitor* article of 13th November 2002, *[See: "We Must Pick Either Free Expression or National Security"]* Mr. Vincent E. Bua reviewed the proceedings of a debate that had taken place at Makerere University-

Kampala. In his review, he said the then *Director of Information* at the ruling NRM Secretariat Mr. Ofwono Opondo said "*...no freedom should be above the freedom of the state to exist*" before adding that "*...we must protect the security of the country even if it means treading on some freedoms*".

So if Vincent Bua indeed quoted Ofwono Opondo accurately, {and I have no reason to doubt him} then good old Ofwono Opondo did not disappoint me there. He did exactly what I tried to explain earlier. In other words he, in his subjective wit and wisdom, as an officer of State, decided that it was "*acceptable*" to put the *freedom of the State to exist* above an individual's human rights.

Not only that, in Ofwono Opondo's view, it was also "*demonstrably justifiable to tread on some freedoms*" if that was indeed what it would take to protect the "*security of the country*". That is despotic unilateralism at its very best. Full of illegitimate authority; it must be added.

But I will say one or two more final things. For those of you who are, or might in future be faced with the dilemma of balancing "*national security*" with the fundamental demands of modern democracy, I urge you to spare a moment to absorb the lessons from the ruling in this United States case, *The New York Times Vs Sullivan*.

Briefly, as the *New York Times* and *Washington Pos* newspapers went to press in 1971 with excerpts from the so-called *Pentagon Papers* {*Intelligence reports on America's involvement in the Vietnam War*}, President Richard Nixon's government sought a restraining order against publication the papers; arguing that their publication would be harmf to [yes, you guessed right] "*National Security*".

In this case however, the US *Supreme Court* ruled that the government had not met the requisite constitutional burden and held that: "...*Security is a broad, vague generality whose contours should not be invoked to abrogate the fundamental laws embodied in free speech constitutional guarantees whose dominant purpose is to prohibit the practice of governmental suppression of embarrassing information*".

And, perhaps to make sure its message was fully hammered home to present and future American politicians, the Supreme Court also added, in no uncertain terms, that "...*the US Constitution tolerates absolutely no prior judicial restraints of the press predicated on surmise or conjecture of untoward consequences in the name of national security*".

It really can't get any clearer than that. And while we are still with American jurisprudence, it might also do us no harm to consider these very clear and politically impartial warnings about the dangers of State repression. They were poetically captured in the observations of Justice Louis Brandeis of the United States in the *Whitney Vs California* case.

In his opinion, "... *the framers of the American Constitution knew that order cannot be secured merely through fear of punishment for its infraction; that it is hazardous to discourage thought, hope and imagination; that fear breeds repression; that repression breeds hate; that hate menaces stable government; that the path of safety lies in the opportunity to discuss freely supposed grievances and proposed remedies ...*".

Of course these precedents, instructive as they may be only carry persuasive authority outside the US. No truly sovereign State should in ever opt for a blanket adoption of another country's laws; that would boarder on total capitulation. That said, if the Judiciary in countries ruled by modern despots is to play a constructive role in delivering the type of freedoms that are said to be inherent, then one of the very first things for them to do should be to fully appreciate the wise counsel dispensed by the American Judges in the cases that we just saw. That, in my view, is the proper approach that should inform any development effort; be it judicial or democratic.

But the modern despot's political insecurities often make the temptation to clamp down on the enjoyment of human rights and other freedoms irresistible for him. And it is for this very reason that Museveni's regime in Uganda has over the years lost countless cases of torture filed by torture victims. Consequently, it was forced to pay out huge sums of taxpayers' money {in damages} to victims of torture; money that would have been better spent on fighting the abject poverty prevailing in most parts of the country.

"Rights abuse cost govt Shs1b" was the perfect newspaper headline that summed it all up for me. It was the headline for a review of the 2005 *Uganda Human Rights Commission* report; a report which found that the biggest percentage of complaints registered and determined by the Commission that year were against State security agencies; who else? And the most common phrase in the report? Yes, it was *"…violation of freedom of…; violation of the right to this; and the right to that;* one after the other in quick succession!

And typically, whenever such a judicial tribunal convicts an oppressive regime of such rights abuses, the modern despot at the helm of it will usually waste no time in accusing those judicial officers of being *"corrupt"* and failing to *"cooperate"*.
Of course, you and I both know that the only reason the despot accuses those institutions of failing to *"cooperate"* is because the Judiciary, for instance, could have stood its ground and resisted all pressure to join in the regime's evil conspiracy to legally oppress its selected victims. If further proof of that were to be needed, then it lies right here in this statement attributed to Uganda's very own modern despot

Gen. Yoweri Kaguta Museveni. We are in the millennium year 2000; or thereabouts. The President of the *Democratic Party* {DP}Dr Paul Ssemogerere had just defeated Museveni's regime. He had successfully challenged the legitimacy of the *Referendum and Other Provisions Act 1999* in the *Constitutional Court*. Thereafter, all heavens brook loose. Unable to contain his anger, an infuriated Museveni described Uganda's judges as *"...lacking patriotism and a proper understanding of NRM's revolutionary methods of work"*.

In that simple utterance, Museveni had made it known to all that the so-called *"revolutionary methods of work"* were actually not *de jure* methods of work but ones premised upon illegalities and violence. As all who worship the rule of law will indeed appreciate, that is a mindset that is seriously deleterious to efforts to entrench the rule of law in any country. Of course, that is not something that the *"revolutionary"* General Museveni cares a great deal about.

So to wrap up this bit, perhaps I should simply say this. In my view, the most reasonable and perhaps even politically judicious course of action to be taken in order to remedy the deficiencies discussed above has to run in sharp contrast to the typical depot's so-called *revolutionary* approach.

And it is, as it must indeed be, that when a government has considerable influence over the law making process as most regimes under modern despots do, then it should strive the hardest, *in its own self interest in fact*, to enact laws that would allow it {as the incumbent government of the day} to not only exist but to freely operate if the roles were to be reversed. History has taught us that except in countries that are under the firm rule of a constitutionally unchallengeable Monarch, any incumbent government is likely to end up in opposition at some point. So a move to enact pro-democracy laws while still in power demonstrates political judiciousness and foresight on the part of the incumbent.

Sadly, it is also the kind of foresight that has somehow eluded the typical modern despot; yes, that one who may be masquerading as a democrat in your country right now.

But it's strange. Strange because no one needs reminding today that the consequences of such recklessness have been shown to be catastrophic for the despots as individuals! Innocent citizens of the countries they rule get caught up in the ensuing mess too. So until both sitting and aspiring political leaders appreciate that very simple fact of politics, I fear that the incessant political upheavals that have bedevilled some of the world's most volatile regions will remain undiminished for generations to come.

Post Script Development

As I have already said, the stubbornness of modern despots never ceases to amaze me. Several months after this debate about the use of *law as a tool of political oppression* was considered wrapped-up, news broke in Uganda of what I can only describe as a re-incarnation of the *Movement Act 1997*. With the adoption of a multi-party system of governance, the *Movement Act* that had conscripted all Ugandans to belong to Museveni's *Movement* party died a *"natural death"*; or so it was thought. Well, it's rearing its ugly head again.

Perhaps sensing that its support base was fast dwindling and shifting towards the opposition parties, Museveni's regime, during a retreat at its ideological school in Kyankwanzi, hatched and announced a *"new"* plan to re-conscript all Ugandan students entering higher education into the NRM-O party; an offshoot of the old *Movement* system. The main thrust of their plan was to make sure all students are forced to undergo compulsory military and ideological training at Kyankwanzi before they could be allowed to progress further with their academic careers.

And the excuse that the regime deployed to defend and justify its plan to re-conscript Ugandans into the NRM-O party was of all things, the law again! *Article* 17{1} {e}of the constitution to be precise; according to NRM-O *Secretary General* Amama Mbabazi at least! The article itself provides that, "*...it is the duty of every citizen of Uganda to defend Uganda and render national service when necessary*".

Reading that article at face value, it may appear that Amama Mbabazi was right on the money. But look deeper into it and you will be amazed at the sheer audacity of Mbabazi's claim.

As a cursory observation for the cynics among you, I say it was not for nothing that it was the NRM-O Secretary General, a man whose job it is to build the capacity of his party, who in the end took it upon himself to defend the conscription of students into fresh military and ideological training. And there may be one more crucial observation to be made here.

I have said this before. As a generally accepted rule of thumb, if a law is designed to achieve something specific, or remedy a specific problem, the only way you can use it to do what it wasn't designed to do would be to misinterpret it and apply it in a manner that does not reflect the true intentions of its framers. That, in my view, is exactly what Amama Mbabazi was attempting to do. To defy the true rationale behind that article for partisan political interests!

And why am I convinced that that was indeed what he was trying to do? Well, for starters, Uganda does not and has never had a tradition of routine national military service. So clearly, in this case, the true intention of the framers of *Article* 17{1} {e}could only have been served by such forceful conscription if it had been objectively deemed to be absolutely *"necessary"*.

The use of the word *"necessary"* at the end of *Article* 17{1} {e}was not by some freak accident. It was intended to have a literal meaning. Therefore, only pure *necessity* could be the proper trigger for it to be invoked. So the question then is: When would it be deemed to be absolutely *"necessary"* to conscript Ugandans into routine national military service? Was there an acute shortage of personnel in the army to the extent that it posed a national security threat? Of course not!

It could only have been the intention of the framers of Uganda's Constitution that such service be required of Ugandan citizens when, for instance, an urgent need to defend the sovereignty and territorial integrity of Uganda arose. And clearly, as far as it could be discerned at the time of that Kyankwanzi announcement, there was no indication whatsoever that Uganda was facing an eminent threat to its sovereignty and territorial integrity. What was under serious threat was the political support base of the modern despot at the helm of the ruling NRM-O party.

Secondly, the fact that another supplementary resolution to recruit NRM-O sympathisers to teach political education in schools was passed at the same Kyankwanzi retreat clearly suggests that the need to rescue the ruling party's support base from serious erosion was indeed the real reason behind the decision to conscript students into the party's ideological school at Kyankwanzi. And it is easy to see why Kyankwanzi, of all places, was the regime's preferred venue for implementing its re-conscription plan.

As in any typical politico-military institute, students would be easily indoctrinated and conscripted into the NRM-O party using a mixture of persuasion and the unquestioning *"indiyo afande"* [*or Yes Sir*] military discipline. Those who have experienced what military discipline is like will tell you that it can be a deterrent like no other. No student can easily identify with opposition causes and views after they have been *told militarily* that it's wrong to do so.

Chapter Four

Despotic Politics & the PRA Treason Case

This is nothing short of an oxymoron; a strange but true case if you like! And it goes like this. From my own Ugandan experience, I have found that one of the most beautiful things about being involved in a peaceful political struggle against a modern despot is the near certainty that it will only be a matter of time before he gives up {sometimes inadvertently} all pretences and comes out clean to show the world his true tyrannical colours. Interesting too is the fact that sometimes, the event, or series of events that finally expose the dictatorship for what it really is, may emerge from the least expected quarters.

What I mean here is that in some cases, those involved in peaceful political opposition to such a dictatorship may not even have to initiate {as you would ordinarily expect} the activity or event that finally strips the modern despot naked. As it blows itself up into a fully fledged dictatorship, everything you ever said in your often frustrating efforts to point out the tyrannical tendencies of the modern despot is totally vindicated without you the fatigued messenger even lifting a finger to pull the final trigger.

In other words, to the messenger's great relief, it is often a typical case of your political opponent fighting your battles for you, against himself! That is the beauty I am talking about here.

So sit back, put your feet up with a cup of tea, or coffee, or a cold beer on a stool next to you, and enjoy the story. The story of how a government that launched a bloody guerrilla war under the false pretence of fighting to restore democracy and the rule of law is finally stripped naked by a single treason case. A very *ordinary* treason case by Ugandan standards in fact!

And, as this bizarre story unfolds, you will see the Museveni dictatorship finally coming of age. You will see all the high sounding values that Museveni claimed to have fought for being thrown out of the window by the very people who allegedly fought and pledged to protect those same values.

A hitherto unblemished image; one of a *"modern democratic"* government crumbling under the weight of its own contradictions is what this is. So here we go then!

In late 2002 or early 2003, barely two years after Museveni *"won"* the 2001 general elections, it was reported in the media that Lieutenant Colonels Samson Mande and Anthony Kyakabale had declared war against Museveni's government from neighbouring Rwanda.
For those who don't know, Lt. Colonels Mande and Kyakabale had actually fought alongside Museveni in the 1981-1986 guerrilla war that brought Museveni to power. But it gets even better. Like Museveni before them, the two Colonels also cited the lack of, and or abuse by Museveni of the very things that they had fought for and pledged to restore. Things like political tolerance, democracy, constitutionalism, the rule of law, human rights observance etc.

And the similarities and contradictions don't end there. Again, like Museveni in 1981, Colonels Mande and Kyakabale were no way near the list of those who had given the incumbent a stiff challenge for the office of President of the Republic of Uganda. In fact, none of them had even contested for the Presidency.

Dr. Kizza Besigye, the man who had given Museveni the toughest challenge in the explosive 2001 presidential elections, had, in a remarkable display of civility, honourably decided to take his grievances to the courts of law. He of course never got the redress that he had sought and perhaps deserved; which was the nullification of the election results declared by the beleaguered Ugandan *Electoral Commission*.

The best he got for his civil efforts was a unanimous concurrence by the Supreme Court Judges that the elections were indeed riddled with serious irregularities, state inspired violence, and that the *Electoral Commission* had not conducted the elections in accordance with the law. Nothing new there! The Supreme Court Judges merely confirmed what you and I expect from an election organised by a modern despot.

In fact, a lot of what we expect from a modern despot had already been documented in Dr. Kizza Besigye's 14-page political critique of Museveni's regime. That critique had already triggered a political avalanche; an avalanche that was already stripping Museveni's regime naked before the PRA case even came to light.

Just to give you a taste of the political avalanche that Dr. Besigye had already triggered, let me tell you this humorous and politically potent analogy from the 2001 Ugandan general elections. Major [Rtd] Okwiri Rabwoni was the *Secretary for Youth Affairs* in the *Elect Kizza Besigye Task Force* [EKBTF] that had been hurriedly put together to respond to the political challenges unfolding.

At one of the campaign rallies in *Kidongole*-Eastern Uganda that I attended and addressed, Rabwoni, speaking through a certain Mr Odea, one of the most charismatic translators I have ever come across, told his keen and attentive audience that Dr. Besigye had finally *"Belled the Cat"*. A few of us on the campaign team immediately burst into hearty fits of laughter. But there was dead silence from the rest of the audience; nothing, nothing at all. The village folk of *Kidongole* simply hadn't grasped the significance and sensationalism of what they had just heard. Rabwoni noticed it too.

So to demystify his devastating political analogy, he went for a more pedestrian approach. And he had to; because the illiteracy rate in parts of rural Uganda is simply shocking. Anyway, Rabwoni then told the *Kidongole* audience that the *Cat* Dr. Besigye had *belled* was in fact called Yoweri Museveni. And the reason Besigye had *belled* it, [or put a bell around Museveni's neck] was to fore-warn Ugandans to run for dear life when they hear the bell around Museveni's neck chiming from a distance.

With that, the place immediately came alive. The crowed, a healthy mixture of young and old village folk, loved every moment of it. In fact, strange as this may sound to you, I got the feeling at the time that they were laughing about it in their local *Ateso* language. It had sunk that deep; believe me.

To this day, I don't know that anyone could have put it any better than Okwiri Rabwoni; coming as it did, at that defining moment in Uganda's politics. It was the most fitting description of what was happening to Museveni's *"democratic"* credentials. Indeed, some political analysts have since argued that at the time, with the process of stripping the Museveni regime of the democracy rags that had been wrapped around its *despotic body* well underway, the regime knew that its fraudulent cover had finally been blown.

Secondly, that Museveni's regime knew deep down that had it not been for the vicious violence it had visited upon Dr. Besigye's supporters, the State resources it had used at will, the ballot box stuffing, plus many other electoral irregularities criticised by the Supreme Court, things might have been very different for candidate Museveni. .

In fact, I think without the absurdity in the law which required the challenger [Dr. Kizza Besigye] to prove that the irregularities had *"Substantially Affected"* the outcome of the election, Museveni would not have been handed the mantles of State power by a 3-2 majority decision of the Supreme Court. In other words, Museveni was an undeserving winner. I think the regime knew it too. And because they knew it, they must have concluded that it was only a matter of time before someone does exactly what they did in 1981.

That was of course the time when Museveni & Co decided to wage a *"Protest War"* against Milton Obote's government; a government Museveni had accused of doing exactly the same things he is now being accused of doing. The only difference, a significant one worth noting in fact, was that this time round, it was the Supreme Court of Uganda that had found against Museveni *"the accused"*. The inherent legitimacy of that Court decision surely sets it apart from Museveni's own unilateral decision of 1981.

So considering all that, I don't think it's terribly difficult to see that the regime could have easily concluded that because of its illegitimate victory, it urgently needed to find ways of pre-empting and or discouraging the possibility of politically aggrieved Ugandans taking up arms to fight an illegitimate government; exactly as they had done themselves in 1981. Yes, these are mere theories.

But if they come anywhere near the truth, which I think they do, then it would also be easy to see that to the Museveni regime, the media report of an alleged plot by Colonels Samson Mande and Anthony Kyakabale to wage war against the government was the perfect excuse they needed to start cracking down hard on dissenting voices within and outside the country. In the words of Dr. Tajudeen Abdul-Raheem [RIP], the news of an alleged rebellion was *"a truly God sent gift"* to Museveni.

In the end, Dr. Besigye and many of his political assistants and supporters took the painful decision to flee the country in search of freedom in foreign countries. From just across Uganda's boarders, to lands beyond the African continent; the political exodus was on! And it was from one these places of exile, the volatile Democratic Republic of Congo {DRC} to be precise, that the BBC *World Service* programme *Focus on Africa* broke the news that some 22 Ugandan dissidents had been arrested by Ugandan soldiers based in the DRC.

Museveni's regime of course quickly concluded that the captured men were rebels belonging to the PRA that was under the command of Colonels Samson Mande and Anthony Kyakabale; the two renegade UPDF officers who had allegedly declared war against the government of Uganda. *"A truly God sent gift"* indeed!

I had actively contributed to Dr. Besigye's campaign. So naturally, I received the news of the DRC arrests with incredulity and great sadness. Great sadness because the voice of one of the captured men being interviewed by the BBC's Anna Bozelo sounded very familiar to me. And, as it later turned out, he was indeed my very close personal, political and professional friend.

I vividly remember that as the news broke, it was a fine afternoon and I was sitting on the bed staring out of the fourth floor bedroom window of a flat on Horn Lane in West London. My companion at that moment didn't even know the significance to me of the news we were both listening to. And before I told her what it was all about, my thoughts immediately turned to my friend's wife who also, believe it not, was by now in exile having been forced to flee Uganda because of her own and her husband's political activism against Museveni's regime.

The skills to calmly deliver bad news to people you love and care about do not come naturally to most people. The tension in me was almost unbearable. My heart was threatening to jump out of my less than broad chest. I started shaking. How would she take the news of this tragedy that was yet to be confirmed beyond doubt, I wondered? How? In the end, I instinctively opted to tow the strategy that most people would have probably opted for. I reached for the phone, called up the poor woman living alone exile, and I tried my very best to prepare her for the worst in the best way I could.

Naturally, *"Jennie"* [as I call her] greeted the news with a very loud silence along the phone line. It was a silence that lasted for what seemed like eternity to me. And yet, in reality, it probably was for no more than two seconds. Those few seconds were weird; very weird in fact. None of us was able to say a word to each other; nothing!

And then, after a deep and heavy breath, she simply said: *"Oh my God Charlie; is he alive"?* To the best of my knowledge, yes; I said. And then, with great relief, she simply said *"that's what matters. He will be okay. That brother of yours is a hard nut to crack"*. To say that I was astonished would be the understatement of the century. I simply couldn't believe my ears. Her strength and ability to quickly absorb and cope with such devastating news is one thing; but that she also seemed to be consoling me instead is quite another. *"What a woman, what a woman"* was all I could quietly say to myself; with great relief!

Anyway within days of that DRC news incident, the group of 22 were flown in a military transport aircraft from the DRC to the North Western Ugandan town of Arua. They were then paraded before the media; even though I thought the legality of such action was highly questionable. Nonetheless, it was at this media parade that the identities of many of the captured men became known. A sizeable number of them, it turned out, were in fact young Ugandan professionals; Doctors and Lawyers included.

According to one of the many theories that were flying all over the place at the time, these were Dr. Besigye's supporters who had been abducted by Ugandan intelligence operatives from the DRC; a neighbouring country where they had sought political asylum. Fits nicely within my earlier explanation doesn't it? But as you can imagine, in the heat of those emotionally charged moments, it was a near impossibility for anyone to verify the abduction claims with certainty. Neither could the association of the 22 men with the shadowy PRA rebel group be verified with any easy.

It was also at the same media parade that my worst fears were confirmed. Not only was my close friend among the group of 22, but other friends whom I had come to know fairly well during the 2001 election campaigns were also in the published group picture. Highly educated professionals that you would ordinarily expect to see in neat Western suits and ties. Not anymore.

They were now in rags; their hair unkempt! Seated on the red Ugandan soil, they looked every bit like chicken thieves; petrified, totally humiliated by the Ugandan State; their own State! What a shame! It is a sight that will remain vivid in my memory as a permanent reminder of what man can do to man.

From the humiliating *Photo Opportunity* in Arua town, the poor souls were taken to the capital city Kampala and held in illegal *"Safe Houses"* for months without charge. Tales of horrendous and mercilessly torture to extort confessions from the captives have since emerged from the blood stained walls of those infamous *"Safe Houses"*. Scores of other people who had supported Dr. Besigye's candidature were also arrested from around the country and brought in to join the initial haul of 22 from the DRC.

For months on end, these men were held incommunicado without charge; all in spite of the fact that article 23{4}{b}of the constitution of Uganda expressly provides that: *"...A person arrested or detained upon reasonable suspicion of his or her having committed or being about to commit a criminal offence under the laws of Uganda shall, if not earlier released, be brought to court as soon as possible but in any case not later than forty eight hours from the time of his or her arrest".*

This is precisely the conflict between legal *theory* and *practice* that we talked about earlier. In the end, it took a Writ of Habeas Corpus for a production warrant to be issued by the High Court. That is how the suspects ended up before a Judge to take plea on the charge of treason. And we must not forget that the *"State"* in this case was dominated by the very Museveni lot who went to the bush under the guise of fighting to restore the *rule of law*. So for the same people to be compelled by a Court order to obey the law is a very sad commentary indeed.

Anyway, with the so-called PRA rebel suspects *safely* tucked away in a remand prison, Museveni's regime wasted no time in fabricating a link between the PRA rebel suspects and Dr. Kizza Besigye; claiming that Dr. Besigye was the overall political leader of the *"PRA rebels"*. However, to this day as I write, the *"PRA"* treason case is still lying dormant in court.

Like many Ugandans, I wait with bated breath to see if the State will produce sufficient evidence to prove that there was such a thing as the *Peoples Redemption Army*; that it had the necessary *"intent"* to wage war against the government of Uganda; and that it actually *"did"* something to put into effect that alleged intent. Interesting times ahead indeed!

But, knowing what we now know about the propensity of modern despots to use the law to oppress their political opponents, I think a question has to be asked: Can the offence of treason really ever be a politically *innocent offence* in a country ruled by a modern despot?

In Uganda, as is the case in many other countries, the offence of treason is one that is deemed to have been committed against the State. That presumption raises the gravity of the offence of treason significantly. What that means is that treason then becomes an offence that can only be tried by the High Court of Uganda.

Originally, *clause* 6{c} of *Article 23* of the constitution of Uganda had this to say about offences of that nature. *"...Where a person is arrested* {and charged of course}*in respect of a criminal offence triable only by the High Court, the person shall be released on bail on such conditions as the court considers reasonable, if the person has been remanded in custody for three hundred and sixty days before the case is committed to the High Court"*.

That was Museveni's law as it stood at one point. In fact, even when independent human rights organisations petitioned against the apparent injustice inherent in the length of the remand period for the offence of treason, Museveni's regime only accepted to reduce it from 365days to 180days. I think the difference of a few months, although terribly important for anyone who is desperate to regain his freedom, is still a lesser issue in terms of gravity compared to the net implications of the clause.

What worried me the most was the fact that technically, if a despot were to deem it appropriate to slap the offence of treason on your head, then you would definitely have to spend some considerable time cooling off in a filthy remand prison somewhere before you become eligible for release on bail.

With such a lethal and above all legal weapon of political oppression at the disposal of a modern despot, I think he would have no difficulty whatsoever in directing his hand-picked *Director of Public Prosecutions* {DPP}to charge the most formidable political opponents with treason. That way, the particularly *stubborn* ones would be kept out of action for some time; allowing the *"big man"* to rule happily in peace. It serves the modern despot very well doesn't it?

Is it any wonder therefore that the majority of people who have been charged with treason under Museveni's rule have in fact been opposition politicians? Evaristo Nyanzi, Zachery

Olum, Professor Isaac Newton Ojok, Daniel Omara Atubo, [now in bed with the devil], and FDC's Dr. Kizza Besigye were all opposition politicians at the time they were charged with treason. That is just a snap-shot. The full list, were it to be published, could be embarrassing.

In fact to add credence to the hypothesis that such oppressive criminal laws are largely used by modern despots to cripple their political opponents, there are claims that similar provisions exist under Zambian criminal law too. It is said that where the offence of treason plays the role of a political magic wand for Uganda's Yoweri Museveni, in Zambia, the equivalent offence is, of all things, car theft! Anyone charged with car theft becomes an automatic candidate for remand in custody for a mandatory period of not less than twelve months before they can apply to be released on bail. Again, like it is in Uganda, it is claimed that the majority of people charged with car theft in Zambia have been opposition politicians.

In Nigeria, it is also claimed that a mere indictment for *Corruption* is to Nigeria's modern despots what *Treason* and *Car Theft* is to Ugandan and Zambian despots. The only difference is that in Nigeria, the sanction is not remand in custody for one year but an automatic disqualification from offering yourself for election to any political office.

To this day, some Nigerians still swear on their ancestors' graves that this is exactly what Mr. Atiku, Nigeria's former Vice President, got for his role in opposing his boss President Olusegun Obasanjo's failed bid to amend Nigeria's constitution to allow himself a third shot at the presidency.
Uganda's Yoweri Museveni had of course, with a mixture of bribes and dubious parliamentary manoeuvres, already set that most obnoxious political precedent that I suppose Obasanjo thought he could ride on. Thank God he never got his way. But here is the other important observation about what modern despots appear to have achieved.

When you look at Uganda's treason law and its counterparts in Zambia and Nigeria, it is pretty difficult to resist the conclusion that the sheer need for political survival by modern despots has also put the very philosophy of law on trial. And the reason I say that is because there is absolutely no doubt in my mind that *injustice* has been written into those laws.

In those circumstances, you then wonder whether the law doesn't actually need saving from itself. In fact, it reminds me of the ancient revolutionary maxim which states that *"When Injustice Becomes Law, Resistance Becomes a Duty"*. So could resistance be a justified course of action [even today] to protect and preserve the *"public good"* element that is said to be inherent in the philosophy of law? I don't know. You be the Judges of that!

What I know for sure is that if such a pathetic state of affairs is left unchallenged, then people living in such countries would be risking a lifetime of legal and political servitude. In the case of Uganda, for example, with all those ghastly and despotic things going on legally, I believe Ugandans may have reached that critical point in time when they have to take some very tough and painful decisions to save their country.

Indeed, as a friend of mine once put it in a newspaper article, *"...to save Uganda today, we may need to destroy it first"*. Very radical thoughts, you might think. Yes, perhaps! But it is also a very good hint of the sort of things that run through the minds of an oppressed people. It shows that there is an instinctive urge in all humans to do whatever it takes to untie themselves from the shackles of legalised political oppression whenever they are faced with one. *Desperate times call for desperate measures*; so the saying goes.

And to see where my friend was coming from when he made that radical suggestion, you need look no further than a few utterances attributed to Uganda's ruler. Sometime in September 2007, the media reported that Museveni had said some things that I think brought out his true undemocratic credentials.

During a visit to a place called Dwaniro in Kiboga District, {a former base camp that his NRA guerrillas once used}Museveni confessed to having had some dangerous intentions during the 1996 presidential elections between himself and Dr. Paul K. Ssemogerere. Addressing the locals who had turned up to listen to him, he said, "...*had you elected Ssemogerere we would have gone [back] to the bush. What else should we have done?*

I am not sure that warrants any further comment or emphasis. It is clear. The will of the people, delivered in accordance with the law, is not something that modern despots like Uganda's Museveni recognise and respect. Not even when their loss comes in spite of all the unfair political benefits of incumbency that they naturally enjoy in such contests.

Fast forward to February 2009! Museveni is at it again. This time, the *Daily Monitor* newspaper of February 18th {see *No Votes, No Cabinet Posts-Museveni*}reported that while addressing residents of Arua town, Museveni, sent another chilling warning to his listeners and said, "...*if you vote for Besigye, you will have voted for a civil war. It is not a joking matter but a serious thing that you vote for NRM*".

That despotic warning prompted Mr. Omar Kalinge Nnyago, a regular political commentator, to conclude that "...*while President Museveni's unfortunate remarks disturbed every civilised Ugandan, they exposed his regime for what it was- a rogue regime bent on causing and spreading death and destruction unless it is allowed to ruin the country without challenge. It shamed his Western supporters, especially the United States and Western Europe, who have sold him as the best thing that ever happened to Uganda. Now they know they were wrong..."*

I don't think I, you, or indeed anyone for that matter, needs any further proof that there are modern despots out there. And for those of you who value your personal liberties, worship your full democratic rights, and treasure good governance, the question I have for you is this: What, in your opinion, would be the best course of action for oppressed people if they wanted to deal with the scourge of modern despots decisively?

Several years ago, Kenya's legendary General Kimathi made it clear that there was only one way of dealing with oppression. *"...I would rather die on my feet than live on my knees";* he said. Anything short of that could have meant *"life on knees"* {before British colonialists} for several generations of Kenyans. If not physically, then certainly psychologically; struggling to live with a nasty feeling of perpetual inferiority.

Now then, having seen the political utility value of the law of treason to the typical modern despot that Uganda's Yoweri Museveni represents in this book, I hope, with reflection, it will now become that little bit easier for you to see how, and perhaps even why, the PRA suspects were safely tucked away in prison on remand. But the drama in the PRA case did not end with the slamming of the remand prison doors. It unfolds and deteriorates in a most dramatic fashion with Dr. Kizza Besigye's return to Uganda.

The Second Coming of the Devil

March 2nd 2007. It's just after dusk, around 20:00hrs *East African Standard Time.* We are at *Sippers Bar* in Hurlingham; one of Nairobi's many entertainment districts! Soothing African songs of local and regional origin are ruling the airwaves here tonight. The volume is just perfect. And

who are the other guests in the house tonight?
Well, I would say it was a very healthy *"united nations"* mix. Ultra skinny-chain-smoking and slightly crazy behaving young African girls of average beauty in the company of greying pony-tail wearing European men; you know, the type of men who, thanks to the Western media, would perfectly fit many people's imagination of a typical paedophile or sex tourist.

On the other hand, you could see middle aged black men [mostly Kenyans] with loosened neck ties, looking big and twiddling nonstop with their latest gadgets; just to impress the obedient, shy looking and thoroughly intimidated girls sitting next to them. By this time of the evening, many are probably on their third or fourth bottle of beer, wine or cocktail glass. It is also unimaginable that the true *"Kenyan Institution"* that is *"Nyama Choma"* {Swahili for roast meat}will have survived this sitting. All in all, it is a very *ordinary* evening in Nairobi town, Kenya's capital city.

Approximately 600miles to the west of Kenya, the atmosphere in the suburbs of Uganda's capital city Kampala is probably no different from Nairobi's. Beer, roast pork, giggling girls and music in the background was what I could imagine and hear when an ecstatic sounding Lawyer, a former colleague, decided to drop me a line to break news of the momentous events of the day; a different kind of day. With more than just a slight touch of triumphalism and defiance coming through his voice, he said, *"...Counsel, we have laid down our tools in protest. Enough is enough"*.

Before I even got the opportunity to ask why they had laid down their {legal practice}tools, my friend, like a man possessed by some kind of *"Eddie Murphy"* talking demon, had already launched straight into the details of what had transpired at the High of Uganda the previous day; March 1st 2007.

March 1st 2007 was of course *"Black Thursday"*; the day when, for the second time in less than two years, over fifty fully armed State security personnel stormed the High Court to re-arrest some of the PRA suspects who had just been granted bail. The only difference was that this time round, the media chose to describe the High Court invaders as *"...men dressed in police uniform"*.

And who could blame them; because ever since the infamous *Black Mamba Urban Hit Squad* turned up at the High Court poorly disguised in police uniform, no one could be sure anymore that men dressed as police officers were actually police officers. In other words, trust in the *Uganda Police Force* as an institution of State had completely broken down; thanks to a despot's decision to abuse the independence and integrity of an institution that should have been totally impartial. Sad; really sad!

But as I said, that was the second invasion. The first time the High Court was raided by the *Black Mambas* was on the 16th of November 2005. That very sad incident had prompted Justice James Munange Ogola, Uganda's Principle Judge no less, to famously declare that *"...the siege constituted a very grave and heinous violation of the twin principles of the rule of law and Judicial independence [and] sent a chilling feeling down the spine of the Judiciary, and left the legal fraternity and the general public agape with disbelief and wonderment"*.

The Second Coming of the Devil, as I prefer to call it, had also elicited a most epic poem from the same Principle Judge. It was a poem in which the Judge, as a *"witness"* this time, [what an irony] explained with poetic eloquence what had transpired at his sacred seat of judgement. That poem should be available in the public domain. I say hunt it down and read it as if your very life depended on it. You will not regret it.

Now back to Nairobi's *Sippers Bar* on the night of March 2nd 2007. It is just over fifteen months since the first siege on the High Court. In a strange if slightly tragic coincidence, unbeknown to the friend calling from Kampala to give me the *"breaking news"* about Lawyers downing their tools, Samuel Nathan Okiring, a very close friend who I can't even bear to call *"an ex-PRA suspect"*, had just arrived from Uganda to meet me.

In fact, he was seated right next to me; narrating the gruesome story of his horrendous torture at the hands of almost certainly the very State security operatives who had just raided the High Court to re-arrest his former co-accused PRA suspects. The mixture of emotions I went through at that material time is still difficult to explain. In fact, it is impossible to explain; not if you are or were in my position.

Sam Okiring, the *"Attorney General of the Rebels"*, [as one Kampala friend once called him jokingly] was totally unaware that I was now faced with a very uncomfortable situation; a dilemma in fact. Here was a visibly traumatised friend, a great friend, a brother to me in every sense, sitting very humbly in front me, not knowing what the Kampala friend on the other end of the telephone line had just told me. In fact, to show you how traumatised Okiring was, I will tell you a very sad little story.

On this hot, windy and unusually dusty Nairobi afternoon, Sam Okiring, myself, and another friend were walking on the paved footpath of *Ngong Road* towards *Adams Arcade* to catch a *Citi Hoppa* bus. Then, out of nowhere, a Ugandan registered vehicle with heavily tinted windows came from behind and suddenly pulled up in front us. I hadn't even noticed it. But Okiring's reaction on that day told me something fundamental and unchallengeable about what he had gone through at the hands of Museveni's merchants of death.

First of all, he froze dead in his tracks; right there! He then quickly, almost instinctively, turned his face away from the vehicle to avoid being recognised. That didn't seem to help. He then tried to flee, but quickly decided against it. Finally, with a torrent of sweat rolling all over his face, his shoulders dropped and he said, *"Oh my God"*. That was it, Okiring had resigned. All within a matter of seconds! That *"Oh my God"* exclamation, as I understood it, was Okiring asking God why; why are you taking me back there again? What did I do to deserve this? It was sad; very sad indeed to see a close friend in that state!

But that is exactly what your typical modern despot, like his ancient ancestor, is capable of *"achieving"* in his quest to silence any form of civilised political dissent. Depending on how the modern despot judges the level of threat you pose, he could treat you harshly and then release you; but not before he has instilled so much fear in you to make you think and believe that you are being watched and listened to all the time. In fact, after he regained his composure, Okiring told me over a drink that "*...Museveni can make you stop trusting your own shadow"*. Now that is a terrifying prospect; even to merely think about!

That car incident gave me a glimpse into Okiring's state of mind at the time; a state of mind that gave me real cause to worry about his health. In fact, it made me appreciate, perhaps for the first time, what sustained physical and psychological torture can do to a man. But let us go back to that telephone conversation I had at Sippers Bar with the Kampala based Lawyer; a young man whose security I will not compromise by disclosing his full names here. What a tragedy! Before I hanged-up on the Kampala friend, a number of disturbing questions were already racing through my slightly intoxicated mind. How prudent, I wondered, would it be for me to reveal all to Okiring there and then when all seemed to be going well for him that evening?

I imagined, perhaps out of fear that Okiring may still be in the very early stages of his recovery from the psychological trauma he had endured at the hands of the nasty *"Men in Black"* who had just raided the High Court. In a nutshell, my dilemma was essentially about how he would react to the news? The poor old chap didn't even know that in those few seconds and minutes, I was having a very serious internal debate about his fate.

In the end, even though I was still totally unsure, I took the risk and told him what I had been told by our learned friend who had just called from Kampala. The gamble paid off. The news didn't affect him; at least not visibly and in the manner I had feared. On the contrary, he looked jubilant. Even in the dimmed and slightly promiscuous lights of *Sippers Bar*, I could see that he was fighting bravely, as usual, to hold back some tears of joy in his eyes.

Then, as if by magic, we moved closer to each other and went for one hell of a hug; a big fat hug that went on in total silence for what seemed like eternity. We were like kids who had just been re-united at their father's funeral.

And yes, our father's funeral it was; because for Sam Okiring and I, as Lawyers, our beloved *father* was the rule of law that Museveni's regime had just murdered in cold blood by the second siege on the High Court. The same siege also forced Uganda's *Deputy Chief Justice* Laetitia Kikonyogo to declare that, *"...all judicial business for all courts in Uganda is suspended with effect from March 5th 2007"*.

Still speaking on behalf of and with the Judiciary's full authority, Justice Kikonyogo further accused the regime of among other things, the*"...repeated violation of the sanctity of the court premises, disobedience of court orders with impunity and the constant threats and attacks on the safety and independence of the Judiciary and judicial officers"*.

With those very simple words coming from the *red-hot* judicial lips of Justice Laetitia Kikonyogo, national, and possibly world judicial history had been made in a far off corner of the world that had not been known for its great judicial precedents. In fact, that was the second time Justice Laetitia Kikonyogo was making national judicial history. The first time was when she became the very first woman to conquer the *Judicial Service Mountain* to the office of *Deputy Chief Justice* of Uganda. Not an insignificant achievement in a profession that had hitherto been largely masculine in outlook.

In the same statement, the Judiciary also complained bitterly about what it called *"...the savage violence exhibited by security personnel within the court premises"*; violence that saw one of the Defence Lawyers [for the PRA suspects] assaulted and left with blood gushing out of his head. Absolutely astonishing!

Finally, the Judiciary also complained about *"...the total failure by all organs and agencies of the state to accord to the courts assistance as required to ensure effectiveness of the courts, and the recognition that Judicial power is derived from the people, to be exercised by the courts on behalf of the people in conformity with the law, the values, norms and aspirations of the people of Uganda"*.

I think there can be no doubt that the Judiciary's grievances touched on almost every conceivable aspect of the administration of justice in Uganda. In fact, I think the regime's actions amounted to nothing less than a complete overthrow of the constitution. That in its own right must be seen as sufficient justification for the protest action taken by the Judiciary. Therefore, the clear lesson from this Ugandan mess for other countries ruled by modern despots is this:

As soon as it becomes apparent that the despot's regime has embarked on a treacherous course of lawlessness, then that should be the perfect time to nip that lawlessness in the bud with such crippling protest action. You see, the typical modern despot, by his very nature, knows that he cannot hang on to power indefinitely [as he wishes] without laying claim to a certain degree of democratic civility. And the functioning of the Judiciary, as a crucial arm of any democratic State, gives him the perfect excuse and authority to claim some civility and legitimacy.

Some political commentators have always argued that *"...democracy has no values"*. That as a concept of political governance, *"...it is only as good as the liberal principles of those who practice it"*! So unless the modern despot carries a disproportionate amount of his autocratic ancestor's genes, he will have no choice but to pay heed to the Judiciary's protest. After all, that is the only way he can continue claiming some pseudo democratic credentials.

But let's go back to Uganda's PRA case. As I said earlier, after their second arrest from the High Court, the PRA suspects were driven off at break-neck speed to unknown destinations. Like experienced urban thugs, Museveni's political thugs too, perhaps in the interest of *"operational efficiency"*, decided to take full advantage of the power cuts and attendant darkness that routinely descends upon the capital city Kampala.

Under the cover of darkness, they whisked their victims off to face the wrath of bloodthirsty red-eyed men. And as they were being whisked off, one of the PRA suspects I spoke to said they were still being beaten mercilessly; even as they sat obligingly on the back of the speeding military Pick-Up trucks.

The next thing the world knew of these poor souls was that the regime had decided, perhaps for the sheer fun of it, that *"Murder"* charges would suit the PRA suspects best. Very serious capital offences [which attract a death sentence in

Uganda] were being played around with as if they were costumes that theatre actors wear and remove at will. That is exactly what a modern despot is capable of. He will make the rule of law a complete farce if that is what it takes for him to secure some sort of political advantage.

After the *Murder* charges had been slapped on the bowed heads of the PRA suspects, Museveni's regime then decided to split the group of six into two and flew them away from the capital city [the seat of the High Court] to up country prisons in Bushenyi and Arua; towns that are located several hundred kilometres to the South and North West of the Uganda respectively. That way perhaps, the *"bad"* publicity that the regime was getting from city Journalists would be momentarily halted. The modern despot is very weary of *bad* publicity; he is a *Public Relations* showman in fact! So instead of maintaining the gag on the media's coverage of the PRA case, [which could have tripled the negative publicity it was already getting] Museveni's regime opted for the safer option. It took the *"stars of the show"* away from the city. How ingenious!

But there is one crucial fact that you must take note of in this whole PRA mess. All these bizarre criminal charges that kept popping out of thin air were not for nothing. And the proof is here: The *Daily Monitor* newspaper published a report that contained Museveni's reaction to the disgraceful events that had unfolded at the High Court on March 1st 2007. The paper said that according to some MPs from Museveni's NRM-O party who attended one particular meeting, Museveni insisted that *"...it was illegal for the High Court to grant bail to the PRA suspects".*

The same Museveni is then reported to have added that, *"...as far as the government is concerned, the PRA suspects will never be released because they are still a security threat to this nation. If they are released, they shall be re-arrested. If they want to be free, amnesty is the only way for them".*

Charles Ochen Okwir

So my strong suspicion is that Museveni, as the *Commander-in-Chief* of the High Court siege thugs, had long decried that the PRA suspects would never be released on bail except on his own terms. In other words, the PRA suspects' right to liberty, as provided for by the supreme law of the land, would not be determined by *"mere"* Judges sitting in courts of law. So the bizarre criminal charges that seemed to be coming from a ruthless but invisible conveyor belt were really an effort by Museveni's legal handlers to put some sanity into what was effectively an illegal despotic decree.

PRA Suspect: *"I am a Guest of the Head of State"*

It was approximately 3pm *East African Standard Time* on a glorious, sunny, Sunday afternoon when another good friend from Kampala called me for what I thought would be an ordinary lad's chat. I was at a family entertainment centre near Nairobi Hospital. Can't remember what it was called. Beautiful place it was though! Graced, almost literally, with the performance of a live band that played mostly gospel songs! Happy noisy kids ran riot around the sandy compound with their fun painted faces; all in their Sunday best of course!

Under the large *Tusker* beer umbrellas on the other hand, nearly all the adults, like a pride of African Lions, seemed to be munching away at something meaty; as only Kenyans know best. It was from this lovely setting that I excused myself and stepped aside to take the call from the second Kampala based friend. What this chap told me on phone triggered a massive contest between my senses.

Here I was; my eyes fixated at the beauty all around me, my nose smelling the delicious smoke from roasting meat, and my ears were hearing a cocktail of great gospel music and rib cracking jokes from the Kampala friend on the phone. The human body is a great machine!

But there were also moments of great sadness as we discussed the *Museveni Vs PRA* debacle. For both its deep sadness and extraordinary funniness, one particular joke stayed with me and will do for a very long time to come. My friend told me that during a visit to one of the regime's ghastly detention facilities, one PRA suspect told him something very interesting.

In both resignation and as a veiled reference to the break down in the rule of law in Uganda, this PRA suspect joked and said: *"...I am a guest of the Head of State and I travel with full military escorts. I can't just leave this comfortable State Lodge at the behest of a mere Judge when my host His Excellency the President of the Republic of Uganda hasn't bed me farewell".*

How a man who has suffered so much torture, trauma, and injustice over several years can retain his courage and sense of humour to come up with such a rib cracking joke, a joke that many stand up comedians would kill for, is beyond belief. Simply incredible!

It just goes to show that while modern despots like Museveni may have the crude power to physically incarcerate and even humiliate great men, they can never, ever, take full control of their great minds. Because in great minds resides an even mightier power; a more superior power; one that can privately dissect and ridicule even the most fierce despot like Museveni to shreds.

Viewed differently, the PRA suspect's joke can, and must be seen as an absolute triumph of the human spirit over evil. But most importantly, if viewed in its proper context, then it is also the most damning indictment on Uganda's due process of law and the *Presidency*; a *Presidency* that is constitutionally supposed to be the *"Fountain of Honour"*. What an irony!

Judicial power in almost every country "...*is derived from the people...and* "*exercised by the courts on behalf of the people*". So the Judiciary's order to the State to release the PRA suspects on bail couldn't have been *illegal* as Museveni disdainfully claimed.

On the contrary, it was Museveni who breached a lawful High Court order by decreeing that the PRA suspects should "...*never be released because they are still a security threat*". What that also means is that once again, Museveni had effectively {to use his own words}"*usurped*" the powers vested in the Judiciary and in the process, probably overthrown the Constitution for the tenth or even twentieth time. Now here is the juicy bit. Only a few months earlier, Museveni had accused the Judiciary of "*usurping*" the people's power when it legitimately ruled against his regime and nullified the *Referendum Act 2000*. The twists and turns of a depot's politics eh! Very interesting to the disinterested observer; although not, I imagine, quite as interesting to those bearing the brunt of its ugly traits.

But I also have a very big quarrel with oppressed people in some parts of the world. Their conviction and courage to stand up against despots in every way possible is still seriously wanting. That really has to change if they value the benefits that can accrue from a strict adherence to the rule of law and full democratic governance.

In the meantime however, our bleeding hearts must go out to those who *invented* democracy and its support mechanisms. Because whereas Museveni's actions and utterances may appear to be mind blowing abuses of those support mechanisms, the reality is also that actually, Museveni's behaviour is fairly typical of what you would expect from the typical modern despot; the type who allocates too much power to himself for even his own good. "*Absolute power corrupts absolutely*"! If you want hard evidence of that, I say be my guest.

While responding to concerns by Ugandan MPs about the increased use of teargas in the country, Museveni, being a man who is totally detached from the realities of life as ordinary men and women know it, said "...*teargas shall continue to be used because it's the only method that is effective in handling those who challenge the Constitution*". That statement, even in its current form, already sounds insane. But it becomes even more ridiculous when you think that by his decision to overrule the High Court which had granted the PRA suspects bail, Museveni was in fact the *Chief Challenger* to constitutional order in Uganda.

So if his latest statement were to be taken as *"law"*, [as the police and army often do] then he would have been the very first person to receive a decent dose of teargas. But that, believe it or not, is not the real reason I suggested that absolute power has indeed corrupted Museveni absolutely. The real reason is this. And you have to read his follow-up statement very carefully for it to sink in!

In a most contemptuous way, the invincible General Museveni, the *"All Caring Father of the Nation"*, is said to have added that "*...this* [meaning teargas] *is not something to worry you. It only itches for a small time and someone becomes normal again"*.

Clearly, the fact that he is the *Commander-in-Chief* of the teargas men has so blinded him that he even refuses to acknowledge the gravity of its effects on adults. In fact, there is tragic evidence to show that if used in large quantities, teargas can cause death to children. That is exactly what happened to an innocent child who had been exposed to Museveni's beloved teargas on the streets Kampala. And to appreciate the insensitivity of Museveni's teargas statement even more, I can tell you that he made only a few days after the child's death from teargas. Absolutely incredible!

Charles Ochen Okwir

As far as the PRA case is concerned, I think there are very few people out there who are better qualified to comment on it than a certain David Mpanga. *"Daudi"*, as he calls himself, was the man who, together with his colleagues, constituted what in my view was the *pro bono* defence legal team for some of the PRA suspects. So, with his express consent, I will reproduce his views on the PRA debacle [in two parts] hereunder:

PRA 22: All Ugandans be Afraid (Part One)

On January 5, 2007, the *General Court Martial* commenced the trial of 22 *People's Redemption Army* {PRA}suspects on charges of unlawful possession of firearms contrary to the *Firearms Act*. The continued detention of 14 of the 22 suspects on the orders of the *General Court Martial* and the commencement of the trial in the *General Court Martial* represents a creeping and dangerous challenge to the Constitution of the Republic of Uganda as well as constitutionalism and the rule of law in this country. The 22 suspects were arrested in November 2004 and were charged in the civilian courts with treason. In November 2005, the *Forum for Democratic Change* President, Dr Kizza Besigye, was arrested and joined to the 22 suspects as Accused No. 1.

In November 2005, 14 out of the 22 were granted bail by the High Court. This grant of bail so incensed the powers that be that they unleashed the, hitherto unknown but since often sighted, *Joint Anti-Terrorism Task Force Urban Hit Squad* {aka the *Black Mambas*}to lay siege on the *High Court* so as to ensure that all the bailed suspects were taken back to Luzira Prison. Then, for no apparent reason other than to obtain an assured remand in custody, the State commenced parallel terrorism and firearms charges proceedings in the *General Court Martial* against Dr. Besigye and the 22 suspects.

The *Uganda Law Society* challenged the Court Martial proceedings against Dr Besigye and the 22 Suspects in the *Constitutional Court*. The *Constitutional Court* ruled that those proceedings contravened the Constitution and infringed upon the suspects' basic human rights. But despite that judgement, the *General Court Martial* refused to release the Suspects, other than Dr Besigye. They remain in illegal detention up to date.

In May 2006 the 22 suspects went back to the *Constitutional Court* to challenge their continued detention and the fairness of their trial in the High Court whilst in unlawful detention. This prompted the State to amend the charges in the *General Court Martial*, in June 2006, by dropping Dr Besigye as an accused person and dropping the terrorism charges.

Then in November 2006 {a whole two years after the suspects were arrested} the 22 suspects were charged with new firearms offence relating to events that allegedly took place in 2001. This was clearly in order to ensure that there is some pretext to continue the detention if their May 2006 challenge should be successful. The 22 suspects launched a second petition in the *Constitutional Court* to challenge the constitutionality and fairness of the new charges and seeking an order banning the State from manipulating the *General Court Martial* in such a way as to defeat judicial orders made in favour of the 22 suspects in the *Constitutional Court* and the *High Court*.

The Constitution is the supreme law of the land and the Bill of Rights contained therein is supposed to be the ultimate guarantee of the human rights of all Ugandans. The *Constitutional Court* is given the duty of interpreting the Constitution and determining whether the action of any person or authority is in contravention of or is inconsistent with the Constitution of Uganda. Appeals from the *Constitutional Court* lie with the *Supreme Court*.

No other person or authority has the power to interpret the Constitution and everyone in Uganda is bound by the decisions of the *Constitutional Court* unless and until they are overruled by the *Supreme Court*. Every person and authority, in the land is therefore expected to respect the judgements of the *Constitutional Court*.

It is also settled law, having been pronounced authoritatively by the *Supreme Court*, that where the constitutionality of any action of any person or authority has been challenged in the *Constitutional Court*, the person or authority whose action has been challenged must stop all further action pending the decision of the *Constitutional Court*.

A good example of this principle in action is the fact that Honourable Mr Justice Vincent Kagaba stopped the treason trial in the High Court as soon as he was informed by counsel that Dr. Besigye and the 22 suspects had challenged the constitutionality of that trial while the 14 bailed suspects were still in illegal custody. It makes sense to err on the side of caution and wait for an authoritative statement as to the constitutionality of any action rather than to move glibly ahead with a course of action that may be found to be unconstitutional.

The case of the 22 Accused has set a very dangerous precedent on a number of fronts. First of all in the *Black Mamba* raid on the *High Court*, the Executive showed that it is willing to use military force against the Judiciary if the Judiciary makes a decision that is not to its liking. This was a shocking violation of the independence of the Judiciary and one doubts whether the Judiciary will ever really be as confident as it was before the raid, the epic poem by the Principal Judge notwithstanding.

The raid also showed that certain sections of the military are willing to act upon unconstitutional orders without question. So if the Judiciary can be laid under siege and its decision thrown out of the window, how safe is Parliament? How safe is the Executive itself, if it should cross this brazen section of the military? How safe is the Constitution itself?

Clearly, abrogation of the Constitution by use of military force remains very feasible today! The *Black Mamba* raid was, in fact, one third of a coup-de-etat; for if the military had gone ahead to challenge Parliament and the Constitution on that day the coup would have been consummated.

Secondly the ham-fisted attempt at getting legal cover for the illegal acts perpetrated during the *Black Mamba* raid through the commencement of the *General Court Martial* proceedings has created what can only be described as a legal and constitutional conundrum.

PRA 22: All Ugandans be Afraid (Part Two)

What is the remedy for people whose rights are being infringed as a result of an unconstitutional action of a public authority if that authority will not respect the decisions of the *Constitutional Court* and the *Supreme Court*? The law does not clearly set out any enforcement procedure for the judgements of the *Constitutional Court*.

The principal remedy sought there is the declaration, a pronouncement upon the meaning of the Constitution or the constitutionality of any action, which is supposed to be binding on all persons and authorities in Uganda. Of what value is a declaration of the *Constitutional Court* if the military can simply look at it and sneer? The continued detention of the bailed suspects is illegal and the commencement of the trial while there is a challenge pending in the *Constitutional Court* are both illegal acts. The *General Court Martial* knows that but it has thrown respect for the Constitution to the wind.

Thirdly, this case threatens to set a dangerous precedent in respect of what can be called *"tribunal shopping"*. The State appears to be saying that it can pick and choose which tribunal is more likely to give it the result that it wants. The use of Military Courts to try cases that have already been commenced in civilian courts just because the civilian courts look like they may not remand or convict a suspect is very dangerous.

It means that the goal posts can be shifted mid-way through the game after the suspect has revealed his or her defence just to ensure that he or she is not acquitted and to give the State time to regroup and re-organise its witnesses. This *tribunal shopping* risk will be faced by all Ugandans, and not just the politically active ones.

For those of you who may not know or recall, in 1976 the late Archbishop Janani Luwum was considered a treason suspect and taken before a Military Tribunal. If it could happen to a Bishop, it could certainly happen to you. There is reason for all Ugandans to be very afraid. The case of the 22 PRA suspects is the tip of a very deadly iceberg. If the Executive, in general, and the military, in particular, is allowed to thumb its nose at the Constitution and get away with it then the Constitution is no longer supreme.

The President, the military or a section of the military will be supreme. They will only abide by the Constitution when they feel like it and opt out when they do not. Everybody will live at their mercy for they alone will be the final arbiters of which rights can be enjoyed when and by whom. We shall then be governed not based on laws but on personal and changeable whims. Uganda has been very close to the bottom of that slippery slope before in the 1960's through to the 1980's. It was not a pleasant experience. Those who have no idea of what it was like should refer to Wod'Okello Lawoko's *The Dungeons of Nakasero* for a detailed description of the kind of hell that disrespect for the Constitution, constitutionalism and the rule of law can unleash upon a country and its citizens.

Whenever the military or any section thereof is allowed to take short cuts through the Constitution and to bend the rule of law, be assured that political and constitutional instability, tyranny, oppression and exploitation are not far behind. Therefore all Ugandans who love peace, democracy, constitutionalism and the rule of law must denounce the continued manipulation of the *General Court Martial* process against the 22 suspects.

Today it is their turn. Their luck may turn and enable them to emerge scathed but alive. Tomorrow it may be you or your loved ones. It could be bad luck or being in the wrong place at the wrong time. If you do not do something now it will be too late then. If you think this is alarmist, then just pause to consider the following facts.

Many Cabinet Ministers and prominent UPC members who cheered when Milton Obote used the Army to overthrow the 1962 Constitution and did not bat an eyelid when several prominent politicians who opposed the move were deprived of their liberty lost their lives soon after the takeover by Idi Amin in 1971. Several people who thronged the streets to celebrate the Idi Amin take over lost their lives later on during Amin's reign. These are extreme examples to make a simple point.

If the Executive and the Military start picking and choosing when they will and will not obey the Constitution be afraid, be very afraid. It is nothing short of a creeping attempt at overthrowing the constitutional order and it is the right and duty of all Ugandans at all times to defend the Constitution. Exercise your duty before we have to call on others to do the same for you. **END.**

For now, that is it from *Daudi* Mpanga. A very powerful argument presented with patriotic passion; that's how it sounded to me! So rather conveniently, I would say that Mpanga's arguments are proof that it's no longer the solitary rants of a one Charles Okwir; a man who is a self confessed and unapologetic critic of General Museveni and his perverted brand of "*democracy*".

On the contrary, with the additional weight of Mpanga's arguments, I think it's probably safe to say that in Museveni's Uganda, it is Museveni himself who acts as the complainant; it's Museveni who is the real *Director of Public Prosecutions*, the trial Judge and Jury, the Court of Appeal, and the Supreme Court of Uganda all rolled into one.

In fact in his own words, Museveni bullishly declares in the *Daily Monitor* Newspaper of 16th April 2007 that "*...as to the courts, the judges are not the ones who liberated Uganda. Their vision cannot be superior to the one of the freedom fighters*". And he adds: "*...if the judges were a stumbling block, the political class has the legislative power to sort that lacuna out*".

This is the real tragedy of a despotic mentality. How a man who was previously thought of very highly could quickly turn into a medieval beast is a subject that probably warrants rigorous research from the world's leading Psychologists. Only then might we begin to develop mechanisms that will hopefully put an end to that despotic mentality; a mentality that is tragically all too common among Africa's post independence leaders.

That said, I also struggle to reconcile that very grim reality with the beautiful fact that the same African continent also happens to be home to some of the greatest statesmen that ever roamed planet earth. Men like Oliver Tambo, Walter Sisulu, Jomo Kenyatta, Kenneth Kaunda, Milton Obote, Nelson Mandela, Julius Nyerere, and Kwame Nkrumah among many others. Even the great Indian pacifist Mahatma Ghandi is believed to have had his critical formative years in South Africa. Anyway going back to the *Second Coming of the Devil* and Judiciary's protest that followed, Uganda's Judges were followed in solidarity by the *Uganda Law Society*.

It mobilised its members to go on a three day sit down strike that commenced, for maximum impact, immediately the Judges called off theirs. Their strike then ended with a symbolic but spectacular *"Cleansing Ceremony"* at the High Court. With their heads bowed, hundreds of Lawyers, fully clad in their black professional robes, marched very slowly, silently, and solemnly in single file around the High Court premises. Many never raised their heads even once. It was an amazing spectacle!

A *20th Century* philosopher once said, *"...a revolution only shifts the burden of tyranny from one shoulder to another"*. Indeed, if Museveni's *Governance Disasters* that we have seen so far are anything to go by, then I think this philosopher was spot-on. It appears the success of Museveni's so-called *Revolution* of 1986 merely shifted the debilitating burden of tyranny from one Ugandan constituency to another.

On the whole however, I think the world should occasionally show a cautious degree of understanding towards those who choose, for the most patriotic of reasons, to take matters into their own hands to fight an incumbent despot. It is not a decision that the well-meaning ones among them take lightly. And they shouldn't. Its justification must only be derived from a genuine and pressing *need*; not a mere *desire*.

Indeed, I suspect that it was in that very spirit that the FDC party President Dr. Kizza Besigye described the High Court siege incident as *"...an ongoing expression of the break down in the rule of law"* before declaring [even as a treason suspect] that *"...we are going to ask the citizens of this country to stand up and challenge the assault on constitutional order in this country"*. Truly amazing courage!

But the most important thing to note here is that although Dr. Besigye stopped short of actually asking Ugandans to rise up in arms and fight the Museveni dictatorship, he had, quite cleverly in my view, also articulated the *need* for such action. So the message to Museveni's regime was crystal clear: *"If things don't change, then expect some aggrieved Ugandans to pick up arms to fight for the values and freedoms that you have taken away from them"*.

And quite rightly, the outrage from concerned citizens didn't end with Dr. Besigye's statement. Out of nowhere, and into the tension filled political ring, came the fiery judicial voice of the controversial law Professor and Senior Supreme Court Judge Justice George Kanyeihamba. *"...I am deeply disturbed by what is happening in the country"*, he said. *"These are very serious matters and it seems that people don't appreciate what is happening in this country. The country could be heading to a crisis"*...because of what he ably described as *"...the near break-down of the rule of law"*. He then added that, *"...it is unthinkable that this can happen under the NRM government"*.

Clearly, from their reactions, both men appeared to be having considerable difficulty recognising any of the democratic ideals and values that they, at different times, once diligently tried to entrench into the Ugandan political psyche. For Dr. Besigye, a man who not only sacrificed his medical career but also put his life on the line to fight alongside Museveni, the frustration must have been even more excruciating. In fact that may explain why he went further than Justice Kanyeihamba in his condemnation of the High Court siege.

So the warning from these two eminent sons of Uganda is simple: Uganda under Museveni's stewardship may be heading for some very turbulent political times. Faced with such a possibility, any prudent leader would have immediately embarked on an aggressive programme of action to set the country back on a path of constitutionalism; action that could also, as a bonus, have repaired his regime's battered image.

But the modern despot is not that sort of person. He has a convoluted perception of both reality and his own popularity; all because his opportunistic advisers tell him what they think he wants to hear. So the despot pushes himself deeper and deeper into public disaffection on the strength of such selfish advice.

In fact, at the time of writing this bit, Museveni's regime had just dreamt up something that must have seemed to them like an *ingenious* way of maintaining their repression of political dissent. *Ingenious* it most definitely was not. It had been tried, tested, and found to be counter-productive. It is what I like to call the *"Ibingira Phenomenon"*.

In that case, Grace Ibingira, the *"Chief Architect"* of a motion to amend the law to make it even more oppressive to Milton Obote's political opponents, ended up becoming the very first victim of the *"Emergency Detention"* law that he had vigorously helped push through Parliament.
So with absolutely no lesson learnt from that very instructive political precedent, Museveni's regime announced that it was in the process of drafting amendments to the law to make it difficult for Ugandans to be released from prison on bail. No prizes of course for correctly guessing who these *"Ugandans"* were! Everyone knows. But that did not stop the regime from describing it innocently as a measure to curb what it called *"...lawlessness and the rampant release of wrongdoers"*.

But why did the regime choose that particular moment to propose amendments to bail laws? For me, the answer is simple. Since November 16th 2005 when High Court Judge Sempa Lugayizi ordered the release of some PRA suspects, the laws governing the right of suspects to be released on bail as they await trial had become a subject of serious controversy. The Judge had ruled then that bail was an automatic right because it was provided for by the Constitution.

Of course, Museveni's regime, like that of any other modern despot, didn't like the sound of that one bit. The reason being that for the modern despot, matters concerning the right to personal liberty, especially for his political opponents, are also matters of great political significance; not legal significance!

Indeed, David Mpanga, the man who as you will recall was one of the Lawyers defending the PRA suspects, reacted immediately to the regime's proposals to clamp down on the so-called *"lawlessness and the rampant release of wrongdoers"*.

He argued that the government was moving towards *"selective legislation"* and that the planned amendments *"...could be targeted at political opponents"*. He then summed up his submission with a warning to the regime. *"...You could set a trap for Ken Lukyamuzi or Dr. Kizza Besigye today, only for your children and loved ones to end up being victims"*, Mpanga counselled.

It is quite interesting that David Mpanga, a man with a great legal mind, also found it necessary to express his fears about selective use of the law to achieve ill political ends. This, you will recall, is the same subject that I attempted to deal with earlier in this book with reference to Lt. Magara's and Brigadier Tumukunde's case. But this legal tragedy may even have wider implications.

A modern despot's natural pre-disposition to enforce the law selectively to further his own political objectives is not just bad for his primary targets; namely, his political opponents. It may also have deleterious consequences for the ordinary man's confidence in the notion of equality before the law; a fundamental principle of justice that no judicial system worth its name can afford to dispense with.

In fact, I don't mind sounding radical in a way by suggesting that without a credible and respected judicial system, there can be no such thing as a viable and modern democratic state. Indeed, Fred Brigland, a veteran Journalist and author of a book called *The War of Africa* once said that *"...applying the rule of law selectively is the recipe for creating a banana republic"*.

I don't know what you make of that. Personally, I have no difficulty whatsoever in saying that Museveni's persistent, ruthless and merciless desecration of everything that is supposed to define statehood has brought this once rising and shining *"Pearl of Africa"* crumbling to its knees.

Uganda's head is now bowed between its crippled legs. A Republic that was once proud of itself can't bear the shame brought upon it by its own children. What a tragedy? A tragedy that has seen the pillars of the State crushed to pieces; the very pillars on which Uganda's most majestic *Crested Crane* once stood proudly. This is sacrilege most foul. Who will rescue this land from the predatory jaws of this feral beast; I wonder? It is only in hope that we must retreat; hope that Uganda's womb will in time produce its own saviour. Of that there can be no doubt; no doubt my friends!

But there may be something else buried in the regime's proposals to tighten up Uganda's bail laws. I think they represented a very real attempt to further erode the constitutional powers vested in the Judiciary. That way, the Judiciary would have no room to manoeuvre even if the justice of a particular case demanded a degree of judicial activism or flexibility.

In the eyes of a modern despot, justice is an inconvenience that stands in the way of his favourite *modus operandi*; one that is premised upon illegalities. Just sit back and enjoy the free circus of how Museveni's regime inadvertently exposed the evil intentions behind its proposals to tighten bail laws. Here we go!

The regime's Deputy Attorney General Mr. Fred Ruhindi, perhaps conscious of the political implications of revealing the real motive behind the move to amend the bail laws, attempted to put a spin to it by suggesting that the *"...prevailing circumstances justified some new legislation and any reasonable government would pass such legislation regardless of what people thought about them. We are looking at the circumstances of the day. Something is rampant, how do we go about it"*, he wondered.

Well, fair enough. However, the most astonishing, and yet unsurprising aspect of Ruhindi's argument was the way in which he attempted to use a precedent from a time in Uganda's history that many would rather forget. He cited the *Aggravated Robberies Act* that was enacted in the 1970s to tame growing robbery. In Ruhindi's view, the government of the day, Idi Amin's government that is, believed that the prevailing spate of robberies justified the introduction of the *Aggravated Robberies Act*. Museveni's regime too, Ruhindi argued, was proposing amendments to bail laws *"...in the same spirit"*. Does he really mean the same spirit with which Idi Amin ruled Uganda?

The answer lies right here. We must not forget that Ruhindi had earlier said that *"...any reasonable government would pass such legislation regardless of what people thought about them"*. So by referring to Idi Amin's *Aggravated Robberies Act,* Ruhindi was effectively endorsing Idi Amin's murderous regime as a *"reasonable"* one? But wasn't Idi Amin's *"reasonable"* government the same one that Ruhindi's boss Museveni said he fought hard to oust so as to liberate Ugandans from tyranny? Contradiction upon contradiction; Museveni's *Movement Bus* of deceit powers on at full speed!

But I feel sorry for poor old Ruhindi; just as I feel sorry for all those who offer themselves into the service of a modern despot's ideals. Ruhindi's problem was that he had neither the courage nor the authority to reveal the true intentions behind the proposed amendments. That is why he wasn't exactly explicit in telling the world what that *"rampant something"* was. His boss Museveni however, as the *Alfa Bull* in his regime, of course didn't have such encumbrances.

So while discussing his regime's proposals to amend the bail laws on a radio talk show, the decorated General of the *"1986 Revolution"* wasted no time. He threw a big fat spanner in Ruhindi's poor work of spin. The planned amendments to the bail laws, Museveni said, *"...will cause the chaotic opposition groups to tread more carefully"*. Bang! Right on cue; just as we had expected! And with that, the proverbial cat was finally out of the bag.

Obviously, tightening bail laws makes a lot of good sense to modern despots. After all, if left to roam freely, opposition leaders riding on moral high grounds would quickly gain ground and favour with the electorate and cause the despot to lose his most valued political asset; namely, the fallacious perception of him as the most superior political player. Besides, a modern despot would never want to see detained opposition leaders quickly bouncing back on the streets [on bail] to milk even more political sympathy than they had before their arrest and detention.

That said however, there are encouraging signs that even with the oppressive bail laws, the regime may not be totally out of the woods. The Judiciary's residual ability to assert itself in the face of such a ferocious Executive assault on its independence can still be detected in Uganda. Yet again, the same PRA treason case provides us with ample evidence of that.

In a truly courageous ruling, Justice Eldad Mwangusya said that after the *Constitutional Court's* decision to uphold the bail granted to the PRA suspects in November 2005, the *High Court*, as a subordinate court, had absolutely no powers to review a matter that had already been determined by a higher court. With that, Justice Mwangusya had effectively dismissed [with costs] the regime's application to have the bail granted to the PRA suspects cancelled.

But while the PRA suspects could not now be held on remand on account of the treason charges they were facing, they were still sent back to prison because [as we saw earlier] they still faced some frivolously fabricated murder charges that had been brought to ensure that they remained in prison. That is the pathetic reality of despotic lawlessness.

But at the very least, with those judgements, the Judiciary had sent a clear message to the regime that Ugandans cherish their liberties and that those liberties should be safeguarded on their behalf by a Judiciary that operates independently without Executive interference. That final message of defiance to modern despots is in my view the most fitting way to end this debate about a modern despot's *use of the law as a tool of political oppression.*

Chapter Five

"The Return of the Hammer"

The most dramatic set of events started to unfold with the news in 2004/5 that Dr. Kizza Besigye had indeed finally taken the decision to return to Uganda from his place of exile in South Africa. One of the reasons for his return, as we now know, was to enable him contest again for the presidency of Uganda in the elections that had been scheduled for February 2006. His supporters were of course ecstatic. The more creative ones among them even called the impending return of their hero *"The Return of the Hammer"*.

Those who are familiar with Ugandan politics will recall that Dr. Besigye had declared during the 2001 presidential elections that he was the *"hammer"* that would dislodge Museveni from power. His supporters at the time wasted no time. They exploited the political symbolism of Besigye's declaration to the max. In no time, they had bought inflatable dummy hammers and were swinging them at political rallies in gestures that suggested that they were trying hammer out something. Some even glued the dummy hammers on the front bumpers of their vehicles and drove around the streets hooting and waving the "V" [for victory] sign. It was an exciting spectacle to say the least.

But as news of Dr. Besigye's inevitable return spread, the shaken regime immediately raised the stakes and sent out a chilling message. *"...Dr. Besigye is welcome to return home but he may have some cases to answer"*, the regime said. That threat was almost certainly designed to scare Dr. Besigye from ever setting foot on Ugandan soil while Museveni was still in power. Nothing new there; typical modern despots doing what they do best! But it wasn't to be. The good old Doctor was going to have none of it. And true to his word, on the 26th of October 2005, Dr. Besigye, accompanied by his wife Winnie Byanyima, sons Anselm and Ampa, political confidants at hand, and a host of foreign Journalist, roared almost triumphantly into *Entebbe International Airport* aboard a Kenya Airways flight from Nairobi-Kenya.

With the mid-morning African sun piercing through the dark clouds of oppression in the background, Besigye emerged from the Boeing 737 Kenya Airways aircraft with his wife and flashed the "V" sign on his fingers. The smile on his face spoke volumes. It was as if the uncertainty of not knowing whether he would ever set foot in Uganda had just been lifted off his shoulders.

And he couldn't stop smiling as he descended onto Ugandan soil to be met by a beautiful little girl carrying a bouquet of flowers. Also on the airport tarmac were party officials from the *Forum for Democratic Change* [FDC]; the brand new political party that Dr. Besigye had been presiding over as *de facto* President from exile.

Now wearing a *"Welcome Home Dr. Besigye"* scarf given to him by FDC officials, he marched straight into the VIP lounge of *Entebbe International Airport* to address a press conference. There, he defiantly, in his deep, crackling, fierce, and very unique trademark voice, refused to condemn rebellion and instead re-affirmed that the people of Uganda had an inherent right to determine their own political destiny *"by any means"*.

The authorities in the capital city Kampala had by now, even before Besigye left the terminal building, already taken their first oppressive decision; a decision that I suspect was designed to dampen the political impact of Dr. Besigye's return. And right on cue, an order came from the regime declaring that Besigye's supporters would not be allowed anywhere near the airport terminal building.

While Besigye's supporters behaved and complied with the banning order, the scenes just outside the precincts of the airport terminal building did not make easy viewing for Museveni's henchmen. Nothing; absolutely nothing would come in the way of the mammoth crowd of cheering supporters who had patiently waited outside the airport to welcome their hero.

Just to give you an idea of the situation that prevailed on the day, the 43kilometre journey from Entebbe airport to Kampala that would ordinarily take a mere forty five minutes took Dr. Besigye's convoy a whole three and a half hours to cover. Thousands upon thousands of hysterical supporters had lined the entire length of the highway to catch a glimpse of their hero. So Besigye really had no choice but to respond with intermittent stops along the way to greet and address them.

Soon, the *"Bad"* news about the *"Great"* events unfolding in Uganda had travelled 7,000miles to London where Museveni was addressing Ugandans. Let me give you some brief facts about Museveni's London meeting. At that time, Museveni's reputation and popularity among Ugandans at home and abroad had dropped rock bottom.

In fact, it took the intervention of an infamous London based PR Firm [that is known for its unethical work with despots] to work out a strategy to literally lure Ugandans in the UK to attend Museveni's meeting. That is how bad things had become for Museveni.

As soon as he got the *"Bad News"*, a panicking Museveni cut short his UK tour and dashed straight back to Uganda to deal with the *"Besigye threat"*. Officially however, the lame excuse that he gave for his sudden departure was that he was *"...allergic to foreign holidays"*. Nonsense! All we know is that as soon as his plane left London, Uganda's greatest political epoch was well and truly underway.

The Greatest Political Epoch of the Century

- *October 26th 2005:* Besigye returns to Uganda.
- *November 14th 2005:* Besigye arrested and charged with treason and rape and remanded in custody; sparking off massive riots in the Capital City Kampala.

- *November 15th 2005:* Besigye committed to the High Court for trial. Riots continue in Kampala and the military is unleashed onto the streets of Kampala; but the riots spread to upcountry towns.
- *November 16th 2005:* The so-called *"Black Mamba Urban Hit Squad"*, an illegal commando offshoot of the Ugandan military storms the High Court immediately Dr. Besigye and his 14 co-accused PRA suspects are granted bail by the High Court. The gang re-arrests all of them and drives them off to unknown destinations. General Museveni warns foreign diplomats accredited to Uganda to keep their noses out of Ugandan affairs.
- *November 17th 2005:* The Chief Justice of Uganda His Lordship Benjamin Odoki condemns the November 16th military siege of the High Court.
- *November 18th 2005:* Justice Edmond Ssempa Lugayizi, the trial judge in the Besigye case withdraws from hearing the case citing military interference. The Principal Judge, Justice James Ogoola also condemns the military siege at the High Court.
- Over 20 policemen and intelligence personnel raid *The Daily Monitor* newspaper offices demanding to know the source of posters in the city calling for contributions to the *"Dr. Kizza Besigye Human Rights Fund".*
- *November 20th 2005:* British Members of Parliament demand that their government makes a statement about the arrest of Dr. Besigye.
- *November 21st 2005:* The *Forum for Democratic Change* {FDC} accuses Gen. David Tinyefuza of planning and executing the arrest of its leader Dr. Kizza Besigye. He of course, denies the accusations flatly.

- *November 22nd 2005:* **Internal Affairs** Minister Dr. Ruhakana Rugunda announces a government ban on all public rallies, demonstrations, assemblies or seminars related to the trial of Dr. Besigye.
- *November 23rd 2005: Information Minister* Dr. James Nsaba Buturo bans all radio talk shows and media debates on Dr. Besigye's case. Delegates to the 2005 Commonwealth Summit in Malta mount pressure on Museveni over Besigye's case.
- *November 24th 2005:* Dr. Besigye is charged with a fresh offence of terrorism based on the same set of facts before the General Military Court Martial {GCM}that is meant to try only serving soldiers. Dr. Besigye refuses to recognize the jurisdiction of the GCM.
- On the same day, *November 24th 2005,* Journalists from *The Daily Monitor* newspaper expose some members of the *Black Mamba Urban Hit Squad* around the High Court dressed in police uniforms in a poor attempt to disguise themselves.
- *November 25th 2005:* Dr. Besigye alone, and not his co-accused, is granted bail by the Principal Judge Justice James Ogoola but the authorities in Luzira remand prison refuse to release him on the orders of the GCM.
- *November 26th 2005:* Seven PRA suspects forced by government to apply for amnesty are eventually released by the GCM after they *"confessed"* to involvement in armed rebellion. They are then paraded before the press by the *Information Minister* Nsaba Buturo. In a most embarrassing twist for the *Information Minister*, they denied knowledge of any links between Dr. Besigye and the shadowy PRA that Dr. Besigye is accused of leading.
- *November 28th 2005:* The *Uganda Law Society* goes on strike at the High Court in Kampala protesting the break down in the rule of law.

- *November 29th 2005:* Dr. Besigye is forced back to Luzira prison even after he satisfied all the conditions for release on bail.
- *November 30th 2005:* The African Parliament passes a resolution calling for an immediate and unconditional release of Dr. Besigye. The Netherlands withdraws Uganda Shillings 13billion in budgetary support to Uganda in protest over the Besigye case.
- *December 1st 2005:* Dr. Besigye's Lawyers file an application challenging their client's continued trial in the GCM.
- *December 2nd 2005:* High Court Judge Justice Remmy Kasule issues an order restraining the GCM from further hearing Besigye's case.
- *December 3rd 2005:* The authorities at Luzira remand prison reject Dr. Besigye's request to have his passport photos taken from prison to facilitate his nomination as a presidential candidate.
- *December 4th 2005:* The UPDF's Chief of Legal Services Col. Ramathan Kyamulesire, in a flagrant breach of the High Court order issued by Justice Remmy Kasule on December 2nd 2005, declares that the GCM will continue with the trial of Dr. Besigye and his co-accused.
- *December 5th 2005:* The authorities at Luzira remand prison confiscate Dr. Besigye's election nomination papers.
- *December 6th 2005:* Dr. Besigye is finally allowed to sign nomination papers after Adolf Mwesige, a government Minister of State who happens to be a lawyer, said there was no law stopping Dr. Besigye from contesting for the presidency.
- *December 7th 2005:* The Attorney General {AG} of Uganda, Prof. Kiddu Makubuya attempts to block Dr. Besigye's nomination as a presidential candidate by offering the Electoral Commission a most dubious legal opinion which came very close to actually suggesting that in Dr. Besigye's case, the automatic

"presumption of innocence" before trial and conviction or acquittal should be set aside.
- *December 9th 2005:* The infamous *Black Mambas* are deployed at Luzira prisons to guard Dr. Besigye.
- *December 12th 2005:* The Electoral Commission ignores the AG's dubious legal opinion and declares that Dr. Besigye is eligible for nomination as a presidential candidate.
- *December 13th 2005:* All his attempts finally defeated, General Museveni, in a face saving move, decides to back Dr. Besigye's nomination saying the AG's legal opinion was based on what he now called *"political values"*.
- *December 14th 2005:* While still in prison, Dr. Besigye's *"Election Campaign Poster"* is finally nominated in lieu of his physical presence as a presidential candidate for 2006 presidential elections. A strange absurdity indeed, I hear you saying!
- *December 17th 2005:* Museveni's government denies knowledge of any plot to poison Dr. Besigye from prison.
- *December 19th 2005:* Both Dr. Besigye's treason and rape cases are adjourned to 6th January 2006.
- *December 20th 2005:* Britain cuts Uganda Shillings 64billion worth of aid to Uganda citing Dr. Besigye's arrest and the State inspired problems afflicting the transition to full multi-party democracy.
- *December 22nd 2005:* The High Court orders the Commissioner General of Prisons to appear in Court on December 28th to explain Dr. Besigye's continued detention in breach of a court order granting him bail.
- *December 23rd 2005:* Still finding it difficult to accept the full impact of the operation of the rule of law, the Museveni regime accuses Uganda's Judges of supporting Dr. Besigye.
- *December 25th 2005:* Dr. Besigye and his co-accused spend Christmas in Luzira remand prison and their families are denied access to them.

- *December 28th 2005:* Dr. Besigye is produced at the High Court to attend the hearing of an application for *habeas corpus* filed by his Lawyers.
- *December 30th 2005:* Dr. Besigye's party the FDC claims that Justices Leaticia Kikonyogo and Remmy Kasule had been bribed by the State over the Besigye case; a claim the Judges flatly denied. The Chief justice Benjamin Odoki promises to investigate the claims.
- *January 2nd 2006:* High Court Judge Justice John Baptist Katutsi rules that Besigye's continued detention is illegal. Amidst massive excitement from supporters and well-wishers, the FDC leader is finally freed and he hits the campaign trail immediately, several weeks after his main opponent, the cowardly Museveni had hit the countryside campaigning for re-election while Dr. Besigye was still under lock and key in Luzira prison.
- *April 2006:* The Museveni regime hires the services of private prosecutors from *Kampala Associated Advocates* for a colossal sum of Uganda Shillings 2.5billion {approx 1.4million dollars}to team up with the Director of Public Prosecutions {whose capacity they probably doubted now following Besigye's acquittal in the rape case} to prosecute Dr. Besigye in the treason case.

So there you have it! That is just a snapshot. But I hope it will finally lay to rest any doubts that may exist about my earlier suggestion that in Museveni's Uganda, should the authorities detect a real or even perceived threat to their stranglehold on power, the dynamics of even the most ordinary of treason cases changes. The above *epoch* has indeed shown exactly that with the re-entry of Dr. Besigye onto Uganda's political arena.

The rest as they say is now history. Just like in the 2001 presidential elections, Dr. Besigye petitioned the Supreme Court contesting the result of the 2006 presidential elections. In that petition, the Supreme Court, again relying heavily on the same absurd legal technicality they relied on in 2001, by a majority of 4-3, ruled in favour of and handed State power back to General Yoweri K. Museveni Esq.

If it is any consolation at all, then perhaps I should say this to all of you citizens of the free world who sit in judgement at the equally powerful *"Supreme Court of Public Opinion"*. The same Supreme Court of Uganda led by the same Chief Justice Benjamin Odoki, also upheld 99% of all the irregularities that by Dr. Kizza Besigye had cited in his petition. How it then failed to nullify Museveni's "re-election" is a matter that will be debated for generations.

The most critical, and perhaps even deliberate omission in the law, is that it fails to prescribe *Specific Benchmarks* for election malpractices to be deemed by the presiding Court to have *"Substantially Affected"* the outcome of any election. If the law had been changed, then I think Dr. Besigye would have got justice. But I am also realistic enough to acknowledge that in countries ruled by modern despots, it is very unlikely that such a change in the law can happen under the despot's watch.

Chapter Six

The Final Assault on State Institutions

State institutions across the globe are established to serve specific needs at any one given time. And those needs vary significantly. From the defence of the realm, to the delivery of public services; from the regulation of public order, to the delivery of justice; and from the efficient and effective functioning of the national economy, to the efficient and effective functioning of government; to name but just a few!

The midwifery role for all that often falls squarely within the remit of the political leaders of the day. And its success or failure in turn depends on the democratic values of those very leaders. Leaders whose job it is, or at least ought to be, to address the aspirations of the people that those institutions are supposed to serve within any given jurisdiction.

However, the full genesis of institution building in Uganda is a long and complex subject that is beyond the scope of this book. Nonetheless, the earlier discussion that touched on the nature and strength of the institutions that were bequeathed to Uganda by Britain at independence should serve as the context within which to approach this next debate. So let's revisit that earlier discussion.

Just to jog your memory, I said my Makerere University law lecturer once attempted to link the continued restriction on the enjoyment of human rights in Uganda to the fact that *"...some of the cardinal principles of law and democracy enjoyed by Englishmen, who are said to be born free, were, by commission or omission, systematically excised from the main body of law during transportation to its new exotic location in Africa"*.

So what exactly were these great principles of law that were in the *"Main Body"* of law? In my view, they could only have been the principles that inform the administration of justice, the observance of human rights, equity, and the entrenchment of democracy.

These are the principles that guide the proper functioning of the State institutions through which those rights, services, and privileges are enjoyed. It can't be too far off from that. In fact while the principles of equity hardly ever feature in the decisions of Ugandan Judges, in England, equity is said to be "...*the flesh that covers the dry bones of the law*".

It embodies humane considerations of fairness; considerations that I think ought to define the very concept of justice. Therefore, the most logical conclusion must be that actually, far from intending to entrench those principles, values, and institutions in Uganda, the British colonialist's attempt was at best half-hearted; and at worst, non-existent. In other words, it wasn't part of their strategic game plan to see successful States crop-up all over Africa. That would have threatened the pursuit of their objective to colonise and exploit large parts of Africa.

Indeed as we saw earlier, quite often, when cornered, Museveni himself has been quick to point the finger of blame at the British colonialists and his own predecessors. And he does that in spite of the fact that he has ruled Uganda for nearly a quarter of a century as I write today.

As a country, more than 45yrs of relative political independence must surely have been sufficient time for Uganda's political elite to cure the country of the deficiencies it was born with. Instead, far from having the requisite patriotic goodwill, Uganda's post independence rulers have only succeeded in desecrating the nascent State institutions whose full development could have lifted the crippled Republic back to its feet.

Indeed, in a newspaper article under the title *"Betraying Africans like the Chief's"* in which he criticised Museveni for failing to sort out Uganda's structural problems, FDC's *Deputy Secretary General in Charge of Research*

Mr. Augustine Ruzindana appeared to agree when he said, "*...building systems and institutions could have been the main outcome of a long uninterrupted administration*".

I say *"appeared to agree"* because I believe Ruzindana, like me, must have been alluding to the fact that a 25yr reign was indeed sufficient time for Museveni to build strong institutions if he had the political will to do so; but he didn't. In fact, if ever there was any doubt in your mind regarding the ideological base from which this book derives its inspiration, then Ruzindana's candid views below provide the precise answer. It is that the typical modern despot is fundamentally sacrilegious in both portrait and character!

Anyway to prove his point, Ruzindana posed a question that was without doubt loaded with frustration. "*...But what do we see*", he asked; before finally saying that "*...even the institutions and systems that were already in place have either been destroyed or are under threat of destruction*".

That in my view is Ruzindana talking about the merciless sacrilege being visited by the regime against a nascent and fragile culture of institutionalism. He then concludes his remarks by saying that "*...the attack on institutions and systems is unfortunately usually spearheaded by the highest authority in the land*".

And the highest authority in the land is none other than General Museveni himself! For me, with that, the case against General Museveni in the court of public opinion was sealed. Therefore, for emphasis and a bit of satirical fun, I suggest we take a quick look at how *Count No 1* on the *Charge Sheet* of Museveni's {pending}trial might look like in a few years time from now.

Uganda Vs General Yoweri T. K. Museveni

<u>Count No 1:</u> Visiting Sacrilege upon Uganda's State Institutions

So how might the further and better particulars of this offence sound like? How about this: "Accused No 1 {A1} General Yoweri T. K. Museveni, you and others still at large, between 1986 and the time you were forced out of power, conceived, plotted and callously executed and or visited fundamental sacrilege and desecration by force of arms upon the sacred Constitution and Institutions of the Republic of Uganda as by law established contrary to Section......of the..........Act and the Oath of Office for the office President of the Republic of Uganda"

How do you plead, Museveni would then be asked? With an unkempt grey beard on a tired and wrinkled face, looking every bit dejected, Museveni struggles with severe arthritis, walking stick in hand, and gets to his feet. And, with a shaky voice full of fear, he looks towards his now frail wife Janet; looks to the packed courtroom in search of old friends and some signs of sympathy and there is none.

Then he turns and looks straight into the piercing eyes of a former PRA suspect who, as it happens, is now the trial Judge at the High Court. Not guilty My Lord", Museveni says in resignation. The hitherto invincible and all powerful General will finally have returned to planet earth! But it's not over yet.

Leading the prosecution team, would you believe it, is the eldest son of Patrick Mamenero {RIP}, another PRA suspect who was tortured to death during interrogation at the Chieftaincy of Military Intelligence {CMI} HQs in the capital city Kampala by Museveni's security operatives. With a sense of great urgency in his voice, and his body language wanting to get on with it, Mamenero Jnr turns to the Judge {the former PRA suspect} and says "My Lord, we would like to call prosecution witness No 1 {PW1}.

Approvingly, the Judge, now quietly loving every moment of the unfolding drama, says: "Mr. Augustine Ruzindana, will you take the stand please". Ruzindana of course happily obliges. He then launches straight into his damning evidence against General Museveni and his co-accused. And the pattern continues; with a host of other prosecution witnesses itching and falling over themselves to give evidence against their former tormentor in chief.

But jokes aside, the simple point being made here as Ruzindana so rightly put it is that even the semblance of State institutions that were already in place have been desecrated by Museveni's neo-patrimonial style of leadership. And that makes him nothing less than the latest neo-colonial and or imperialist agent. Admittedly, I have to say that is not an indictment that should be attached to anyone lightly. Not least against a man like Museveni who has himself, for different reasons, been quite critical of the same imperialists. That said, the evidence so far points to only one logical conclusion. And it is that contrary to popular perception, Museveni's attempts at entrenching State institutions in Uganda through the 1995 constitution were largely designed to win praises and favours from the West.

At best, his attempt, like the British one before it, was half-hearted. More than anyone else, Museveni knew that strong State institutions that are independent of his despotic influence would be counter-productive to his grand plan to rule Uganda for as long as he wished. If you set your sights firmly on an unpatriotic political objective, then the means of achieving that objective will by necessity also be deleterious to good democratic governance. I am wholly convinced that both Museveni and the British colonialists failed in their attempts to build strong institution because of that.

Of course, I am aware that there will be people out there who will argue that my criticisms of Museveni's neo-patrimonial style of leadership are inspired by partisan prejudice. Well, fair enough. They may have a point. In the circumstances, I think the best way to settle the debate would be to take a random look at the available evidence of how some State institutions [in Uganda] are *actually run* and how *the law says they should be run*.

The Judiciary Vs a Modern Despot

So here is the deal. Let's start with what the law says and then check the actual practice for any consistencies or flaws. Under Chapter eight of the Constitution of the Republic of Uganda, article 126{1}thereof declares that: *"Judicial power is derived from the people and shall be exercised by the courts established under this Constitution in the name of the people and in conformity with the law and with the values, norms and aspirations of the people"*.

With that simple declaration, a new judicial era was supposed to have been ushered into being. The courts created as a result would be required to dispense justice *"...to all irrespective of their social or economic status"*. The constitution also declared that *"justice shall not be delayed"*; that *"adequate compensation shall be awarded to victims of wrongs"*; that *"reconciliation between parties shall be promoted"*; and that *"substantive justice shall be administered without undue regard to technicalities"*.

Whether or not that is what it turned out to be is a matter that is seriously debatable. And it elicits varied views depending on who you put the question to. The respondents' political leanings will almost certainly be a big determining factor. The pro-government respondent will obviously argue that Museveni's regime has strengthened the administration of justice in the country. On the other hand, the opposition will no doubt point out some serious flaws in the assertions of the pro-government respondent.

But there are some hard facts that are impossible to contest. For example, the *Daily Monitor* newspaper of February 27th 2004 ran a story under the title, *"I Will Shake up the Judges-Museveni";* a story that, to the best of my knowledge, has never been contested by Museveni's regime. In his reaction to the loss that his government had suffered in a politically charged case filed by the then *Democratic Party* President Dr. Paul Ssemogerere, Museveni was reported to have said that, *"...Ssemogerere's* [court] *victories do not change any big thing"*.

He then added that, *"...these Judges shall be shaken....now that the Movement has stayed longer in power, it has now got its cadres go through schools and some have mastered; we shall shake these Lawyers"*. On the face of it, Museveni's utterances appeared to be merely reckless; typical; characteristic; the sort that you would expect from a bitter bad loser.

It's also very easy *not* to read too much into Museveni's utterances. After all, they are consistent with the usual political sound bites that emanate from State House every so often. Like most people who are ruled by modern despots, Ugandans are also accustomed to such despotic utterances. They know that they are crafted to intimidate society as well as to score cheap political points from hastened headlines the day after. And all because the modern despot has everything to fear from a detailed and informed debate!

However, a forensic examination of the context within which the remarks were made reveals a worrying intent that would drop the jaws of democracy enthusiasts and raise the hair on the back of the necks of all who worship the rule of law. It was a very strong statement that was intended to project both defiance and intent. After all, the regime had by now lost a number of politically significant cases to the opposition.

Secondly, it was also, in many ways, Museveni's way of sending a chilling warning to the Judiciary that their days of relative independence to do as they deemed fit were numbered. That the *Movement* had now bred its own ultra loyal Lawyers who will, at every available opportunity, take over from the few non partisan Judges who are on the bench.

For me, that was the exact essence of the statement Museveni had just made. And I wasn't going to sit back quietly. So incensed I was that I in turn, for whatever it was going to be worth, decided to author an opinion article as a reaction to Museveni's comments. Thankfully, the *Daily Monitor* newspaper published it almost immediately under the title *"Executive Threatens Nation's Civil Defence"*.

The gist of my argument then was, and still is, that as a result of Museveni's comments, the Judiciary that is supposed to be the very last line of civil defence for all citizens was now under threat from the Executive arm of government. And all for doing nothing other than what it was in fact constitutionally charged with doing; namely, to administer justice impartially and fairly according to the law.

Later political developments in the country, especially those that came after a court ruling that nullified the *Referendum Act 2000,* certainly showed Ugandans that modern despots do keep their promises; be it at the expense of national efforts to strengthen institutions of State. To show that he meant business, Museveni went on national television and rejected the unanimous verdict of the *Constitutional Court*.

Not only that, he also accused the Judiciary of "...*usurping the people's power*". Dear Oh dear!

Clearly, from that tone alone, it was easy to see that Museveni had either not bothered to seek professional advice from the regime's legal experts, or he had sought their advice but simply ignored it. If he had taken legal advice, he wouldn't have accused the Judges of usurping the people's power because as article 126{1} cited above clearly states, "*...judicial power is derived from the people and shall be exercised by the courts established under this Constitution in the name of the people*".

This typical despotic blunder should serve as the clearest warning about the futility of undermining State institutions. State institutions are established and manned by expert technocrats whose job it is to support politicians like Museveni in the discharge of their official duties. If you ignore expert opinion, then that is exactly what you end up with; embarrassing outbursts that have *"ignorance"* written all over them.

Secondly, if he had sought advice from the regime's *Public Relations* experts, he would also have known that such an ill informed outburst was bound to discredit him in the eyes of the world. The popular perception that it was his *Movement* government that fought for and restored democracy and the rule of law will have also been exposed as a complete fallacy; and it was.

Almost immediately, Major [Rtd] Okwiri Rabwoni, a young man who fought alongside Museveni in the 1981-86 bush war, told me over a drink as we discussed this subject that, "*...Museveni has completely failed to dispense with his bush war mentality even after years of rubbing shoulders with civilised world leaders*".

What Okwiri was saying was that Museveni had failed or refused to *"unlearn"* his bush war habits. That also means he had failed to adjust to the modern demands of working within a formal institutional framework. Whenever he deemed fit, he still preferred to rule with an iron fist; just as he did when he was still a rebel leader years ago.

Going back to Museveni's outburst on national television, there is no doubt in my mind that by his outright rejection of the *Constitutional Court's* decision, it was actually Museveni who had *"usurped"* the power of the people vested in the *Supreme Court* to which he should have taken his grievances by way of appeal. So what then, does Museveni's unilateralism and rejection of the due process of law tell us? Well, it tells us that as far as a modern despot is concerned, courts of law are only tolerated if they deliver judgements that favour or further the despot's political objectives.

If that and many of his other unilateral decrees do not constitute a fully blown dictatorship, then Idi Amin might as well be canonised as a Saint. There is simply no other way of looking at it. And we are not done with the Judiciary yet. There is further evidence to suggest that Museveni may in fact be on course to making good his promise to *"shake up the Judges"* and turn the nation's Judiciary into the *"judicial arm"* of his NRM-O party.

A partisan arm that will sit in judgment in all cases brought before it; including those with great political significance. Because from then on, the regime could simply say to the aggrieved parties that *that is the due process of rule of law and there is nothing we can do about it*! Those are the sort of unfair and *"semi-legal"* advantages that modern despots cherish and thrive on.

Secondly, at the time of writing this book, there was an impending decision by Museveni's government to amend the law to lower the qualifying period of consistent legal practice required for one to be considered for appointment as a Judge. That decision was only shelved after serious concerns were raised by the opposition about the underlying reasons for the proposed amendments.

But you have to give a despot's regime credit for swift opportunism. Soon after the opposition *victory* over this matter, one NRM-Party cadre seized the opportunity and turned it on its head; arguing with delight in fact, that the opposition's *victory* showed that democracy was flourishing in Uganda. Fair enough. But that does not take away the regime's unpatriotic political values that informed the proposal to amend the law in the first place. If passed, it would have meant that even the most inexperienced NRM *Cadre Lawyers* would have qualified for appointment to the Bench. And you can be sure they would have been appointed; because the all powerful General Museveni had already declared that they would.

But it wasn't only Museveni who was showing signs of a burning desire to undermine the Judiciary. Soon after his embarrassing outburst on television, Ugandans were treated to another comical debacle. Perhaps taking cue from his boss, the media reported that the then *Minister of Information* Dr. Nsaba Buturo had taken it upon himself to, and I quote, *"investigate"* a Magistrate's judgement to find out the grounds upon which the judgement was based.

And yes, you guessed right; that judgement had gone against an NRM-O party leaning litigant in Masaka town. That was that! Now let us, *"Without Prejudice"* of course, consider something else that may raise eyebrows about the independence of Uganda's Judiciary. *Mr. Steven Kavuma:* He was a well known NRM-O party ideologue. He even served as *Minister of Defence* in Museveni's government. Today, Kavuma is as a Judge in the *Court of Appeal;* a court that doubles as Uganda's *Constitutional Court* and determines a lot of politically sensitive cases.

Portrait of a Despot

M/s Margaret Oguli: She once served as the *Director of Legal Affairs* at Museveni's *Movement* Secretariat. Today, Oguli is a *High Court* Judge.

Mr. Bart Katureebe: Another well known NRM-O party ideologue. He served as *Attorney General* in Museveni's ruling *Movement*. He was then appointed to serve as a Judge of the *Supreme Court* just before the sham 2006 presidential elections which ended up before the same *Supreme Court*.

Mr. Peter Kabatsi: A long serving *Solicitor General* in Museveni's government; appointed to serve as a Judge of the *High Court*.

Mr. Simon Byabakama: He was *Acting Director of Civil Litigation* in the Attorney General's office. He led the State's prosecution team in the politically motivated rape case against Museveni's leading political opponent Dr. Kizza Besigye. Today, Byabakama is a *High Court* Judge.

Mr. John Arutu: A professional and impartial career judicial officer who served as Chief Magistrate of Nakawa Magistrates Court. He was nominated for appointment as a *High Court* Judge but was unceremoniously dropped at the very last minute. Make what you will of those appointments and the one unfortunate disappointment! But after the appointments and disappointments, comes the inevitable questions. I leave that to you. All I can say is that as a Lawyer, I have some grave concerns about some of the judgements that these Judges have passed in politically sensitive cases that they have presided over.

The Directorate of Public Prosecutions

Like the Judiciary, the *Directorate of Public Prosecutions* also has its guiding principles enshrined within the constitution of Uganda 1995; article 120[1] to be precise. The functions of the *Director of Public Prosecutions* [DPP] are clearly set out in clauses 3{a-d} of article 120. No problems there.

But it is not to the functions *per se* that one must look if one is interested in studying how the *Directorate* is run. Rather, the focus ought to be in the manner in which the DPP exercises the powers vested in him as he goes about discharging the tasks assigned to his office by the constitution.

And to do that, we must look at the article and clauses of the constitution that prescribe the manner in which those powers ought to be exercised. Article 120; and clause {5}in particular, expressly provides that, *"...in exercising his or her powers under this article, the DPP shall have regard to the public interest, the interest of the administration of justice and the need to prevent abuse of the legal process"*. Nice! Clause {6}of the same article on the other hand provides that, *"...in the exercise of the functions conferred on him or her by this article, the DPP shall not be subject to the direction or control of any person or authority"*. Even better! Now, with reference to one or two typical cases, let us put the key issues in clauses [5] and [6] above to the test. And they are the *"...the public interest"*, *"...the interest of the administration of justice"*, the need to *"...prevent abuse of the legal process"*, and the need for the DPP to avoid being subjected *"...to the direction or control of any person or authority"*.

Test case No.1: (The Trial of the Century)

The first, and arguably most high profile case that tested the DPP's ability to adhere to the principles enunciated in clauses [5] and [6] above was the prosecution of opposition leader Dr. Kizza Besigye; President of the *Forum for Democratic Change* [FDC].

You will recall that Dr. Besigye was arrested and charged with the rape *[among other things]* of a one Joanita Kyakuwa soon after his return from exile. Dr. Besigye himself of course maintained from day one that it was a *"fabricated"* case that Museveni's regime brought to court simply to persecute him.

I think a quick trip down memory lane should be perfectly in order for this one; just to bring you back into the picture. Dr. Besigye's violent arrest occurred on the 14th of November 2005; bang in the tense heat of the 2006 general elections in which he participated as FDC's candidate for the presidency of Uganda. Party political activities were nearing their peak and the political temperatures had risen dangerously high to match the occasion; day in, day out in fact.

Predictions and conspiracies were rife; especially in the evening social joints where city dwellers retreat to treat themselves to the few remaining *"politically correct"* pleasures of life. Expectations of political power for opposition leaders and their supporters were high too.

For the rest, and especially those who had been trapped in the disease ridden concentration camps of northern and eastern Uganda, salvation and the hope of a better future seemed only days away. Almost visible from around the corner! The uncertainties of a modern despot's sham elections on the other hand, also made that *salvation* and *hope* of a better future seem far off; in a fantasy land in fact!

But Museveni's camp was not having a party either. They had their own worries. Different kind of worries! Dr. Besigye was attracting huge crowds at his *"Meet and Greet the People Tour"*; a national tour that he had embarked on soon after his return from exile. So the threat and anxiety at the possibility of losing power to Dr. Besigye and his FDC party was difficult for Museveni's strategists to shrug off.

Their fear was premised upon the fact that such a loss would inevitably come hand in hand with the loss of the lucrative jobs, contracts, and all the political favours that they had become accustomed to over the years. So understandably, emotions were running high across the political spectrum.

Dr. Besigye's arrest in such circumstances therefore meant that the stage was surely set for what the creative newspaper Editors perfectly described as *"The Trial of the Century"*. And it was not for nothing that it was described as such.

In its first few months, *The Trial of the Century* had, almost without precedent, already caused the dramatic withdrawal of two trial Judges; one after the other in quick succession. While one of them cited *"State Intimidation and Interference"* as the reason for his withdrawal, the other settled for the safer *"Medical Reasons"* excuse. You make up your own minds.

Personally, I will stick my neck out and say that at the very least, the Judges may have felt compelled to withdraw because of too much pressure from the State to *"deliver"*. And that may have meant a demand from the very top that the Judges *"do everything"* possible within and perhaps even outside their powers to ensure that Dr. Besigye is convicted. The actual merits of the prosecution's case count for very little in such circumstances.

In the end, the *Besigye case* only took off when His Lordship Justice John Bosco Katutsi, a brave High Court Judge, took over the trial. And as soon as he did, the circus, in the form of a modern despot's politico-criminal justice system, unfolded and gripped the entire nation; thanks to the wide media coverage the case attracted. And it wasn't just ordinary Ugandans who were glued to their newspapers. There was an unprecedented interest from diplomats accredited to Uganda too; many of them actually taking time off to attend court proceedings.

In this politico-criminal trial, the prosecution's case [officially] was that Dr. Kizza Besigye had *"raped"* a one Joanita Kyakuwa. I have put the word *raped* in quotes with good reason. As you will see, from the modern despot's closet will emerge the big one; the one that I hope will shed some light on and perhaps even put to rest the myth that the DPP under Museveni's regime exercises his powers without subjecting himself *"to the direction or control of any person or authority"*. So here we go!

It is January 12th, the year of our Lord 2006. In her testimony as prosecution witness number 6 [PW6], none other than the *"whole"* Director of Uganda's *Criminal Investigations Directorate* [CID] Mrs Elizabeth Kutesa told a fully packed court presided over by Justice J.B. Katutsi that she had indeed received Museveni's directive to investigate the rape case against Dr. Besigye. The directive, she confessed, had come through the then *Inspector General of Police* [IGP] Major General Katumba Wamala. Bingo! A devastating bombshell by any standards; even for the decorated Generals involved, I suspect!

And to help you appreciate the gravity of this whole mess even better, I think it is important to note that Major General Katumba Wamala, the *IGP* we are talking about here, was still a serving military officer. So Katumba Wamala would have had very few *"cheap"* options open to him. Either way, he would have paid a heavy price. So let's explore his options. The first is that he could have opted to offer his resignation in the hope of bowing out of the mess with honour. But that too, by its very implication, would have been quickly interpreted as a straight slap in Museveni's face. And as we know, modern despots don't take such things lightly. Harsh reprisals often follow in one way or another.

The second option, which Katumba Wamala took, was to obey his *Commander-in-Chief's* orders to *"...investigate the rape case against Dr. Besigye"*. And by so doing, he totally soiled himself in Museveni's muddy political battles. The moral of the story is this: When an otherwise reasonable man chooses to serve a modern despot, sadly, that is exactly what he gets.

But let's go back to Mrs Kutesa's testimony. Can it really get any worse than her earth shaking confession about Museveni's directive to investigate Dr. Besigye? Oh yes it does; and it goes like this. Under the ferocious heat of cross-examination from a very able Defence Counsel, Mrs Kutesa was left with no option but to spill even more smelly beans. She admitted in court that she assigned Florence Okot, a police investigating officer, to go to *State House* [Museveni's official residence] to carry out *"investigations"* into the *"rape"* allegations. So let's get this straight first.

Other than the fact that the directive to investigate the *"rape"* allegation had come from *State House*, how else does the official *Presidential Palace* come into this politico-criminal investigation? Well, it's because that is exactly where Kyakuwa [the so-called *rape victim*] was residing at the time! Was she a very special *rape victim?* You bet! She had to be. And we are not done yet. The theatrical circus of a modern despot's politico-criminal justice system continues.

Before Mrs Kutesa's testimony, another state witness going by the names of Aisha Nakiguli had taken the stand in the witness box. Her claim to fame in this *Trial of the Century* was simply that she had once worked as a *Housemaid* at Dr. Besigye's residence. In her testimony, she told the same court during cross-examination that she had not only lived in a house provided by the CID Director Mrs Kutesa [possibly at taxpayers' expense] since her interrogation in 2004, but that the same Kutesa had also helped her start up a chicken rearing business.

The irregularities were simply staggering; it was all soothing music to a Defence Counsel's ears of course. So Dr. Besigye's Defence Counsel David Mpanga had a field day tearing the prosecution witnesses apart. In fact, he was so confident about the hopelessness of the prosecution's case that he even opted not to lead Dr. Besigye [the accused] through the defence evidence. So let me share with you a beautiful excerpt taken from Mpanga's final submission.

With confidence, Mpanga said: "...*My Lord, we submit that this whole case is, and was a fabrication from beginning to end, calculated to embarrass Col. {Rtd.} Dr. Kizza Besigye. This sad case was born in the deluded mind of Ms Joanita Kyakuwa; it was nurtured and developed in State House; it was cooked to imperfection in the Criminal Investigation Directorate of the Uganda Police; and it was presented into full inadequacy by the Deputy DPP. Now it's court's time to dismiss it*".

And so it was. In fact, I think even a smart first year law student could have dismissed this case. So how could Justice John Bosco Katutsi, an experienced, brave, and most able High Court Judge have failed to! Accordingly, in acquitting Dr. Kizza Besigye on March 7th 2006, Justice John Bosco Katutsi, perhaps sensing the great significance of the occasion too, roared straight into action and ruled thus: "...*the investigations were amateurish. The best way to describe the way the investigations were conducted and carried out is that it was crude and amateurish and betrays the intentions behind this case*".

Yes, that's it; "...*betrays the intentions behind this case*" were the words that revealed what the Judge thought were the real motives behind the regime's push to prosecute Dr. Kizza Besigye for "*rape*". It couldn't have been a *bona fide* pursuit of justice for a *rape victim*. It was the pursuit of power by a cowardly modern despot; one that called for the deployment of every conceivable tool of oppression at his disposal; including the law itself!

Still agreeing with the Defence Counsel, His Lordship Justice J.B. Katutsi, perhaps not wanting to be outshined by his junior David Mpanga, decided to craft his own immortal John Grisham style set of words to set forth his historic judgment. He said, "...*the evidence before this court is inadequate even to prove a debt, impotent to deprive [one] of a civil right, ridiculous for convicting [one] of the pettiest offence, scandalous if brought forward to support a charge of any grave character, monstrous if to ruin the honour of a man who offered himself as a candidate for the highest office of this country"*. So there you have it. Forget my humble views about what I thought were the actual motives behind Dr. Besigye's prosecution. There can be no clearer indication than this that the Judge, like most Ugandans, saw right through the wicked intentions behind Dr. Besigye's arrest and prosecution. Pure political persecution executed very poorly using the due process of the criminal justice system of Uganda. The most important point to remember in this case review is that we are trying to examine how the DPP in a modern despot's regime exercises the powers vested in him/her by the Constitution.

So cast your great minds back to clause [5] of article 120 of the Constitution of the Republic of Uganda. That article enjoins and or requires the DPP to *"...have regard to the public interest"* among other things. You will then find that the DPP, by sanctioning prosecution on the basis of the bogus evidence described by the Judge, did *not*, as required by that clause, have any regard whatsoever for the *public interest*. On the contrary, he may have had full regard for Museveni's *"personal political interests"*. Secondly, with the falsification of documents that the CID Director Elizabeth Kutesa confessed to under cross-examination, it is probably safe to say that the DPP also didn't have any regard for the *"...interest of the administration of justice and the need to prevent abuse of the legal process"*.

And finally, when the CID Director confessed that it was indeed Museveni who directed that Dr. Besigye be investigated for alleged rape, it became clear that the *Director of Public Prosecutions,* by sanctioning Dr. Besigye's prosecution under false pretences, did in fact ignore the *public interest* and also subjected himself *"...to the direction or control"* of another person and authority in the form of **Yoweri Kaguta** Museveni.

Therefore, with the *Criminal Investigations Directorate* and the *Directorate of Public Prosecutions* totally compromised, I think it is now safe to say that a modern despot's unrelenting quest to retain does indeed cause a country's criminal justice system to be considered partisan, corrupt, and totally untrustworthy. Hardly the ideal scenario!

And it was precisely because of that collapse of confidence that when the time came for Dr. Besigye to seek justice for the politically motivated ills that had been visited upon him, he saw no merit whatsoever in involving the CID and DPP. After all, both of them had already been shown to be under the *"direction and control"* of his main political opponent General Museveni. So to stand any chance of getting justice and perhaps redress, he decided to institute a private criminal prosecution [led by his own Lawyer] against the CID Director Mrs Elizabeth Kutesa.

Of course, a private criminal prosecution is neither unusual nor new to Uganda's criminal justice system. But the greatest significance of Dr. Besigye's decision to take out a private prosecution [to seek justice for himself] was that like many other Ugandans involved in opposition politics, he too had now lost confidence in the ability of the very institutions of State that are supposed to render impartial service to all Ugandans. That sad and most unfortunate reality will be further compounded by what you are about to see next.

Under most constitutions, the DPP is [if he so wishes] empowered to take over any privately instituted criminal prosecution. And to no one's great surprise, Uganda's DPP, probably acting on strict instructions *"from above"*, immediately took over the private criminal prosecution that Dr. Besigye had instituted against CID Director Elizabeth Kutesa. And then, for the final twist in this circus, he immediately entered a *nole prosequi* before court. In other words, he miraculously *"lost interest"* [as he is entitled to] in prosecuting his former witness in the shambolic rape case that was thrown out by Justice J.B. Katutsi!

But the DPP's more than suspicious *nole prosequi* business was now irrelevant; too late! Dr. Besigye had already made his point loudly and clearly. That under modern despots like Museveni, institutions of State are nothing but modern extensions of their primitive instruments of political intimidation, persecution, and even elimination in extreme cases. Whether or not the despots themselves appreciate the grave implications of such a catastrophic collapse of confidence in the criminal justice system is a different matter.

Test case No. 2: Uganda Vs the PRA Suspects

Yes, the old PRA case. It is back; again! I am not sure I know how to start discussing it here but discuss it I must. You would have thought that having been thoroughly humiliated by the revelations of prosecution witnesses in the rape case that we just discussed, Museveni would have prevailed upon his DPP to enter a *nole prosequi* in this PRA treason trial. He didn't. Instead, a new chapter of targeted political persecution opened with the resumption of the PRA treason trial.

Of course, for many of you who enjoy the luxury of rational thinking without the daily pressure to dream up *"ingenious"* ways to sustain a modern despot's unending quest to hang on to power, the PRA suspects probably committed no greater crime than to support Dr. Besigye's candidature for the presidency of Uganda in the 2001 general elections.

In other words, their *"crime"* was that they had the audacity to exercise their democratic right to choose, campaign for, and vote for Dr. Kizza Besigye; Museveni's most formidable political opponent. For most modern despots like Museveni, such a decision probably amounts to nothing short of *high treason*; a crime punishable by death! Therefore, in the despot's mind, such audacious people need to be dealt with harshly.

So, after the bruising defeat that Museveni and his DPP had suffered at the hands of the defence team in the rape case, this time round, in this PRA treason case, they seemed determined not to take any silly chances. There was a lot at stake; the despot's political power inclusive.

Therefore, for this *"very noble"* task, nothing would deter them, and nothing would be spared. If it meant soliciting for the help of private legal experts outside the *Directorate of Public Prosecutions*, then so be it! With that of course, the prospect of wasting obscene amounts of taxpayers' money for an illegitimate political cause loomed even closer. But Dr. Besigye had to be nailed with a criminal conviction and tucked away in prison; that is what mattered most to his tormentors. After such a conviction, only a humiliating plea for mercy by Dr. Besigye would have bought him back his freedom. And guess what! Oooh yes, constitutionally, only Museveni, as *"President"*, would have had the power to entertain such a plea for mercy from Besigye *"the would-be convict"*. Thereafter, at his own time and pleasure, he would then decide whether or not to exercise the *Prerogative of Mercy* to release Dr. Besigye. That would really stroke a depot's larger than life ego wouldn't it?

And with that, the all powerful General Museveni would have succeeded in portraying Dr. Besigye as a weak leader. After all, some political analysts have always argued that Dr. Besigye's appeal to the electorate is premised upon the perception that he is a *brave* man who can stand up to a vicious modern despot. And as we all know, in politics, a discredited leader stands little or no chance at all of winning an election. Besides, that would have made real the possibility that the invincible General Museveni would never have to be ruled by a man who was *"only"* one of his physicians during the bush war struggle that brought him to power. That way, and only that way my friends, would everyone live happily thereafter. Sadly for Museveni, it was never to be.

The good old Doctor had a more scientific prescription to cure the evil plan to kill him politically. To the chagrin of the architects of this evil political plan, Besigye out-rightly rejected the option of applying for amnesty to secure his personal liberty at the expense of Uganda's democracy.

Call me what you like, I really don't mind; but I would like to think that it is precisely this demonstration of selflessness, nationalism, and political foresight that appeals to many Ugandans. Not the mere perception of Besigye's *bravery* that some political analysts like to sing about. But let's move on.

Like I said, in this PRA treason case against Dr. Besigye and others, the regime was determined to leave nothing to chance. The humiliating defeat they had suffered in the *"rape"* case would not be repeated. So it came as no surprise at all when the media reported that Museveni's regime had indeed hired private prosecutors from *Kampala Associated Advocates* [a firm of *well connected Lawyers*] for a colossal sum of 2.5billion *Shillings [approx 1.4million dollars]* of taxpayers' money. After all, the DPP's capacity to deliver the impossible had been found to be seriously wanting in the *"rape"* case.

I am sure you have already noticed one crucial act of shameless hypocrisy in the regime's decision to hire private prosecutors. It was doing exactly what it had fought hard to ensure Dr. Besigye doesn't do; namely, to prosecute a criminal case [against the CID Director Elizabeth Kutesa] privately without the help of the DPP. But let's leave that for a moment and look at something else concerning the DPP's actions in this PRA treason case.

Earlier in my discussion of the *"rape"* case, I concluded that as a presidential appointee, the *Director of Public Prosecutions* had in fact subjected himself *"...to the direction and control"* of his boss Yoweri Kaguta Museveni.

That, I argued, had caused the DPP to contravene clause [6] of article 120 of the constitution which prescribes the manner in which the DPP should exercise the powers vested in him. So in the same spirit of my *"rape"* case analysis and conclusion, we must now ask ourselves a few more questions regarding this PRA treason case:

- *Knowing what I hope we all know now, do you think it was in the "public interest" [as required by clause [5] of article 120 of the Constitution] for Museveni's regime to sanction the payment of almost $1.4million of taxpayers' money to a firm of private Lawyers just to ensure that Museveni's political opponent Dr. Kizza Besigye is convicted of treason and possibly sentenced to death?*

- *Wouldn't the wider "public interest" have been better served if that money had been injected into the Directorate of Public Prosecutions to sharpen skills or improve salaries and morale?*

- *How many standard rural hospitals could have been constructed and reasonably equipped with a 1.4million dollar health fund?*

- *How many life saving drugs would 1.4million dollars have bought to save Ugandans from dying of curable diseases?*
- *How many Doctors would have been fully trained with a 1.4million dollar education fund?*

- *How many Teachers would have been fully trained with a 1.4million dollar education fund?*

- *How many roads of reasonably good quality would have been constructed with a 1.4million dollar infrastructure fund?*

- How much would 1.4million dollars have contributed to Uganda's national struggles against poverty?

- How many children would have got quality education if 1.4million dollars was ploughed into their education?

Over to you! Not even the mighty modern despot who roams your streets can intimidate you as you consider your verdict in the privacy of your mind. For that most beautiful fact of life, I say woe unto the modern despot! You and I must now turn our attention to another crucial State institution. In fact, for its unglamorous role at the epicentre of some of the world's worst political upheavals, it may even be considered to be *"Most"* deserving of close scrutiny.

A Modern Despot's "Personal" Army

In Uganda, the *Constituent Assembly* [CA] delegates who debated and promulgated Uganda's 1995 Constitution had, in their wisdom, deemed it fit that Museveni's rebel *National Resistance Army* [NRA] should be formally transformed into a national army. Their resolution was then enshrined in article 208[1] which stipulated that, "*...there shall be armed forces to be known as the Uganda Peoples Defence Forces*" [UPDF]. With that, the UPDF was born and required by clause [2] of the same article to be "*...non-partisan, national in character, patriotic, professional, disciplined, productive and subordinate to the civilian authority as established under this constitution*".

Clearly, the wording of cause [2] reflects a very strong desire and resolve by the CA delegates to transform the NRA from a rebel army to a *"national"* armed force that would be professional and pro-democracy. And this *new national army* was, on paper at least, supposed to be *fundamentally* different from all others before it that had been credited with wrecking havoc in the country.

But as they say, *"the proof of the pudding is in the eating"*. In other words, only, and only the manner in which the UPDF would henceforth conduct itself would determine whether it indeed turned out to be what the CA delegates intended it to be. And to be fair, for a few years, the UPDF was relatively disciplined and productive in most parts of Uganda that enjoyed peace and stability. But that's just about it.

North of the political fault-line that is the *Karuma Bridge* on the great *River Nile*, the story was very different. There, there is absolutely no doubt that there were numerous incidents where the UPDF fell far short of being what the Constitution had envisaged and required it be. No arguments there; I hope! So to put the UPDF through its constitutional test, we must look beyond its conduct situations of peace and stability.

It is the year of our Lord 2001. The UPDF's *Commander-in-Chief* General Museveni is due to face a general election. Dr. Kizza Besigye, a serving Colonel in the UPDF at the time, had just authored a stinging 14page critique of Museveni's ruling NRM government. It is for all intents, an insider's account; exactly as he sees it. Therefore, the general presumption is that it is authoritative. Believable; if you like. And the overriding message in the *"Besigye missive"* was that Museveni's regime was now rotten; totally incorrigible. And for those reasons, it was considered to be the most damaging disillusion of a modern despot's deceit.

The Monitor newspaper that is publishing the *"Besigye missive"* is quite simply the hottest selling commodity in town. The eyes of the nation are suddenly popping open. There is disbelief at the sheer scale of the rot that had been glossed over for years by the regime's powerful *Public Relations* machinery. A good number of people *south* of the *Karuma Bridge* are beginning to wake up from the deep political slumber; for it is they who used to say *"kacita twebaka"* or *[at least we can sleep]*.

To understand the significance of this *kacita twebaka* phrase better, I think it is important that I lay down a fair context of the circumstances under which it was being used by those who were enjoying relative peace and stability. Perhaps some valuable lessons will be learnt from it. So here we go!

When corruption started taking root in the country, many Ugandans south of Karuma Bridge simply turned a blind eye and said "kacita twebaka". When opposition activists from the Democratic Party and Uganda People's Congress were being harassed, beaten and persecuted by Museveni's security operatives, many Ugandans south of Karuma Bridge hardly bated an eyelid because "kacita twebaka". When NRA soldiers were executing civilians by firing squad in northern and eastern Uganda, south of the Karuma Bridge, the chorus was "kacita twebaka". When innocent children were spending their precious nights wide awake in the jungles of northern and eastern Uganda to avoid abduction by the murderous Lord's Resistance Army [LRA], south of the Karuma Bridge the near unanimous consensus was "kacita twebaka". When independent Journalists and media houses that were trying to hold Museveni's regime to account were being persecuted and prosecuted, the word in the bars, offices and living rooms south of the Karuma Bridge was "kacita twebaka".

If I wanted, I could have gone on and on until the proverbial *"cows come home"*. But I won't. Besides, this time round, as soon as Dr. Besigye published his missive, things began to change; and I mean really change. And for that, I think even those who used to sing "*kacita twebaka"* should be forgiven.

Because now, from the capital city Kampala, to the fertile and hilly plains of Western Uganda; from the gorgeous and mountainous eastern parts of Uganda, to the majestic and yet wild hinterlands of northern Uganda; very serious questions were now being asked.

Questions that were becoming awkward for both those asking them and those supposed to answer them. They were also questions that demanded straight myth busting answers about the so-called "*1986 Revolution*" that brought Museveni to power.

In the flashy confines of *State House*, there is every chance that no one was feeling the discomfort of those awkward questions more than General Museveni himself. And with good reason too. He was being stripped naked in the press by a Colonel who should have been saluting him unquestioningly.

It was therefore inevitable that the regime was going to do something about it; and do it without kid gloves. A sense of foreboding was truly hanging in the air. General Museveni was about to go native. And he did. From the heavily fortified *State House* in Nakasero hill, a most powerful-irritation laden voice rang out in the same way it does at military parades.

It virtually filled the dust clogged air hanging above the capital city Kampala. And, given Uganda's turbulent political history, city dwellers panicked and held their breaths; not knowing what would happen next. Before the dust settled, as it usually does at dusk, city dwellers had already found out what had happened when that powerful military parade style voice rang out.

It was of course, and could only have been, a sound emanating from the powerful vocal Chord of the supreme *Commander-in-Chief* of the UPDF Lt. General Yoweri Kaguta Museveni. His order was clear and unequivocal. Colonel Besigye must face the *Court Martial* for "*...airing his views in the wrong forum*".

Hang on! *"Airing his views in the wrong forum"?* I think not. What Museveni should have said was that Col. Kizza Besigye should face the *Military Court Martial* for his temerity. That would have made more sense. How could he, a mere Colonel, have let out a General's biggest political weapons? Nepotism, cronyism, patronage, deceit, corruption, and dictatorship among many other things!

All lethal [offensive and defensive] weapons that had been smartly dressed in whiter than white democratic colours! And, like smartly dressed sweet little girls on their knees, heads bowed before the White Priest, [read Western donors] these *lethal weapons* were christened the *"Movement System"* of governance. One that would be based on *"Individual Merit"*; not political parties!

But his tough orders notwithstanding, Museveni had waited too long to nip the Besigye tirade in bud. The eyes of the nation were now open. And to show it, the nation, led by elders from Rukungiri where Dr. Besigye hails from, launched a campaign to dissuade Museveni from pushing for the *Military Court Martial* trial that would have resulted in the conviction of *"their"* son Dr. Kizza Besigye. At least that was how the media and the public perceived it then. But I have news for them. They were both wrong; very wrong in fact!

While on an official visit to London in October 2007, Dr. Besigye told me that while he was at *State House* with Museveni and the Rukungiri elders, he had vehemently opposed the elders' plea to Museveni to forgive him. That he insisted that the *Court Martial* trial should go ahead so that he gets the opportunity to defend himself.

Besigye said he had also asked that if he was found guilty, then he should be punished appropriately. Such punishment, Besigye insisted, would serve as a powerful deterrent to other UPDF officers who might consider airing their views *"in the wrong forum"*. Now what do you make of that?

Over a humble cup of tea in my flat, I had sat there listening to Dr. Besigye in utter disbelief as he casually narrated this hitherto unknown twist in the *Court Martial* story. So captivated I was that my tea actually went cold. What was the source of this mind-boggling bravery and confidence, I had quietly wondered to myself? For me, it seemed as though he really was at the mercy of the all powerful General Museveni.

So I couldn't quite figure out why he had confidently demanded that his *Court Martial* trial should proceed as planned. But Besigye's confidence was not without basis. He had something up his sleeve. It was something that would have been unpleasant; nasty in fact, even for the all powerful General. So what was it?

Well, he told me that had Museveni dared push ahead with the *Court Martial* trial as he was urging him to, he would have produced evidence that would have embarrassed and damaged Museveni even more. Even more interesting, Besigye said, Museveni himself knew that more than anyone else in attendance at that *State House* meeting. So as we shall soon find out, this may just explain Museveni's later change of heart.

Back then, and with no knowledge of these intricate facts that have just emerged about the tripartite *State House* meeting, the media was of course quick to grab a slice of the action. Its interest in the case had ensured that the debate on whether or not Dr Besigye should face the *Military Court Martial* dominated public political discourse for weeks.

Newspaper sales shot through the roof on the streets of Kampala and across the county. And with that of course, the newspaper shareholders, like the great scavenger that is the African Hyena, laughed all the way to their bank managers with maximum returns from minimum investment.

To the unsuspecting public at the time, it was difficult to see why the order from the *"great"* Commander-in-Chief appeared to be faltering in its effect. Something had shifted from under his feet; surely. And to his credit, perhaps sensing the mood of the nation, Museveni changed his mind. Dr. Besigye never got anywhere near the *Military Court Martial* for *airing his views in the wrong forum.*

So it was a win-win situation for shareholders of media houses; for Dr. Besigye; for his now massive army of supporters and admirers; for the elders of Rukungiri; and for the nation as a whole. But with every win, there must be a loser. And for the very simple fact that the world had now started having serious doubts about what a modern despot's *"fundamental change"* actually means, I think Museveni, the champion of that most fallacious political sound bite, became the net loser.

And the loss didn't end there. Museveni was on the verge of losing even more grip over Dr. Besigye; a man who was under his firm command only a few days earlier. Being the man he is, Besigye quickly read the weight of public opinion leaning towards him. He smelt Museveni's poisonous political blood and was determined to drain out a few more litres. So he rode on the back of that tide and quickly petitioned the army authorities to allow him to retire from active military service. Museveni, as *Commander-in-Chief*, was left with only one sensible option. And that was to let Besigye retire from the army before he could cause more trouble from within. In so doing, Museveni had also, without knowing, set the stage for a gigantic political contest between himself and Dr. Besigye.

As a civilian, Dr. Besigye was now *"free"* to embark on his political activities. One of his first, and perhaps most memorable moves as a civilian political player, was to sensationally blow up Museveni's deceit and myth; the myth that under his so-called and non-partisan *"Movement"*, every Ugandan had the right to contest for any elective office. In fact the fallacy was that even Museveni's own office of *Chairman* of the *Movement* was up for grabs. And how did Besigye blow up the myth? Well, he did it with a very simple declaration of intent to challenge Museveni for the leadership of the ruling *National Resistance Movement* [NRM]. Whether he meant it or not is a different matter. My own guess however, is that Besigye, more than anyone else, knew that there was no way Museveni would allow such a challenge to take place. At least not with a certain Kizza Besigye; the man who had just exposed the regime's despotic pre-disposition!

In a sense, I think Dr. Besigye knew exactly what he wanted to achieve by declaring his *"intention"* to challenge Museveni for the Chairmanship of the *Movement*. And it wasn't the leadership of the NRM; after all, he had already declared in his 14page missive that the *Movement* was now incorrigible. Beyond redemption; in other words!

So I think by declaring his intention to challenge Museveni, Besigye merely wanted to prove a point. A point that the *Movement* was in fact a fully fledged political party and not the broad-based and non partisan system of governance it had been made out to be. And he was proved right; almost immediately in fact. In panic, the NRM passed a resolution declaring that Museveni was going to be its only candidate for the leadership of the NRM; no ifs; no buts! With that, all the razzmatazz about the *Movement* being a new democratic system that allows everyone to compete for any political office at any level on their *individual merit* went through the window too. A modern despot's trickery exposed by a *"dummy declaration of intent"*; how interesting!

From then on, the world knew that Museveni's *Movement* had all along been a disguised but fully fledged political party that secretly sponsored its own candidates. Now that the *Movement* party had slammed its metallic door to the

Chairman's office in his face, if Dr. Besigye still wanted to pursue his political objectives, then he needed to find a new political home and find it quick.

Luckily for him, his audacious and by all accounts historic exposure of the *Movement's* deceit, the humiliating collapse of Museveni's *Military Court Martial* trial, and his controversial quest to retire from active military service, were all tough political battles that he had won convincingly in a very short time against a General who had been considered invincible.

In the process, Besigye had also won the admiration and support of millions across the country. That was the political base he needed to launch his bid for the presidency of Uganda in the 2001 general elections. And in no time, the *Elect Kizza Besigye Task Force* [EKBTF] was born. The rest, as they say, is history.

But what exactly have all these *Museveni-Besigye* political battles have to do with our present discussion about the management of the UPDF as an institution of State? Well, the last few paragraphs were simply a build-up to this moment. The moment at which the character, operation, and management of the UPDF would be put to its constitutional test!

In fact, before we even get to that constitutional test, it has just occurred to me that the *Court Martial* trial drama that we touched upon earlier actually involved two men who belonged to the UPDF as an institution of State. And one of them, General Museveni, had unilaterally declared that Colonel Besigye should face the Court Martial.

Even as a lay civilian, I wonder whether some sort of *"Army Disciplinary Committee"* shouldn't have sat first to decide whether there was a *prima facie* case for Colonel Besigye to answer. But let's move on. As we all remember, the constitution of Uganda requires the UPDF to be a *"...non-partisan, national, patriotic, professional, disciplined, [and] productive army that is subordinate to civilian authority"*. Great isn't it?

Now, in 2001, much in the same way as he had bravely criticised Museveni's *Movement*, Dr. Besigye declared at a campaign rally that he enjoys 90% support in the UPDF. The UPDF, like most national armies around the world, is of course made up of men and women who, although not allowed to participate in partisan politics, are nonetheless entitled to hear what every candidate has to say. Not in a modern despot's world I am afraid!

As soon as he learnt of Dr. Besigye's claim to 90% support in the UPDF, Museveni moved quickly to set the record straight. And, without mincing his words, he responded to Dr. Besigye's claim with a chilling declaration: *"...anyone who tries to mess around with MY army will be sent six feet down under"*, Museveni said. Yes, you heard it. Forget what a *"mere"* constitution says. This is a modern despot's world and he doesn't do constitutional legalities; thank you very much! The UPDF is *"His"* personal army! That is the true Gospel according to *"Saint"* Yoweri Kaguta Museveni.

The truth of the matter is that Museveni never intended to, and in fact, never did cede to the nation the *NRA* rebel force that he had personally founded and nurtured. In the deepest chamber of a modern despot's mind, a national army sits side by side with his personal estate! Therefore, I think deep down, Museveni viewed the UPDF, an institution of State, in the same way as he viewed his expensive suits and shirts.

It was now neo-patrimonial rule; complete with all the ugly flair that comes with it. And there was no stopping it! From then on until the end of the 2001 general elections, the UPDF took full control of nearly everything concerning the policing of polling stations; a function that ought to have, according to the law at least, been that of the *Police Force*.

Charles Ochen Okwir

It was as if Museveni had set out to demonstrate to Dr. Besigye and the country that he was still in full control of *"His"* UPDF. The army's *Red Beret Military Police*, now dressed in full combat gear with assault rifles at hand, commandeered government vehicles at will. They used the high-jacked vehicles to roam the streets; menacingly looking at, threatening, intimidating, harassing, and in some cases, even shooting dead Dr. Besigye's supporters.

In fact, *"shooting dead Dr. Besigye's supporters"* was exactly what happened at a rally in Rukungiri District-Western Uganda where Dr. Besigye's *National Youth Coordinator* Maj. [Rtd] Okwir Rabwoni was campaigning. That was how far the regime was prepared to go if that is what it would take to intimidate Besigye's supporters into submission. The atmosphere suddenly turned tense. The threat of death was very real. You could almost smell it!

In the end, many of Dr. Besigye's supporters were reduced to passive spectators; a very sad spectacle indeed. With their hands on their cheeks, like castrated bulls, they peeped through the windows of their homes and offices powerlessly as General Museveni's *Military Police* ran riot in town. The rest again, is now history. Museveni was declared *"winner"* of the 2001 general elections.

So did anything change in the management of the UPDF after the 2001 elections? Well, actually, yes and no! Yes in the sense that the army's visibility and illegal political activities in the cities reduced considerably as soon as Museveni was firmly back in State House.

That in itself tells its own story. Perhaps that was the order *"from above"*. So what remained unchanged? Well, there was *"no change"* [Museveni's re-election slogan incidentally] because the UPDF was still very much a partisan army that existed for and served at the pleasure of one man; Gen. Yoweri Museveni!

Now fast forward to 2006! A general election is looming large in the horizon again. The prevailing circumstances are strikingly similar to those of the 2001 general elections. So we shall not waste time with that. It is to the post-2006 election period that we must now turn to bring you the next piece of evidence; evidence that I think will finally put to rest any hope of the UPDF ever becoming the *"national"* army that the framers of Uganda's 1995 Constitution had envisaged.

And this is not just any evidence. It is evidence that has its origins at the very nerve centre of the UPDF; its intelligence services. It is essentially a military intelligence assessment; one that shouldn't have bothered anyone who didn't have anything to do with the management of the army. But for its reference to the voting patterns in the army, and its recommendations about what needs to be done to remedy the situation, I will say anyone with even the slightest interest in Ugandan politics needs to pay attention.

The author, a Colonel [at the time] in one of the many intelligence arms of the UPDF, had this to say about the 2006 general elections: "...*the recently concluded presidential elections showed a steadily growing opposition infiltration in the army. A number of Officers and Men were noted to have overtly supported Dr. K Besigye despite the known fact of FDC's links with its armed wing the PRA and LRA…..this clearly indicated the low level of political education amongst our troops*".

Well, well, well! I think the most logical inference to be made from that also happens to be the simplest. And it is that the author of this infamous intelligence assessment clearly thought that it was not acceptable for any officer in the UPDF, man or woman, to vote for anyone other than the *Commander-in-Chief* General Museveni. Who, in all honesty, still believes the UPDF is or can be a "...*non-partisan, national, patriotic, professional, disciplined, and productive army that is subordinate to the civilian authority"*?

Perhaps I should try something else that is not just *slightly* but *totally* different. For the doubting Thomases out there, this is for you; with love from yours truly. The author then makes this ground breaking recommendation to his superiors and says: *"...it is suggested that the CPC [Chief Political Commissar is my guess] organises intensive politicisation courses for the army with emphasis on the Units identified to have performed poorly in the recent elections".*

Yes, *performed poorly!* Should voting for the opposition candidate [Dr. Besigye] in an election really be construed to mean *poor performance*? Of course not! But we may never know for sure what the report's author actually meant. We may also never know if the CPC actually acted on or implemented those intelligence recommendations. But those are really irrelevant factual details in the context of this debate.

The important fact is that the recommendation was made; even when the constitution clearly tells us that it was illegal for the army's intelligence service to make such a partisan recommendation. Besides this, an interesting story that appeared in the *Daily Monitor* newspaper that will be reviewed later in my insight into the *Uganda Police Force* may suggest that at the very least, the possibility that the CPC actually implemented the illegal intelligence recommendations should never be ruled out.

As far as the UPDF is concerned however, I am very clear in my conclusion. Professionalization is a lost cause under a modern despot like Gen. Museveni. If true democracy is to take root in a country like Uganda, then there must be a very compelling case for untying all those in the armed services from the shackles and chains of command that demand total and unquestioning loyalty to their superiors during elections.

In other words, like the rest of the civilian population, the brave men and women in uniform deserve and must at such crucial times be accorded the minimum dignity to obey their conscience to choose a leader that they, in their absolute discretion, deem fit to lead their country. It's a very achievable democratic ambition; with the right political will of course!

That political will should also see to it that any incumbent President or *Commander-in-Chief* who is offering him or herself for re-election completely relinquishes the powers of State vested in him or her for the entire duration of the election campaigns. Yes, there are some imperfections associated with such a move if it's handled poorly. Such imperfections can however be dealt with swiftly by selfless men and women who look beyond their personal political ambitions. The most important thing is that if incumbents were to be stripped of their state powers during election time, then at least they will have been forced into a reasonably levelled political playing field with all others contesting for election to the same office. But don't take my word for it.

In its July-December 2008 report, the *Foundation for Human Rights Initiative* [FHRI] said, *"...Uganda's road to achieving electoral democracy is still bumpy"*. Crucially however, the report went on to add that *"...no matter the number of proposed reforms or initiatives to prepare Ugandans for the 2011 elections, the single largest threat remains the role of the security services in the electoral process. Leaders in politics and civil society fear that the military will, at best, intimidate voters and disenfranchise the representatives of political parties or at worst, invalidate results that favour opposition candidates or violently repress political dissent"*.

The independent evidence is therefore clear. Perhaps the only thing I will add to that is that a modern despot's aggression can never prevail over the power of the human spirit forever. There is clear evidence that in all countries ruled by modern despots, the human spirit has stubbornly remained unvanguished even in the face of the most vicious onslaught.

Like the great *Mt. Etna*, it remains beneath the surface simmering dangerously. And usually, it erupts violently sending the despots scampering for dear life. For evidence of that, I say look no further than what happened to President Zine El Abidine Ben Ali of Tunisia in January 2011. He was forced to flee his country under the cover of darkness by bare-handed Tunisian protestors.

With sufficient courage, the hazardous political walls that a modern despot's opponents struggle to scale on a daily basis can crumble like the proverbial pack of cards. The reason, a very simple one, is that the despot's bulwarks are not built on a legitimate mandate to govern. They are built on shaky foundations; foundations that are only held together by the army's weapons of terror and oppression.

There are many more examples of such possibilities. Uganda's own Idi Amin *"Conqueror of the British Empire"*, Iraq's Saddam Hussein, *"Emperor"* Bokassa of Central African Republic, Ethiopia's Haile Mariam Mengistu, General Sani Abacha of Nigeria, Zaire's Mobutu Sese Seko *"Nkuku Ngbendu Wa Za Banga" [The all-powerful warrior],* General Augusto Pinochet of Chile, Slobodan Milosovic of Yugoslavia, and many others found out the hard way. None of them got a dignified ending. History, they say, has a funny way of repeating itself. Beware modern despots!

The Civil Face of Political Oppression

The propensity of modern despots to hide behind civility is a matter that has already been discussed in this book. It is now time to look at the real face of a modern despot's favourite agency of *"legal"* oppression. Like the UPDF that we have just discussed, the *Uganda Police Force* [UPF] too is supposed to be a "*...non-partisan, national, patriotic, professional, disciplined, and productive force that is subordinate to the civilian authority*". At the time of writing this book however, the UPF was under the brutal leadership of an *Inspector General of Police [IGP]* who is said to be one of Museveni's *"blue-eyed"* boys. So I think it would be a very pleasant surprise indeed if the way it is run turns out to be any different from the way the UPDF is run.

For a start, IGP Kale Kayihura is a military General who previously served as the UPDF's *Chief Political Commissar* [CPC]. Note: "*...it is suggested that the CPC organises intensive politicisation courses for the army with emphasis on the Units identified to have performed poorly in the recent elections*". That is the most crucial clue *[from the military intelligence report I reviewed earlier]* for you to bear in mind as we discuss Kayihura's stewardship of the UPF.
And the reason is simple. IGP Kayihura is first and foremost, a serving Major General in the UPDF. That means he still gets his marching orders from the UPDF's *Commander-in-Chief* General Museveni. What more can we really add to that? Nothing! So, for a different kind of illustration, let us examine an interesting story that appeared in *The Daily Monitor* newspaper.

"*Besigye Shirt Causes Trouble in Army Camp*" was the headline. It is a headline that lends powerful credence to my suspicions. This incident took place at Kasenyi *Presidential Guard Brigade* [PGB] training base; a military establishment where some police officers were undergoing VIP protection training. But here is my worry. By requiring police officers to undergo training in a military establishment, it was clear that the two institutions of terror were not only losing their identities, but their independence from each other too. Secondly, in terms of institutional superiority, well, that is a *"No Contest"*. In a modern despot's world, the army, for its ability to intimidate more, will always carry the day.

Charles Ochen Okwir

Going back to our *"Besigye Shirt"* story, the paper reported that police constable [PC] Kwikirize *"...discovered that it is a wrong career move to wear former presidential candidate Kizza Besigye's T-shirt".......he may now have to wait long before he gets another opportunity to get specialised training in protecting VIP's".*

The report also suggested that PC Kwikirize could have been better off wearing another candidate's T-shirt. The army's PGB boys were of course wearing campaign T-shirts of one of the presidential candidates. As the typical cockney accented British male would say, that for me is a *"no brainer mate"*. In other words, it's not even worth thinking about!

As officers and men of the UPDF's *Presidential Guard Brigade*, the firm suspicion must be that they were openly wearing their boss Yoweri Museveni's campaign T-Shirt. So the PGB boys, perhaps sensing that Museveni's dominance *[even at this UPDF training camp]* was coming under threat, confronted the poor old police constable and ordered him to remove the Besigye T-shirt immediately.

Now before we move on, I think a quick reflection would be in order. Earlier, I had argued that it is the army that usually keeps modern despots like Museveni in power. In my view, this incident partially *[if not totally]* vindicates that stance because we can clearly see that the army is not prepared to accept anyone other than Museveni.

I also argued that even with such vicious levels of repression, the human spirit often remains unvanguished. Well, here it is in action. It was reported that when he was approached by the PGB boys and ordered to remove the Besigye T-shirt he was wearing, PC Kwikirize simply told the PGB boys off; arguing that *"...the country was now under a multiparty political arrangement and therefore he was free to wear an FDC T-shirt".*

I think PC Kwikirize was trying to raise a very important issue; one of natural justice! That if the PGB boys could openly wear a partisan political campaign T-shirt bearing the picture of one of the candidates, then why shouldn't he be allowed to wear one bearing a picture of another candidate. After all, PC Kwikirize argued, the country was now under a multi-party dispensation. If looked at politically, you can see that PC Kwikirize was actually demanding a level political playing field; a fact whose absence in countries ruled by modern despots has often caused bitter civil wars.

Besides, the way PC Kwikirize was treated by the PGB boys also brings back into very sharp focus one of the most important issues I raised while I was discussing the infamous military intelligence assessment. That when a country is undergoing such an important electoral process, the brave men and women in the armed services must be accorded the dignity to obey their conscience and allowed to vote for a candidate of their choice; just like their civilian counterparts.

Commenting on this particular *"Besigye Shirt"* incident, Uganda's Army spokesman Major Felix Kulayigye of course said, "*...no one is allowed to put on party colours......we are supposed to follow the code of conduct we have been given*". But that still leaves open one key question: Why weren't the PGB officers who were wearing partisan colours also given their marching orders like PC Kwikirize? My take on that is that it was simply impossible for Kulayigye to justify such injustice in political terms; hence the empty *Public Relations* response.

But should anyone be at all surprised by the injustice suffered by PC Kwikirize? I think not. We had, after all, long established, almost beyond reasonable doubt, that selective application of the law is one of *the true traits* of a modern despot's rule. Egalitarianism is a norm that is simply alien to them. For them, if political dominance and longevity calls for total desecration of the nation's sacred institutions, then so be it! So Uganda's police force is likely to remain just as it is now; a partisan State institution which does the despot's political bidding.

Uganda Prison Service: The Final Exposure

Uganda Prison Service [UPS] was for a long time perceived to be the least partisan State institution under General Museveni's regime. But this too may have been merely for incidental or in fact, even accidental reasons. Not that the regime had deliberately set out to make it totally non-partisan. And the reason is this. By its very nature, the UPS cannot be as involved as the army and police are in Uganda's frontline political confrontations. Once the police and army have done their bit for the regime, then the UPS merely comes in to make sure the arrested prisoners are securely kept under lock and key.

The assumption in this theory, a very unscientific one at that, is that the regime's security operatives will have taken their political prey through Museveni's schizophrenic judicial system. It is not uncommon for them not to. If and when they do, then perhaps the public would be right to consider the UPS to be at the quiet tail-end of the regime's political persecution chain. And it is only because of that that it somehow managed to escape the relative media scrutiny that the police and army have had to contend with.

But perhaps most importantly, it may also be that the UPS's non-partisan credentials had really never been tested. That may also have been for the simple reason that its role had never attained great significance in Museveni's quest to dominate Uganda's political landscape. But all that changed when the UPS received the so called *PRA* rebel suspects into its detention facilities on the shores of the great Lake Victoria. Its impartiality was immediately called into question when news broke that some of the PRA suspects had been irregularly removed from the gazetted *Luzira*

Remand Prison by military intelligence operatives and spread into un-gazetted *"Safe Houses"*; *houses* that are in reality, pure torture chambers. Just to give you an idea of how bad these *Safe Houses* are, one *PRA* suspect once told me that they often felt *"...a great sense of relief"* while on their way back to *Luzira* prison after receiving what he called *"...our dozes of torture"*. A typical case of jumping *from fire to the frying pan*! In other words, the frying pan *[Luzira Prison]* was not as hot as the fire in the *Safe Houses.* In Luzira, he painfully added, *"...at least we could not be finished off quietly without anyone noticing"*. So the possibility of a quiet painful death in Museveni's *Safe Houses* was a very real prospect.

The *PRA* case, being the high profile case that it was, meant that it would only be a matter of time before the UPS's non-partisan credentials are put through a practical test. And, right on cue, that test came when the *High Court* granted the *PRA* suspects bail and ordered their immediate release from prison pending trial. The rule of law working perfectly; you would have thought. No; not this time! Uganda's *Commissioner General of Prisons* Mr. Johnson Byabashaija was having none of that *"nonsense"*.

The *PRA* suspects, he said, would not be released because he had received *"orders from above"* that they must remain in custody. Any surprises there? I think not. Of course, the so-called *"orders from above"* should under normal circumstances have been the High Court's orders that the *PRA* suspects be released immediately. That would have left the UPS with no choice but to release the suspects as duly ordered by court. But these were not normal circumstances. This was *"Revolutionary Criminal Justice"*; Museveni style!

As I said earlier, Museveni had already decreed that none of the *PRA* suspects would be released *"unless they apply for amnesty"*. His word was law. An admission of guilt by the *PRA* suspects would of course have had to precede that grant of amnesty. So in the circumstances, I find it hard to exclude the conclusion that Museveni's infamous decree must have been bearing heavily on the *Commissioner General's* mind. That is how a modern despot like Museveni deals with *"His"* security agencies.

Desecration of the National Legislature

Democracy is based on the notion that people within a given jurisdiction have the right to freely enjoy their inherent rights and freedoms to associate, assemble, protest, dissent, and express themselves. I would also like to think that the enjoyment of those rights and freedoms invariably means that those enjoying them would, among other things, be accorded the liberty to elect the leaders they want.

Secondly, that those elected into positions of leadership would be held accountable for their actions. If that be the case, then surely the Legislature must be at the very heart of that Western democratic tradition of holding political leaders to account. It is a tradition that has been emulated in many parts of the world. So you would think that it's now settled; wouldn't you? Well, not quite. Not if a modern despot has anything to do with it.

The unshakable claim in this book is that the Legislature in Uganda has been fundamentally desecrated by Museveni's despotic rule. An intrepid claim indeed; I appreciate. So perhaps then, just to aid your appreciation of that claim, I shall attempt to lay down a few basic facts about "a" Legislature by answering some equally basic questions about it. Questions like: What exactly is, and does a Legislature really do? What role does it play in a democracy?

To the non native English speakers like yours truly, the first port of call must be an English dictionary; which I have right here. It is a battered old *Oxford English Dictionary* from my school years; and it defines a Legislature as "*...a body of persons invested with the power of making the laws of a country or State*".

That is what the English think a Legislature is, or ought to be. But how does that compare to what you think the Legislature is, or ought to be? Not very different; I imagine. In Uganda, article 79 of the constitution alluded to exactly that when it said, "*...subject to the provisions of this constitution, Parliament shall have power to make laws on any matter for the peace, order, development and good governance of Uganda*".

The problem I have with article 79 of Uganda's Constitution is that it only appears to be addressing a broad range of activities performed by a Legislature without necessarily distinguishing between the many types of Legislatures that exist around the world. It also, in my view, fails to acknowledge that the Legislature shares its law making function with other organs of the State like the Judiciary. But to embark on an exhaustive insight into the numerous functions of the various types of Legislatures around the world would be a little too ambitious for this book.

o the compromise position I propose is to simply describe the basic functions that virtually all Legislatures in democratic States share; and the ways in which they differ. And the differences in question

Smerely involve the form of the Legislature; the role of the majority or ruling party; the role of the opposition parties; the role of other internal or associate organisations; and finally, the role of civil society groups. In most democratic States, deciding the form the Legislature takes, how to elect its members, what powers to bestow upon it, how to entrench avenues of expression for minority parties, and how to organise its internal functions are some of the most critical issues. They not only determine the credibility of that Legislature, but that of the sitting government and the nation's democracy as a whole. Cultural factors, historical experiences, and political realities in every jurisdiction however make the task of providing a universal answer very difficult.

For example, while some Legislatures may have a strong foreign policy role, others may have none at all. While others may have well defined committee systems, others may not have well defined means by which roles are discharged in Parliament. While others may only have two major political parties, others may have as many as ten political parties with varied levels of representation in the Legislature.

What I think is beyond contention however, is that no country in the world can have a fully functional democracy without having a credible, vibrant, and powerful Legislature; a Legislature with strong opposing voices that check the excesses of the Executive. A Legislature that provides adequate avenues for civil society organisations to be heard! It must also be a Legislature with well defined and predictable rules that govern the conduct of business in the House.

So what makes me say that Uganda's Legislature has been fundamentally desecrated by despotic rule? Well, for a start, it is because there is strong *prima facie* evidence to suggest that there has been a systematic stifling of strong opposing voices of reason in the Legislature. Secondly, there is an obvious luck of accountability from the government. And thirdly, there are inadequate avenues for civil society organisations to be heard. But before we get into the specifics of all that, let's try and work out what exactly Legislatures do.

The Role of a Typical Legislature

It is now a settled view that Legislatures are primarily lawmaking bodies. But it may also be important to appreciate that as an institution, the Legislature has many other important functions and responsibilities. As I said earlier, one of the key weaknesses of the dictionary definition of the Legislature as merely "*...a body of persons invested with the power of making the laws of a country or state*" is that it fails to point out that the Legislature is not the only

State body that makes laws and regulations.

So what unique functions or features, if any, clearly distinguish the Legislature from all the other law making bodies? Naturally, as a representative body, the Legislature is unique because of its intrinsic nexus to the electorate of any given State.

As John Stuart Mills indeed put it in 1862, in a representative democracy, "*...the proper office of a representative assembly is to watch and control the government: to throw the light of publicity on its acts, to compel a full exposition and justification of all of them which any one considers questionable*" and "*to censure them if found condemnable...*" In addition to that, Mills says "*...the Legislature has the responsibility to be at once the nation's committee of grievances; and its congress of opinions*".

In Mill's view, therefore, the Legislature acts as the eyes, ears, and voice of the people. Other than the fact that it gains its legitimacy by representing the public will, the Legislature also has other distinguishing features. For example, a Legislature tends to consist of a large group of individuals who come together for a common cause as equals *[in theory]* on the floor of the House and operate under a system of collective decision making.

The other thing is that although some of its members may in time assume leadership positions or special responsibilities within the House, customarily, each member's vote carries exactly the same weight when it comes to deciding issues on the floor of the House.

The other key feature that distinguishes the Legislature from the other law making bodies is that it adopts policies and makes laws through a process of deliberation that is usually guided by some broad set of principles contained in that country's Constitution. Their decisions need not proceed from the rule of law or specifically established legal precedents. And it is this that sets the Legislature apart from other law making bodies within the State.

Furthermore, most Legislatures also perform a unique educational role. Using their resources and expertise, Legislators digest and simplify complicated issues. They filter information from various sources in order to resolve conflicting ideological positions before presenting their constituents with clear policy choices.

This educational function has in the past twenty years become increasingly important as societies have become more complex and demanding; as the scope of government activity becomes even more extensive; and as the public gained increased access to Legislative proceedings via the various media that now cover such proceedings. So the media does indeed have a fundamental role to play in a democracy.

The other defining characteristic of the Legislature is the dual role of its members; the Legislators. They have a duty as law makers for the good of the nation [as a whole] as well as a duty to represent the unique interests of their constituencies. The tension that no doubt exists between those two roles is unique to representative forms of government that have districts as is the case in Uganda.

As Edmund Burke MP, a lawmaker and great political theorist of his time philosophically put it *[with a touch of poetic eloquence]* in a speech to his constituents in Bristol City- United Kingdom in 1774, the tension between the role of the Legislator as a trustee and as a delegate at the same time is a very real one.

In discussing whether a *Representative* should only be a *Delegate* whose job is merely to present the views and interests of his constituency, or whether a *Representative* should be a *Trustee* who offers his own judgment regarding what is best for the nation, *[even if it conflicts with the interests of his constituents]* Burke, in typical fashion, came down firmly on the side of the Legislator as *Trustee* and said:

"...*Certainly, gentlemen, it ought to be the happiness and the glory of a representative, to live in the strictest union, the closest correspondence, and the most unreserved communication with his constituents. Their wishes ought to have great weight with him; their opinions high respect; their business unlimited attention. But his unbiased opinion, his mature judgment, his enlightened conscience, he ought not to sacrifice to you, to any man, to any set of men living. Parliament is not a congress of ambassadors from different and hostile interests, which interests each must maintain, as an agent and advocate, against other agents and advocates; but Parliament is a deliberative assembly of one nation, with one interest, that of the whole, where not local purposes, not local prejudices, ought to guide, but the general good, resulting from the general reason of the whole. You choose a member, indeed; but when you have chosen him, he is not a member of Bristol, but he is a Member of Parliament".*

On this one, I think very few people out there can fault Burke. The tension between the *"Trustee"* and *"Delegate"* role is one that all Legislators have to deal with. It can be tension that is built around the needs of a smaller geographic constituency versus the needs of a nation; or around the needs of a narrow ideological, partisan or ethnic group versus the needs of a nation. Every country, and every Legislature, has to decide how best to balance those tensions.

For example, in cases where the Legislator's role is that of a mere *Delegate* and the minimum number of votes required for a party to gain representation in the Legislature is too low, *[exactly as is the case with the many tiny Districts in Uganda]* then small and narrow groups can wield disproportionate power at the expense of the majority. Equally, creating districts that are too large, or holding elections at only national level, can disenfranchise minority ethnic and or interest groups and leave them feeling powerless and bitter.

Having gone through the roles and functions of the Legislature, perhaps the time is now ripe to re-focus our minds and start considering a few real-life cases that I hope will demonstrate that Museveni's government did, and continues to desecrate Uganda's Legislature.

The Uganda-Rwanda Invasion of Zaire

The year was 1998; or thereabouts! Uganda and her then ally Rwanda decided that it was right and fitting to invade Zaire; present day *Democratic Republic of Congo [DRC]*. I will not even attempt to go into the reasons the two countries gave to justify their invasion of Zaire because the *International Court of Justice* [ICJ] already did that for me. It was a serious *"...violation of the independence, sovereignty and territorial integrity of the DRC contrary to international law"*; the ICJ ruled. No more arguments about that. Museveni's Uganda was therefore as good as a vicious criminal in the eyes of the *law of nations*.

The concern here is therefore with the manner in which Gen. Museveni, as *Commander-in-Chief*, took the decision to start and or join what was effectively a cross-border war of aggression against a sovereign neighbouring State. So our investigation must go straight into the set of laws that govern the declaration of war against another State. Were those laws adhered to? If they were not, then what was the effect of that blatant act of impunity? Would such impunity help sustain the claim in this book that Uganda's Legislature has been totally desecrated by the Executive? Well, let's see.

A very casual investigation shows us that Uganda does indeed have a set of legal guidelines that govern the declaration of war. The obvious gravity of the decision to declare war also meant that only the supreme law of the land *[the Constitution]* could provide for it. *Article* 124[1] thereof provides thus: *"...The President may, with the approval of Parliament, given by resolution supported by not less than two-thirds of all Members of Parliament, declare that a state of war exists between Uganda and any other country"*.

A proper application of that article therefore means that while the *President* of Uganda does indeed have powers to declare that a state of war exists between Uganda and another country *[in this case DRC]*, his decision can only be validated by a majority resolution of Parliament. Article 124[2] only provides a limited exception to that rule.

It says that, *"...where it is impracticable to seek the approval of Parliament before declaration of a state of war, the President may declare a state of war without the approval [of Parliament] but shall seek the approval immediately after the declaration and in any case NOT later than seventy-two hours after the declaration".*

Very clear and unambiguous! But that is where the legal certainties end. Those who followed or subsequently studied the history of the DRC conflict will tell you that not only did Museveni ignore the legal procedures prescribed by the constitution, but he also, for several months in fact, denied the presence of Ugandan troops in the DRC. That *"several months"* lull before the final confession came was of course a clear violation of article 124[2] which as we saw, requires the President to seek Parliament's approval within seventy-two hours *[latest]* after declaring war without its approval.

Uganda's invasion of *Zaire* was therefore illegal. But that, strictly speaking, is still not a major concern in this investigation. The concern of this book lies with the question of whether or not Museveni's failure to seek the approval of Parliament *[both before and immediately after the invasion]* could sustain the claim that Uganda's Legislature has been fundamentally desecrated by Museveni's regime.

Just cast your mind back, if you may, to the earlier discussion in this book where the role of the Legislature was discussed. If you do, you will clearly find that by avoiding the approval of Parliament before and immediately after the secret declaration of war against *Zaire*, Museveni had deprived

Parliament of one of its most critical roles; namely, to check Executive excesses. It was not for nothing that the framers of Uganda's constitution thought it fit that a resolution of Parliament "...*supported by not less than two-thirds of all Members of Parliament"* should be the minimum requirement to be met before their sons and daughters are sent into harm's way. War, they knew, was literally a matter of life and death.

So clearly, Museveni's unilateral decision to invade *Zaire* without parliamentary approval effectively rendered Uganda's Legislature toothless and irrelevant at the most critical time. A time in fact, when it should have been at its highest level of vigilance, effectiveness, and above all, relevance to the nation!

This sort of impunity is exactly what leads me to conclude that unilateralism, desecration of the most sacred things, contempt for institutionalism and the rule of law, are, *inter alia*, the key features that define a modern despot. You may think, perhaps legitimately, that I am passing judgement on the strength of a single case. Well, fine! Let's look at another one then shall we?

The "American Project" in Lawless Somalia

This is a *Similar Fact* case that I hope will once again bring into focus the unilateralism that informs a modern despot's decision making process within a pseudo-democratic setting. It is a *Similar Fact* case because like the invasion of *Zaire*, it also involved sending sons and daughters of Uganda into harm's way in the war-torn capital of Somalia Mogadishu.

So parliamentary approval was required before Museveni could legally deploy UPDF soldiers to participate in what one *Strategic Studies* analyst suggested was no more than *"An American Project"*. A *project* that was to be executed as an *African Union* [AU] peace mission! The reality, this analyst insisted, was that the project was only of bilateral benefit to Museveni and President George Bush Jnr. of the USA.

And I agree. After the debacle that was the 2006 Ugandan general elections, the now beleaguered despot Yoweri Museveni was rapidly losing Washington's confidence. So to stand a chance of winning back Washington's confidence *[and all the financial, technical and political favours that come with it]*, Kampala, in the form of General Museveni, had to do Washington's strategic foreign policy bidding in lawless Somalia using innocent Ugandan soldiers. The USA was still reeling from the humiliating *"Black Hawk Down"* incident in Somalia during the Bill Clinton years.

Black Hawk Down was of course the time when battle-hardened Somali insurgents shot down a US *Black Hawk* assault helicopter killing a number of US Marines in the process. For the final insult, they then dragged the dead Marines' naked corpses inhumanely on the streets of Mogadishu in broad day light.

Of course, the US wasn't going to risk that sort of humiliation again. So it was more prudent for the world's most belligerent hawks at the time *[Yoweri Museveni and George Bush Jnr.]* to adopt a *"scratch my back and I scratch yours"* strategy. It is a fascinating subject that deserves a separate book. So I shall leave it at that and go back to where our main concern is. Having secretly ordered Ugandan troops into Somalia, I can imagine the regime officials involved in that illegal deployment complementing each other and saying: *"Yes, we have pulled it off again; mission accomplished"*. Accomplished in the sense that they thought they had managed to put on a successful show of playing by rules!

Sam Kutesa, Uganda's *Minister of Foreign Affairs*, went even further and declared on the BBC's *"The World Today"* programme that Uganda would never deploy into Somalia without the approval of Parliament. So we can now confidently say that with such a firm declaration coming from the very top of Uganda's relevant Ministry, Museveni's regime definitely appreciated the constitutional need to secure Parliament's approval. That means if they don't *[in the end]* secure that crucial parliamentary approval, then the all important *"mens reas"* or *"intention"* to undermine the Legislature will have been sufficiently established before the court of public opinion.

But before we even get to the real *"beef"*, as if by magic, *The Daily Monitor* newspaper ran a story on the 1st of February 2007 under the headline *"NRM MPs throw out govt bid to rush Somali deployment"*. The story claimed that Museveni's own party MPs had refused to *"give the go ahead"* for the deployment of UPDF soldiers to Somalia without the full participation of opposition MPs who had walked out of Parliament in protest over the continued *[illegal]* detention of the PRA suspects.

It was simply amazing how the regime's mishandling of the *PRA* treason case was coming back to haunt it at every twist and turn. That said, I also think that the opposition MPs' protest walk-out, and the NRM MPs' decision to throw out the regime's proposal to deploy UPDF troops to Somalia, actually played into the hands of the regime's architects of external misadventures. Because they could now say that the failure to secure parliamentary approval *"...wasn't for want of trying"*. I suspect that was the exact *"Plan B"*.

Indeed, writing in the *Daily Monitor* newspaper of 1st February 2007, the UPDF's Spokesman for the *Somalia Mission* Captain Paddy Ankunda said the Somalia deployment had to be done because it was a matter of *"Strategic National Interest"*. Ruth Nankabirwa, Uganda's *Minister of State for Defence* at the time, also declared that, *"...not even the walk out by the opposition MPs would stand in the way of the Somalia deployment. We will be there within two weeks from now"*.

I think some quick observations will be in order here: First of all, such despotic bullishness from Museveni's regime is neither new nor surprising to people who follow politics in countries ruled by modern despots. Secondly, *"globalisation"* has made our world a very small place. A *"global village"* in fact; as some enthusiasts like to put it! I am not sure whether that is a good thing or not.

What I can say however, is that these technological advancements have ensured that information now travels at such blistering speeds that leave information managers totally bewildered. Now, let me give you what I consider to be the perfect example of what that means in real terms.

As Uganda's *Minister of Foreign Affairs* Sam Kutesa was still trying to convince the world that Ugandan troops would only be deployed in Somalia with parliamentary approval, contradictory news from very credible sources had already reached Somali communities in the world's capitals. They had been told, and I quote, that *"…Ugandan troops were in Somalia long before the Ethiopian soldiers withdrew from Mogadishu"*.

Confirmation of this came when a Somali friend sarcastically introduced me to his countrymen who were gathered in an *Internet Café* run by a fellow Somali in North West London. *"This is my friend Charles. He is a Ugandan; the good people who have sent their "troopisi" [troops with a Somali accent] to our country to help us"*; he said. What followed that very *"generous"* and *"kind"* introduction by someone I thought was a good friend shook me to the bone.

Suddenly, nearly all the Somalis who had been firmly glued in front of a tiny television screen following the tragic events unfolding in their motherland turned around to see who that Ugandan was. Believe me; any Ugandan in my shoes at the time would have loved to disappear miraculously into thin air.

Even the most hard-nosed Ugandan would have been overwhelmed by fear, panic, and perspiration; all triggered by embarrassment. But that wasn't the end of the story; not for me at least. That most uncomfortable encounter had merely solidified my quest for the truth. I desperately needed to hear the facts of Uganda's Somalia deployment from someone else. So I set out on a mission to find that *"someone else"*.

Fortunately, luck was on my side this time round. Confirmation of Museveni's secret and illegal deployment of Ugandan troops into Somalia came from a very senior official in the *Transitional Government* of Somalia. Fresh from Mogadishu, this *Transitional Government* official told me that Uganda had indeed deployed approximately 600 troops to Somalia. Crucially however, he added that the 600 or so Ugandan troops had been deployed several months before the invading Ethiopian soldiers who had dislodged the *Union of Islamic Courts* withdrew.

That was the illusive *"smoking gun"* I needed. In this *Transitional Government* official, I had got myself a very credible witness. So as far as I was concerned, the case was now closed. A guilty verdict against Museveni on the charge of *"fundamentally undermining and desecrating Uganda's Legislature"* was now inescapable. So I shall say no more than what I said in the last paragraph of our discussion about the invasion of *Zaire* [now DRC]. It is exactly the same.

Disciplining "Rebel" NRM-O Party MPs

It is a case that came along in 2007; the same year of the infamous *Somalia Deployment*. For their audacity to offer dissenting views that flew in the face of their official NRM-O party policy position, Ugandan Legislators Henry Banyenzaki MP and Dr Sam Lyomoki MP were labelled *"Rebel"* MPs. As a result, they were dropped immediately from their positions as Vice Chairpersons of their respective *Sessional Committees*.

The broad implications of their sacking were, to put it mildly, very disturbing. As Vice Chairpersons of *Parliamentary Committees*, the implication of their sacking goes far beyond the narrow confines of internal NRM-O party discipline. It becomes, as Hon. Beti Kamya ably put it then, a very *"serious national problem"*. You can't argue with that, can you? If you do, then pay particular attention to this review of her article.

ection [or Rule] 134[5] of parliament's *Rules of Procedure* states that, *"...parties have powers to withdraw and relocate its members from individual committees"*. It was on the strength of this rule, Kamya said, that the NRM-O party Chief Whip decided to punish the *"Rebel MPs"* by dropping them as Vice Chairpersons of their respective Committees. Their crime, in Kamya's view, was no more than that they had taken *"...positions that were contrary to the official party position"*.

I agree. That is precisely why these so-called *"Rebel MPs"* lost their privileged positions. Kamya then argued that while she *"...appreciates the NRM's concern about discipline in their party, they must realise that some situations advance beyond a party's control"*. To hammer her great point home, she cited the position of President of the Republic Uganda.

Her argument, a very solid one in my view, was that while the ruling NRM-O party had chosen a certain Yoweri Kaguta Museveni to be its flag bearer for the 2006 presidential elections, once he got *"elected"*, he became *"President"* of the entire Republic of Uganda.

That meant that under Uganda's presidential system, he would henceforth be beyond the control and reproach of the NRM-O as party. In short, the NRM-O party's constitution becomes irrelevant to *"The"* President of the Republic of Uganda. In the same spirit, Kamya argued, Henry Banyenzaki MP and Dr Sam Lyomoki MP *[as Committee Vice*

Chairpersons] became national servants whose job was now to serve the entire nation. What I find most fascinating in Kamya's argument is that when you think about it carefully, you will find that even after 233yrs of global parliamentary history, the correct appreciation of what a proper Legislature should represent in a democracy has remained largely unblemished.

Like the British MP Edmund Burke [of 1774] before her, Uganda's own Beti Kamya MP was essentially that *"...parliament is a deliberative assembly of one nation, with one interest, that of the whole, where not local purposes, not local prejudices, ought to guide, but the general good, resulting from the general reason of the whole. You choose a member indeed; but when you have chosen him, he is not a member of Bristol"*.

In this *"Rebel MPs"* case therefore, *"Bristol"* is Uganda's ruling NRM-O party; one that is pre-occupied with what Burke called *"local purposes"* and *"local prejudices"*. It is completely irrelevant that Beti Kamya's democratic credentials have since been called into serious question because of her tribal demand to *un-democratically* replace Dr. Kiggundu [RIP] as FDC Party Chairman. At the time, when sanity still prevailed, she had made a very valid point that demonstrated that she fully understood how a Legislature is supposed to work in a democracy.

In fact, upon close scrutiny of the parliamentary *Rules of Procedure* cited by Kamya, it is clear that the NRM Chief Whip, perhaps acting under duress from the top echelons of the party, seriously erred in law by invoking Rule 134[5]. That rule only applies to *"members"* of a Committee. And as Beti Kamya rightly pointed out, the two *"Rebel MPs"* were no longer mere *"members"*. They were now Vice Chairpersons. That also means that like the *President of the Republic of Uganda*, they were now beyond the jurisdiction of their party's constitution.

Kamya then went on to express the exact fears that I expressed. And, rather interestingly, she did so in strikingly similar language to that used by David Mpanga in his article that warned Ugandans about the wider implications of the illegal detention of his clients the PRA suspects. Like Mpanga, Kamya warned Ugandans to be *"very afraid"* for the *"sanctity of Parliament"* and the *"spirit of the immunity privilege for MPs"*; a privilege that insulates them from any form of intimidation that could arise from what they say or refrain from saying in Parliament.

The question of immunity from intimidation that Beti Kamya raised is a very critical one. It's a fundamental privilege in any parliamentary democracy. No parliament in world would be able to function effectively and independently without the freedoms of conscience and expression that the principle of parliamentary privilege accords to them. *"...Isn't it sad"*, Kamya wonders, that *"...the NRM should find ways around national efforts aimed at empowering vulnerable offices and is now in the business of intimidating MPs"*. Exactly! Because that, in the eyes of right thinking members of society, would amount to nothing less than a wicked attempt by a modern despot to desecrate an already crippled national Legislature!

"...What if the Speaker doesn't toe the [NRM-O] party line" when a dangerous precedent *[of sacking "Rebel MPs]* has already been set; Kamya wondered. Would the same Speaker who is constitutionally supposed to preside over Parliamentary business impartially survive the NRM-O party Chief Whip's knife? If not, then what implication would that have on the credibility of parliamentary resolutions if the Speaker [as Referee] is bound by partisan rules?

It is precisely for the deleterious gravity of those implications that Hon. Beti Kamya further argued that, *"...even if the Rebel MPs choose not to seek the Constitutional Court's interpretation of the powers of a party over its members who have assumed broader roles in Parliament, the opposition should do so in order to ensure that the Speaker is fully insulated from the long arm of his/her party".*

The inherent logic in Beti Kamya's call to opposition MPs to petition the *Constitutional Court* for a judicial interpretation on the matter is, as I have already said, very simple. Parliamentary privilege is crucial in any credible democracy. Its protection should therefore, quite rightly, be beyond petty partisan political squabbles; squabbles for cheap political point scoring.

To conclude her argument, Beti Kamya then makes reference to the trite practice in the British Parliament. There, she says, *"...once a person is elected Speaker, he/she hands back his/her party membership card and presides over the British Parliament as an independent person......1,000 years of parliamentary democracy taught the British a thing or two. Shouldn't Uganda pick a leaf from the British"?*

Of course any country should. But just as I warned about the risks inherent in any *"wholesale"* rush to adopt American judicial precedents on the protection of human rights, I also think the same applies to broad *"wholesale"* lessons from 1,000yrs of British parliamentary democracy. On the specific question of parliamentary privilege however, the view held in this book is an absolute *Yes*. Let global democratic activism pick a leaf from 1,000yrs of British political maturity. No second thoughts there!

Militarization of the Legislature

The other serious issue in this Chapter is the obvious *"militarization"* of the Legislature by modern despots; especially in the developing countries of Asia, Africa, andLatin America. Uganda's Yoweri Museveni brought "

Army Representatives" to Parliament under his so-called *"affirmative action"* drive. His argument was, and still is today, that the army is a marginalised constituency that needs affirmative political action to take care of its interests. Never mind that it is the same army that continues to hold its guns at Uganda's head; threatening at every twist and turn to pull the lethal trigger! In July 2007, all NRM-O party MPs were ordered to wear military fatigues during a five day retreat to the party's ideological institute. Located at a place called *"Kyankwanzi"*, the institute has for long, in typical modern despot style, been deceitfully sold to the world as a *"National Leadership Institute"*.

There is absolutely no doubt in my mind that Museveni's ruling NRM-O party has firm political interests behind its push to militarise State institutions; parliament inclusive. And the evidence is right here: While commenting on the grave concerns raised by the public about NRM-O party MPs wearing military uniforms, the party's Spokesperson Ofwono Opondo simply said: *"...for a military uniform, it is just like a bed, mattress and water at Kyankwanzi; just to facilitate training. All the people that have been going to Kyankwanzi have been accessing uniforms"*.

All that is of course utter nonsense! The truth of the matter, which Ofwono Opondo knows very well, is that by law, military uniforms are an *"exclusive preserve"* of the *Uganda People's Defence Forces*. In fact, hearing Ofwono Opondo say that made me remember what a not-so-close friend of mine once said. *"...Ofwono Opondo and Fox Odoi make me ashamed of being a Jap"*; he said. *"Jap"* being short for Japadhola; the tribe to which my friend, Ofwono Opondo, and Fox Odoi all belong! Who can fault the poor old chap for feeling that way? Wouldn't you feel the same if you were a proud, top notch, and intellectually independent *"Jap"* as many are?

Perhaps I should give you a taste of the sort of things that members of the public said so that you appreciate the selfishness of Ofwono Opondo's response. The *Daily Monitor* newspaper published a letter from someone called Peter Sabiiti. In it, Peter said:

"I am confused at the sight of a photo of NRM MPs on a retreat in Kyankwanzi donned in full military uniform...are they soldiers? If they are not, can other MPs from other political parties put on the uniform if they wish to? As far as I know, this uniform is for the UPDF which is a national army and not for NRM party. A soldier who wears it has successfully completed military training. What about those civilians arrested and court-martialled because they were in possession of military wear? Can the responsible authorities give us an explanation please?"

There is no way the authorities would have given Peter a satisfactory explanation without sounding just as silly as Ofwono Opondo. What Peter was actually confused about was something that we have already dealt with in this book. It is the compulsive propensity of modern despots to enforce the laws of the land selectively to serve their selfish political objectives.

But the real significance of this latest episode of public bewilderment is that it shows that the cases of *"selective enforcement of the law"* that I cited earlier were not merely isolated, unintended, and regrettable incidents. They are, as I said then, a modern despot's standard *modus operandi*. All designed to maximise his political advantages.

In this particular case where NRM-O party MPs were forced into military attire at Kyankwanzi, there were persistent rumours of an impending rebellion by NRM-O party MPs inparliament; the same rebellion that I think Beti Kamya alluded to. It is therefore [more than] likely that the NRM-O leadership thought the best way to deal with the impending rebellion was to use the only tried and tested method that a desperate modern despot worships; and that is militarily.

As the age old saying indeed goes, *"in the eyes of a man with a hammer, every problem looks like a nail"*. Sorry about the cliché; just couldn't resist it. But the message was clear: Military-style discipline was now required from all NRM-O party MPs. In other words, you do as you are told and ask questions later. Pure intimidation to achieve a sinister political end! For that reason, I think no despot can willingly give up his militaristic ways of solving political problems without having his arm severely twisted by a national effort. That is the sad reality that I think people who are being held hostage by modern despots must take on board if they want to restore sanity to their State institutions.

The Cold-Blooded Massacre of Article 105[2]

Like most debates these days, the debate over the amendment of article 105[2] of the constitution of Uganda was kicked off by an ordinary newspaper report. As I have said many times already, it is a great testament to the crucial role that the media plays in even a pseudo democracy like Uganda. The report itself said some NRM supporters were working flat out [behind the scenes] to *"convince"* their leader Museveni to run for office again after the expiry of his two five-year terms as *"President"*. The fixed two term limit for service as President of the Republic of Uganda had of course been imposed [patriotically] by Uganda's *Constituent Assembly Delegates* and enshrined in article 105[2] of the constitution of Uganda 1995; the very subject of our debate here. I have to say that the report was staggering for its sheer audacity. Not surprisingly, it was dismissed almost instantly by most people who, in disbelief, thought it was no more than an act of speculative journalism.

But they were wrong! Just picture this for a moment: His head was bent to the left, firmly supported by his clinched fist. He wore a very sad look on his face; a look that said "*please tell me he is not going to do such a thing*". That was before he even opened his mouth. Finally, without blinking, he looked me straight in the eye and said: *"Charles, do you really think Museveni can do such a stupid thing".*

I had no answer; I couldn't have had. In fact, I could easily have asked this great Ugandan friend of mine the same question but he beat me to it. But it wasn't difficult to see where our bewilderment and disbelief was coming from.

In 2001, Museveni had made a firm manifesto commitment to the people of Uganda that he would not run for the office of President again. That 2001-2006 would, as required by the constitution, be his very last term in office. Besides, in his book *"Sowing the Mustard Seed"*, Museveni had been ferocious in his attack on African leaders who overstay in power.

At the time, Museveni's view was that a leader who stays in office for more than ten years will have outlived his usefulness and could become a reason for political conflict. Yes, perhaps for the very first time, I was in total agreement with the youthful *"old"* Museveni of the mid 1980s; not the *"new"* Museveni who has metamorphosed into a 21st Century despot.

The people of Uganda also appreciated what the young Museveni had alluded to [in his book] and agreed with him. So to reverse the tragic *"history of political and constitutional instability"* acknowledged in the preamble of their constitution, they decided in no uncertain terms that no Ugandan President should ever be allowed to rule for more than two five year terms.

It was a patriotic resolve in every sense. In fact, it also reflected the true spirit behind *"The Late"* article 105[2]. So for that most sacred reason, I will say with some degree of profanity that *"The Late"* article 105[2] must never be allowed to *"Rest in Peace"*.

Initially, Museveni himself, in true modern despot fashion, had been careful not to publicly declare that he intended to run for office again. That clearly suggests that he also knew that the crusade to amend article 105[2] was unpatriotic at best, and out rightly evil at worst.

Secondly, he must also have known that if article 105[2] is amended, then in principle, it would make him the first direct beneficiary of the absence of term limits in Uganda's constitution. So he really didn't have to utter a word for as long as he didn't need to. But for how long would he sit comfortably on the fence as fierce debate raged everywhere about his political future? Not very long is the answer! All of a sudden, Museveni threw all caution *[and shame]* to the wind and started arguing that the two term limit prescribed by article 105[2] of the constitution was [would you believe it] *"an impediment to democracy"*. His reasoning, a perverted one in my view, was that term limits deny the electorate the opportunity to continue voting for a leader of their choice.

His *"new"* view was now that what mattered was the *"vision"* to lead. Which begs the question: Who said that *"a leader who stays in office for more than ten years will have outlived his usefulness to the country"*? Wasn't it Museveni himself?

One thing is for sure though: Not only was the debate about the amendment of article 105[2] emotionally charged, it was also quite easily the most divisive political process that Uganda had ever seen. Not only that. When it finally happened, the amendment of article 105[2] actually caused a catastrophic collapse of trust between politicians and the people. That is clearly not a record that any statesman of modern times would want to carry to his grave.

And we are not done yet! As captivating as that historical account may seem, it's still only of contextual value to what is to follow. The crux of the matter is not so much in Museveni's U-turns and betrayal of the trust that the people of Uganda placed in him. Rather, it is the manner in which that betrayal was callously executed.

The hope, once again, is that by examining the manner in which the amendment of article 105[2] was executed, we may be able to gather some evidence to test the claim in this book that Uganda's Legislature has been fundamentally desecrated by Museveni's despotic rule. So let's give it a shot.

We all remember the details of how *The Referendum and Other Provisions Bill* was summarily rushed through parliament. Once again, history was about to repeat itself tragically in Uganda's Legislature. As soon as Museveni declared his views to be in favour of the *"evil crusade"* to amend article 105[2], his political strategists swung into action with murderous zeal like the *"Black Mambas"*. Their mission was to make sure a *'Yes'* vote was extracted *[literally]* from MPs and delivered on a silver plate to a waiting General.

But the sharp divisions in the country at the time also meant that the regime's legal and political architects could not be absolutely sure of sufficient support. Not even with the commanding majority that they had in Parliament! So something drastic and bold needed to be done and done fast. And it was.

Museveni's *"Shy" Political Assistant* Moses Byaruhanga, and the *"Hawkish"* Robert Kabushenga from the State owned *New Vision* newspaper appeared to be the public face of this most *"evil crusade"* to amend article 105[2]. The duo took on the *unpatriotic* task of challenging any *patriotic* view that was being expressed against the amendment of article 105[2].

Of course that was their democratic right; and we must all respect that. But what was later visited upon Uganda's MPs seriously shook my liberal values and faith in politics. It told an all together different story; a story of how far away from democracy Uganda was!

In conformity with a modern despot's policy of impoverishing the population before presenting himself *[with taxpayers' money]* as a philanthropist, news broke that every Member of Parliament would be given 5million Shillings *[approx $2,500]* as *"facilitation"* to *"sensitise"* their constituents about the proposal to amend to article 105[2]. The opposition parties and civil society organisations of course saw the move for what it really was. In fact, no one could have failed to notice that the move had the words *"Political Corruption"* written all over it!

On the wrong side of the politico-moral spectrum, the regime's *"Spin Doctors"* also fought back feverishly. They insisted that the 5million Shillings must not be seen as a bribe but *"Logistical Facilitation"*. Even with that level of madness, the drama had in fact only just begun. Very soon, the regime's argument that the money was meant for *logistical facilitation* began to create its own set of problems. Fresh problems that the architects of the plan had probably not anticipated! And as you would expect, they were also problems that they were woefully ill prepared for.

For a start, when the *"Dishonourable"* Members of Parliament got wind of the *"free"* money from the state, like scavengers, they sprinted to the source of the putrid cash in their hundreds. The mad rush of course overwhelmed the regime. That was when the real fun begun. As expected, some of the *"Scavenger MPs"* came in for very rude shocks. They discovered that there were in fact some very long strings attached to that *"free"* money. All of them who had made that historic *"Walk of Shame"* soon found out that before they could lay their dirty hands on the dirty money, they would have to sign a private *Memorandum of Understanding* with the regime first.

That MOU required the *"Scavenger MPs"* to commit themselves *in writing* that they would support the proposed amendments on the floor of the House. But even that wasn't the full length of the attached string. Far from it! They would also have to declare to the waiting media, and by implication to the country, that they would indeed support the obnoxious amendment.

All heavens broke loose at that point. Those who had actually intended to oppose the amendment but still wanted to *"eat"* the *"free"* money blew the whistle on the regime's fraudulent trap. But that does not make them lesser crooks. In fact, I think they were worse crooks because they had not one, but two despicable criminal intentions. The first was to deceive the regime that they were going to support the amendment when they actually didn't intend to. The second was to *"eat"* taxpayers' money without giving any value for it.

Then finally, the acid-tongued Kahinda Otafire, a Minister in the regime, made matters worse by confessing that he collected the dirty money and blew it all on one or two drinking sprees with his buddies. Well, at least Otafire was honest about his dishonesty. That is probably the best compliment anyone can ever give the good General who fought *"gallantly"* alongside Museveni to bring *"fundamental change"* from *integrity to thuggery* in Uganda.

As for the MPs who collected the money with the hope of wriggling out of the MOU come voting day, it was only a matter of time before they would discover that there is indeed no such thing as a *"free lunch"*. The regime was not about to let them off the hook.

A certain Nyombi Tembo, a diminutive but *strategically* energetic NRM cadre, quickly moved a motion *[which was passed]* to suspend the parliamentary rule that provided for voting by secret ballot when amending *"specifically entrenched"* articles of the constitution like article 105[2]. Voting would now be done by a primitive show of hands. Incredible stuff!

In fact, it all seemed like the final fulfilment of a generational curse. Because Nyombi Tembo, Museveni's *"hero of the moment"*, had done exactly what his NRM *"comrade in crime"* Mike Mukula had done on the day *[a few years back]* the *Referendum and Other Provisions Bill* was put to a vote in the House. It was as if they had a standard political template for handling such cases. And they must have had some very good reasons for maintaining it. So let me take a wild guess at something very obvious.

Naturally, voting by show of hands *[as opposed to a secret ballot]* puts MPs on the spot and forces them to vote for whatever they signed up to. They would then, out of shame, have no option but to meet their part of the 5million Shilling *"bargain"*. History has taught us that these theories are not too far-fetched.

In a book written by G.F. Engholm [*"Elections in Uganda"*] that was published in 1958, a story is told of a bitter argument that had raged in British politics for nearly 40yrs. One side supported open voting while the other side vehemently opposed it. In Engholm's view, the conflict between the opponents and proponents of secret ballot voting was largely about *"...what would happen if open voting were to be abolished while bribery and corruption were still tolerated"* as it was in Britain at the time.

It was essentially a conflict between good old innate human conscience and modern capitalism; with bribery and corruption sadly representing the evils of capitalism. What the British conflict also tells us is that there can be no such thing as a genuine democracy in any country where there is insufficient political will to fight corruption.

And yet, as we know now, corruption is indispensable to a modern despot. It is in his interest to perpetuate it. With it, he can bribe his way to *victory* after *victory* on any issue that is up for democratic determination. But let's go back to G.F. Engholm's bitter political argument in Britain for a moment.

During one particular public meeting, a politically insecure opponent of the proposal to introduce secret ballot voting in the British Parliament shot to his feet and proclaimed:

"...*What is the use of registration if a man is to vote by ballot? And what is the use of enquiring how a man is going to vote when a man may conceal that vote by ballot? Why! A man may register one way and vote the other. Suppose you give a man five pounds. He may receive the money and vote the other way. That goes to make a man disguise his real sentiments and meaning. Even if I purchase a man I may not be able to know how he is going to vote. He may vote against me after he said he will vote for me*".

The passion and bewilderment in that is unmistakable. This poor British chap knew exactly what the introduction of a secret ballot voting system would mean for corrupt and politically insecure politicians; and he didn't like it one bit. However, no sooner had he sat down than he was answered with commensurate passion by a voice at the back of the hall. In a few simple but democratically significant words, the voice from the back of the hall rang out and declared: "...*That is what we want. You will not then have us under your thumb*".

An absolutely fabulous response that couldn't have been put any better! And the voice from the back of the hall wasn't a lone voice. Similar sentiments were subsequently echoed by other proponents of the secret ballot voting system. For its philosophical and biblical touch, this particular one caught my eye: "...*in the ballot box the benign principles of Christianity have taken root; and from the ballot box rushes forth the glorious truth that of whatever colour our skins may be, our souls before God are of one hue".*

The most crucial part of this speaker's view to our debate must surely be the part in which he states that *"...from the ballot box rushes forth the glorious truth"*. In other words, a man says exactly what he wishes to say if he has the secrecy of the ballot box at his disposal. And that, in essence, is really what democracy is all about. The right and freedom to obey your conscience and beliefs without fear or undue influence from outside your own self! Let's leave Britain now and fly back to the Uganda to see how article 105[2] of the constitution was amended. Before I veered off, I had listed two of the three possible reasons that I think explain why Museveni's regime consistently scraps secret ballot voting in parliament whenever there is something big at stake.

The first was the put the MPs on the spot and the second was to send a clear message to the bribed MPs that it was payback time. The third, and perhaps most sinister reason in my view, is that open voting by show of hands favours Museveni's regime because it gives his *"affirmative action"* army Generals in Parliament the opportunity to intimidate weak minded MPs into total submission.

In this case, at least one, or a combination of all my theories about why Museveni's regime often scraps secret ballot voting at crucial times appear to have been at play. For those reasons, the regime's proposal to amend article 105[2] was successfully carried through parliament by a massive majority. With that, the two term constitutional limit for service as President of Uganda was consigned to parliament's *"Special Archive of Shame"*; thanks to a modern despot's insatiable appetite for power and more power.

At the end of the amendment process, the Legislature, a pivotal institution of State, had been rendered incapable of functioning to its full and in fact expected capacity.

The menace of excessive, illegal, and certainly crippling despotic interference just wouldn't let it.

That is exactly how a modern despot wants things to be; a semblance of democracy that works under his firm direction and control! In fact, according Museveni himself, it really doesn't matter if his NRM-O party MPs go to parliament to sleep. The most important thing, Museveni said, was that *"...as long as they wake up in time to vote with the government side"*.

In a nutshell, that is how much a modern despot values the role of the Legislature. No doubt about that! In fact, as the next case will show, there may be further evidence of an underlying resolve to totally undermine the authority of the Legislature and portray it as an unworthy gathering of undeserving idlers.

"I Captured Parliament"

This confrontation between Museveni and the Legislature couldn't have been unexpected. A modern despot's patronage politics meant that it was bound to happen. An *"own goal"* scored by the team Captain himself, if you like! Museveni's patronage policy created a plethora of new parliamentary constituencies in Uganda; all to boost his party's majority in parliament.

With every bogus new District created, *"affirmative action"* demanded a *"District Woman MP"* position. Regular parliamentary constituencies may also have been created in the new District. If you then add the other *"Special Interest Group"* MPs who represent the *Youth, Workers, the Disabled* and the *Army*, the result is a heavily bloated Legislature.
The crucial point to note here is that all of them owe their presence in parliament to the *"Great"* General who ordered the creation of their constituencies in the first place. It's anyone's guess who they will support thereafter.

What is not in doubt is that the number of MPs increases significantly with every new District created! Of course, with such a huge number, all of them then find themselves jostling for office space in an old colonial complex that was never meant to cater for such numbers. In fact, in some cases, as many as four MPs were forced to share one office. Inevitably, several MPs *[including Shadow Ministers]* complained.

Parliament's Administrators were therefore left with no option but to explore new avenues to accommodate all the new *"Patronage Policy MPs"*. And one of the options floated at the time was to rent office space from private landlords who have office premises within the vicinity of the existing Parliament. However, for a desperately poor country like Uganda, the 1.5billion *Shilling* [approx $1million] annual rent price tag also meant that it would be a controversial option.

The Treasury protested that move and argued that renting office space from private landlords would increase the already high cost of public administration. A very prudent argument that no doubt derived its weighty authority from the need to adhere to principles of fiscal discipline; especially in poor countries like Uganda! And the Treasury's argument appealed to both the long suffering Ugandan taxpayer and some level headed Mps.

In an attempt to resolve this impasse, some MPs suggested that Museveni should vacate all the rooms allocated to the *Office of the President* at Parliament so that their colleagues could occupy them. That, they argued, would save the country the burden of renting office space from private landlords at open market rates. Again, a very sensible alternative in my view! After all, Museveni already had the whole of State House to himself.

But the *sensible alternative* didn't go down well with Museveni. It hit a very raw nerve and clearly brought out the amount of contempt he had for the Legislature. An opposition MP who claims to have witnessed that political confrontation between Museveni and the patriotic MPs had this to say: *"His voice was oozing with disgust at the sheer audacity of the suggestion. He vowed never to vacate his offices at the Parliamentary buildings*; this MP said.

Finally, he said Museveni declared that, *"...I captured Parliament. How can anyone want to evict me? It will be unfair for anybody to think that I can move my office elsewhere. I have every right of having my office at Parliament"*.

For the fact that he assumed state power through the barrel a gun, Museveni says he *"captured"* parliament. Therefore, he should be regarded as a more superior authority than the entire Legislature. No regard whatsoever should be paid to the pressing needs and traditional authority of the Legislature. Just to hammer this point home, I invite you, just for a moment, to compare Museveni's bullish attitude towards Uganda's Legislature with that of British Prime Minister Tony Blair; his counterpart at the time.

On this politically dramatic summer's day, The Rt. Hon Tony Blair MP started the day as Britain's Prime Minister. By afternoon that same day, he had resigned and become an ordinary *Labour Party* backbencher. By 5:00pm, he had been appointed *United Nations Envoy to the Middle.*

But it is his resignation speech that we are most interested in; not the day's dramatic role-hopping. In it, Tony Blair made a confession to the world that confirmed the impact that the invisible authority of the British Legislature *[aka The House of Commons]* can have on even he who was considered to be one of the best performers at the *Despatch Box*.

It's approximately 12:32pm on Wednesday 27th June 2007. The *House of Commons* is unusually packed. Blair's final *Prime Minister's Question* [PMQ] time is drawing to a close. Then, in an extremely emotional, touching, and humbling display of humility to his parliamentary colleagues, Blair uttered his final words: *"...from the beginning to the end, I have never stopped fearing this House. That tingling feeling of apprehension at 3mins to midday* [when the PMQ time begins] *has remained the same. It is in that fear that the respect is contained"*; Blair said.

It's that *"fear"* that sets a functioning parliamentary democracy apart from the pseudo democracies that modern despots like to wallow in. One where they, as heads of the Executive arm of the state, have nothing but contempt for the Legislature!

I think this *"I captured parliament"* case has ably demonstrated to us the dangers that can potentially accrue to a country's key institutions if the Head of State assumes power by military conquest as opposed to a popular political mandate. That is of course not the same thing as saying military action can never be justified; because it can in extreme cases of despotic rule!

Post-Script Development

Several months after I closed my case on the fate of the Legislature in a modern despot's country, a screaming single word headline that simply read *"Impotent!"* was the best the *Sunday Monitor* Editor of 30th July 2007 could find to describe Uganda's parliament. This was in the wake of investigations that the paper had carried out into how Museveni's regime was ignoring its constitutional obligations to submit to parliament *[for approval]* several financial dealings that had apparently been struck *"in the public interest"*.

The Great Loot of the Central Bank

To keep the partisan state institutions as well as the patronage and public relations machineries that keep them in power happy and running smoothly, modern despots require a lot of money; money that they, as individuals, often don't have!

But even if they had such humongous amounts of money tucked away in the many foreign bank accounts that they are known to secretly operate, they still wouldn't touch it. The typical modern despot, in his typical perversion, thinks the public owes him a favour for his *"personal sacrifices"* to the nation. And because of that, the public till, in most cases, will be his first port of call.

The other sad, and yet almost natural extension to this despotic perversion is that because the modern despot thinks the public owes him a favour for his *"personal sacrifices"*, in his mind, an unfettered, almost inherent right of access to public funds must also come *"as standard"*. In other words, it's a given! If he wants money from the public purse, then all rules and procedures that govern the allocation of such funds must be set aside. In most cases, it's even done unofficially on the despot's illegal orders!

In Uganda, the country's *Central Bank,* like the *Directorate of Public Prosecutions* that we discussed earlier, is required by article 162[2] of the constitution to be independent and not *"...subject to the direction or control of any person or authority"*.

And to be fair, the public perception had always been that the *Central Bank* of Uganda operates independently and effectively without too much despotic interference. What happens behind the scenes may of course be a different matter. My own suspicion is that the mighty omnipresent despotic hand couldn't have been too far off.

For that reason, I think the romantic view that Uganda's *Central Bank* has been operating *"...independently and effectively without too much despotic interference"* may have been more as a result of ignorance than anything else. Those who know the reality of how things have been working within the *Central Bank* under Museveni's rule have very uncharitable things to say about its independence as an institution of state. In fact, two specific cases that made it into the public domain *[almost by accident]* suggest that there may indeed have been numerous incidents of despotic interference in the way the *Central Bank* operates.

The Bassajja-Gate Affair

Naturally, a tabloid description like *The Bassajja-Gate Affair* often stems from something or someone from which some sort of scandal arose. In this case, it is derived from the surname of a certain Hassan Bassajjabalaba; a controversial and extremely *"successful"* Ugandan businessman.

As it happens, Mr. Bassajjabalaba was also [and probably still is] the Chairman of the *Entrepreneurs League* of Museveni's ruling NRM-O party. Hmnnn! Business *"success"* and Chairmanship of the ruling party's *Entrepreneurs League*! What an interesting coincidence?

Anyway, in this *Bassajja-Gate Affair*, an independent Ugandan media house had published a report about an alleged State bail-out of *Messrs Basajjabalaba Hides and Skins*; a loss making company owned by Hassan Bassajjabalaba; Museveni's money-man! I hope the fact that *Messrs Basajjabalaba Hides and Skins* was actually found to be a loss making company will enable you appreciate why the word *successful* above appears in quotes! According to the newspaper report, evidence had emerged which allegedly showed that on the 10th of February 2004, Museveni had personally *directed* the Governor of Bank of Uganda to use funds from the bank's *APEX Reflows Account* to pay *Standard Chartered Bank Uganda Limited* the sum of 21,091,491,670 Shillings; approx $11,575,500. That payment was, according to the report, meant to clear debts that had been recklessly accumulated by *M/s Basajjabalaba Hides and Skins.*

This massive bail-out apparently caused the *Apex Reflows Account* to be overdrawn by over 7billion Shillings; approx $4million. It was also revealed that no measures had been put in place to ensure that *M/s Basajjabalaba Hides and Skins* repaid the public funds that were used, on Museveni's orders, to pay its creditor *Standard Chartered Bank Uganda Limited*. On the contrary, the grapevine had it *[around July 2004]* that some senior Bank of Uganda officials were considering writing off the debt.

But the sheer scale of this abuse of Executive authority by Uganda's modern despot may not actually make a great deal of sense to you unless you know the source of the funds and understand the laws that purport to govern its disbursement. So let me try and explain it as simply as an economic layman would; after all, that is exactly what I am.

The *European Investment Bank* [EIB] - *Uganda Apex Private Sector Loan Scheme* is a donor funded credit programme administered by the *Development Finance* department of Bank of Uganda. Its aim is to promote economic development by encouraging and facilitating new private sector led investments in the agro-industry, education, fishing, healthcare, horticulture and floriculture, manufacturing, mining, quarrying, tourism, and hotels sectors.

Under the programme, the EIB provides the Government of Uganda with low interest loans. These loans are paid into the *Apex Reflows Capital Account* in Bank of Uganda; an account which forms part of Uganda's *Consolidated Fund*. Article 154[1] of the constitution of Uganda prescribes the circumstances and manner in which funds from the *Consolidated Fund* should be used. It provides that:

Portrait of a Despot

"*No moneys shall be withdrawn from the Consolidated Fund except: {a}to meet expenditure charged on the fund by this Constitution or by an Act of Parliament; or {b}except* "*where the issue of those moneys has been authorised by an Appropriation Act, a Supplementary Appropriation Act, or as provided under clause [4] of this article.*

Clause [4] then sets out the few exceptions under which the President may authorise disbursement of funds from the *Consolidated Fund*. Finally, clause [3] of article 154 provides that, "*…no moneys shall be withdrawn from the Consolidated Fund unless the withdrawal has been approved by the Auditor General and in a manner prescribed by Parliament*".

If these legal requirements are met, the *Central Bank* of Uganda would then "*on-lend*" the *Apex* funds to nine approved financial institutions. Those nine financial institutions will in turn lend the funds to small and medium sized businesses for projects in the sectors listed above.

After that, the financial institutions would then collect the *Apex* loan funds from the businesses [with interest of course] and repay Bank of Uganda under their own private loan arrangements. The funds that are paid back to Bank of Uganda are then credited to the *Apex Reflows Capital Account*. Most of the money in this account is of course used to repay the *European Investment Bank*. But there is some interest income that accrues to the Government of Uganda too.

The most important thing to remember about this complex process is that the *Apex Reflows Capital Account* forms part of the *Consolidated Fund*. And money from the *Consolidated Fund* is not meant to be used as a slush fund that the President donates at will to his cronies who happen to be in financial difficulty. As the constitution provides, both the *Auditor General* and Parliament must have a say in who gets how much from the *Consolidated Fund*.

But according to FDC party President Dr. Kizza Besigye, on the 10th of February 2004, General Museveni wrote a letter referenced PO/10 to the Governor of Bank of Uganda in which he started off by alluding to the financial difficulties that *M/s Bassajjabalaba Hides & Skins* was facing. Museveni then went on to assert, without any objective evidence as required by *clause [4]* of article 154, that this company was *"generating foreign exchange for the country"*. So in a matter of seconds, Museveni had already forgotten that he had just said that the company was facing *"financial difficulties"*. Incredible stuff!

In his reaction to the *Bassajja-Gate Affair*, Dr. Kizza Besigye said at the time that *"...these documents are a glimpse at what has become the preferred method of stealing from State coffers"*. On the evidence, I think it would be very difficult for anyone to dispute his allegations. This *"preferred method"* theft from *"State coffers"* by modern despots involves fronting a rogue proxy investor who then *"invests"* in a qualifying project like Bassajjabalaba's Hides & Skins business for example so that they fraudulently get access to money from the *Consolidated Fund*.

Once that is out of the way, then most of the money borrowed ends up being spent on anything that the despot chooses. More often than not, it ends up being spent on the despot's *Public Relations* activities, on his political patronage activities, as well as on voter bribery during elections. The rogue proxy investor then defaults on the loans and *"surprise-surprise"*, the government pays back the financial institutions owed by the rogue investor under some dubious guarantee arrangements.

But the interest of this book is not so much in where the ill gotten money ends up; the abomination of that notwithstanding! Rather, it is in the illegality of the process by which public funds are disbursed by those with sufficient authority and or political influence to do so.

Therefore, while the *"Bassajja-Gate Affair"* may have been merely one of many cases of financial impropriety within the *Central Bank*, it nonetheless provides us with a clear and disturbing insight into how modern despots abuse lawful working procedures within State institutions to further their political objectives.

And I say "disturbing insight" because the *Bassajja-Gate Affair* was not an isolated case. There was also the *"Tri-Star-Gate Affair*; another similar fact case whose details we can't go into because as I write, it's still a subject of a court case and therefore covered by the *Sub Judice* rule.

The Schizophrenic Watch-Dog

Under article 225[1] of the constitution of the Republic of Uganda, the *Inspectorate of Government* has as its main functions the elimination of corruption and abuse of authority in public offices; the promotion of fair, efficient and good governance in public offices; and the supervision and enforcement of the *Leadership Code of Conduct* among others.

Looking at these functions, there can be no doubt that th *Inspectorate of Government* has a very important role to play in shaping Uganda's public service ethics, good governance, and by extension, democracy. But there is an important cursory observation to be made before we dig deep into how it's run.

For the similarities in their constituting instruments, the procedure for appointing those who lead them, and the provisions that purport to guarantee their independence, the *Inspectorate of Government* and the *Directorate of Public Prosecutions* are virtual twins. So to bring yourself quickly up to speed, I say you need look no further than what has already been stated in this book about how the DPP is constituted, the procedure for appointing its head, and the provision that purports to guarantee its functional independence.

And for very similar reasons, I also think it would serve no useful purpose for us to discuss why Museveni has over the years [mainly] appointed his loyal party cadres to occupy the top most position of *Inspector General of Government* [IGG]. What is worth examining however, are a few unique incidents that show the ferocious consistency with which modern despots undermine the independence, development, and effectiveness of State institutions. Even those established by the despots themselves are not spared. Which then begs the question: Do they set up these institutions as mere public relations gimmicks? Well, let's wait and see.

Clipping the IGG's Wings Legally (Part One)

Earlier, we talked about how modern despots use the *law as a tool of political oppression*. I argued then, that the obnoxious practice had almost acquired the status of a culture among modern despots. Uganda's despot Yoweri Museveni has not abandoned that despotic culture; because he can never do that and also expect to survive politically. The law is still the unconventional tool of choice for furthering political persecution and perpetuation.

For Uganda's *Inspectorate of Government* in particular, I think it's fair to say that Museveni has had a love-hate relationship with it. It all depends on whether the IGG is biting in the *"correct"* political direction or not. If the watch dog mauls down an opposition activist or party, then Museveni will be passionately in love with it. If it bites in the direction of his interest to perpetuate his rule, then you can be sure a *"Decree Nisi"* will be swiftly sought.

And no one could have described the despotic propensity I have just referred to better than Miria Matembe; a former *Minister of Ethics & Integrity* who fell out with the regime when it amended article 105[2] of the constitution to remove the term limit for service as President of Uganda. She said, *"...it is mind boggling why Museveni, who, between 2003 and 2005 sought to reduce the powers of the IGG through constitutional amendments, is now the greatest ally of this department in the fight against corruption"*.

And the ex-Minister was not alone in expressing bewilderment at some the actions proposed and indeed taken by Museveni's government. Scores of other credulous Ugandans who previously bought into the regimes ill intentioned political manoeuvres have also expressed disappointment. The constitutional amendment proposals that the ex-Minister was talking about were contained in a *White Paper* that surfaced in September 2004. The proposal was meant to *"clip the IGG's wings"* by merging the entire *Inspectorate* with *Uganda Human Rights Commission*.

Also included in the regime's *White Paper* were what I think were typical modern despot proposals. The idea was to strip the IGG of powers to scrutinise the manner in which lucrative government contracts are awarded. That way, the despot could then manipulate the process with ease to serve his political patronage interests. It must be remembered that those powers had been deliberately given to the IGG to help him/her identify and hopefully, with time, eliminate corruption and abuse of authority in public offices; exactly as the *Inspectorate* is enjoined to do by the constitution.

So if the regime had succeeded in stripping the IGG of powers to scrutinise the manner in which lucrative government contracts are awarded, then the result would have been even greater corruption and impunity by well connected political sharks within the regime. The regime's sharks, being the in-conscientious creatures that they are, would then have been at total liberty to use their ill gotten wealth to ruthlessly push forward their personal as well as the regime's political objectives.

Charles Ochen Okwir

A modern despot is naturally at peace with such unethical political manoeuvres. Like his in-conscientious cronies, he too feels no qualms whatsoever about such things. On this very rare occasion however, Uganda's main opposition parties, in a spirited show of resistance, succeeded in forcing Museveni's regime to withdraw the obnoxious proposal to *clip the IGG's wings*. It was a rare display of the benefits that can potentially accrue to a people from having even a mere semblance of multi-party democracy.

Clipping the IGG's Wings Legally (Part Two)

In another case where the law was again the tool of choice, the political survival of one of Museveni's most trusted *Political Assistants* was on the line. We are of course talking about the *self-styled* no nonsense Major Ronald Kakooza Mutale; he of the notorious State financed *Kalangala Action Plan* [KAP] militia. The brief facts were this:

The IGG had dutifully recommended that Major Ronald Kakooza Mutale, the *Presidential Adviser on Political Affairs*, be dismissed for failure to declare his personal wealth as required by the *Leadership Code*. Mutale was of course going to have none of that *"nonsense"*; after all, he had the big man's ear right next to him.

So he quickly petitioned the *Constitutional Court* seeking orders to reverse the IGG's recommendations. The IGG too, being the one who had recommended Mutale's sacking, expressed interest in joining the Attorney General's team to boost its capacity to secure victory against Kakooza Mutale in court.

The then *Attorney General* however, in a surprising twist, objected to IGG Jotham Tumwesigye's desire to join the State's legal team. And yes, you guessed it right again! With the mighty weight and authority of General Museveni's duly sworn affidavit, the *Constitutional Court* found in Kakooza Mutale's favour and the decision to relieve him of his duties was reversed forthwith.

Now then! To fully understand what I meant earlier when I said a modern despot like Museveni only tolerates the IGG's work if it bites in the right political direction, you need look no further than John Ken Lukyamuzi's case only a few months earlier. Lukyamuzi was a fierce Museveni critic and *Conservative Party* MP. For exactly the same allegations that Kakooza Mutale's sacking was recommended, Lukyamuzi's constituency seat was immediately declared vacant and a bi-election ordered to replace him. No surprises there!

In terms of overall severity however, Kakooza Mutale's shameful reinstatement is dwarfed by the regrettable fact that his successful Court challenge also resulted in Sections of the *Leadership Code Act* being expunged from the law. The deleted Sections were in fact those that empowered the IGG to recommend the sacking of corrupt government officials. With that, the IGG's wings had well and truly been clipped by a modern despot's legal machinations; all for nothing other than the desire to maintain an unfair political advantage over his opponents!

Clipping the IGG's Wings Verbally

If you push a modern despot hard enough and force his back to the wall, then you can be sure he will throw all his false pretences to the wind and *"go native"* in a desperate bid to hang on to power. As always, a good old Ugandan example should do the honours for us on this one.

In 2004, the IGG, again in the proper exercise of his constitutional duties, ordered the arrest of a one Lucian Tibaruha. Tibaruha was the acting *Solicitor General*. At the time of writing this book, he had however become the substantive Solicitor General; having been appointed by Museveni against the IGG's express advice.

The IGG's order for Tibaruha's arrest had been for an allegation that as acting *Solicitor General*, he had irregularly sanctioned the payment of 13billion Shillings to Mr. James Garuga Musinguzi. Musinguzi had apparently claimed this money from the State as compensation for his farmland which had been irregularly allocated to settlers by the government.

Anyway to cut a long story short, in the end, Museveni, in typical style, intervened and told the IGG to stop interfering with the work of other government officials. For a modern despot, it didn't matter that the constitution required the IGG to do exactly that and do it without the *"...control and direction of any person or authority"*. It will not have escaped the recognition of even the most passive Ugandan reader that this was indeed a very unique case. It was unique in the sense that Musinguzi, the man to whom Tibaruha had allegedly sanctioned the payment of 13billion Shillings, was not exactly known to be a Museveni crony. On the contrary, he was known to be fairly sympathetic to the opposition FDC party.

So why did Museveni appear to be supporting something that was going to benefit his political opponents? Could that be sufficient evidence to discredit my suggestion that a modern despot only tolerates the IGG's work if it bites *"in the right political direction"*? In my view, absolutely not! Museveni was simply being himself. A capricious modern despot; just like that the chameleon that he often likens himself to!

I also think one must never rule out the possibility that Museveni, in his canning political calculations, may have concluded that 13billion Shillings was a small price to pay to retain the services of Lucian Tibaruha; his loyal NRM cadre *Solicitor General*. The added advantage for Museveni would also be that from then on, Tibaruha would feel heavily indebted to Museveni as an individual. He would henceforth have to do Museveni's political bidding in the courts of law with the zeal of a trapped hostage hoping for early release.

In fact, if the crucial role that Tabaruha subsequently played in the numerous political cases against Museveni's regime are anything to go by, then you have to say Museveni was right on the money. It is completely irrelevant to the proper appreciation of this particular Tibaruha saga that Museveni later fell out with Tibaruha and in fact, just as the IGG had recommended, ordered his immediate sacking. As far as a modern despot is concerned, a man like Tibaruha had outlived his political usefulness to the regime. It is also irrelevant to the unconscionable modern despot that such a man had already rolled his name and face in mud as he fought [tooth and nail] to defend the indefensible cases against the rogue regime. As I said earlier, the modern despot is not stupid. In his eyes, men like Tibaruha are no more than *"Useful Idiots"* who, for their naivety, deserve exactly what they get in the end.

But here is the saddest twist in this Tibaruha saga. The regime soon found that it had in fact fallen deep into its own trap. With the threat of dismissal *[on Museveni's orders]* hanging over his troubled head, Tibaruha took full advantage of Kakooza Mutale's earlier Court success which had caused the IGG's powers to be trimmed. Using that judicial precedent, Tibaruha challenged Museveni's order to relive him of his job as *Solicitor General* and won.

So the net result was that Museveni's disgraceful affidavit in support of Kakooza Mutale's petition had, in *Ibingira Case* style, come back like a deranged ghost to haunt him for his wicked desecration of the culture of institutionalism in Uganda. And the lessons of this whole mess are quite simply inescapable for any aspiring leaders.

For them to succeed in the eyes of ordinary men and women today, they will need to do more than just steer clear of a modern despot's brand of politics. The modern despot has done us a great favour. By his obnoxious actions, he has caused ordinary people to demand higher standards of political leadership. Well that is the hope I am hanging onto as I sign off here.

Charles Ochen Okwir

The Trusted Accomplice in Despot Country

In any country where elective politics is supposed to be the means by which individuals and political parties contest for and acquire State power, the significance of the *Electoral Commission's* [EC] impartiality cannot be emphasised strongly enough. It is critical. In fact, the very credibility of democracy depends on the integrity of the EC.

That integrity can only be achieved if the EC is independent enough to carry out the crucial task of organising regular, free and fair elections. In Uganda, the things that the EC must do in order to deliver free and fair elections are set out in article 61[a-h] of the constitution of Uganda. They include the demarcation of constituencies, revising and updating the voters register, supervision of elections, hearing and determining election complaints, conducting civic education, and declaring *[in writing and under its seal]* the results of elections.

So any competence deficit on the part of the EC with regard to the conduct of these crucial functions is likely to have grave consequences for the entire electoral process. In the worst case scenario, it can fatally damage public confidence and even cause political conflicts. History has indeed been consistent in its wise counsel about the prospect of violence and instability when the EC fails in its job. Indeed, the Kenyan and Zimbabwean elections of 2007 and 2008 showed us the catastrophic consequences of such failure.

So it wouldn't at all be far-fetched to suggest that a country's political stability rests heavily on how well the EC does its job. How well that job is done in turn depends heavily on how it is constituted. Besides that, the integrity of the EC's top leadership is the other critical factor. These are some of the biggest challenges for many young democracies. It is therefore right that in this part of our discourse, we pay particular heed to how top EC officials are appointed.

In Uganda today, the manner in which the EC is constituted is not significantly different from the way many other institutions of State are constituted. The President, a partisan politician, is always at the centre of it as the *Appointing Authority*. Thereafter, the men and women he will have chosen would have to be approved by the same Parliament that one newspaper editor described as *impotent.*

For the same reasons I gave in my earlier discussion on how modern despots manage institutions of State, I think it would be foolish for anyone to expect Uganda's EC to do any better against the same despotic onslaught. Just listen to Senator Barak Obama talking about a strikingly similar futility at one of his electrifying campaign rallies for the US presidency: *"...the greatest risk we can take is to try the same old politics, with the same old players, and expect a different result".*

It was a very powerful and logical statement of caution that many US voters clearly found hard to ignore. So in Uganda, I would say Museveni's *"No Change"* politics should be interpreted to mean that Uganda's EC will remain as partisan as it has always been. The overbearing *Portrait of a Despot* hanging over Uganda simply can't allow progressive reforms to take place at the EC. After all, a partisan and incompetent EC is the modern despot's most important *"election theft"* accomplice.

Most Lawyers I have met have great faith in evidence based debates. So let me try and give you some hard facts to prove what may be sounding like the mutterings of a *Voodoo* prophet of doom to you. Whereas article 60[2] of the constitution of Uganda demands that *"...members of the Commission shall be persons of high moral character, proven integrity, and...possess considerable experience and demonstrated competence in the conduct of public affairs"*, the reality often tells its own story. A story that is far removed from the prescriptions of the Constitution!

In the end, what Ugandans have consistently ended up with as Chairpersons, Commissioners, and officials of the EC have been no more than disguised *Polling Agents* who secretly subscribe to and work for the ruling NRM party. But it's also true to say that not all of them would have voluntarily hobnobbed with the ruling party if they had their way.

That means there must be an element of duress somewhere in that whole EC mess. In fact, Eng. Badru Kiggundu who was the Chairman of Uganda's EC at the time of writing this book almost admitted to this when he posed a very interesting *tongue-in-cheek* question to a *Weekly Observer* Journalist who had asked him about the EC's political impartiality: *"...what was the governing philosophy or structure of this country before we came here? Who wasn't a Movement person in this country"*, Kiggundu asked the Journalist.

I think Kiggundu must have been alluding to the fact that not too long ago, all of them at the EC [like every Ugandan] were required by law to belong to Museveni's *Movement* party. So he may have been hoping that the Journalist would join the dots and conclude that there may still be many in the present EC who subscribe to and illegally work to further the interests of Museveni's *"new"* NRM-O party from within.

But that is not all. When Kiggundu was asked to comment on a story that the *Weekly Observer* had run about some EC officials who participate in rigging elections for Museveni's regime, he didn't even attempt to deny it. And that speaks volumes; incriminating volumes in fact!

All he said was that *"...these people we rounded up on polling day, we never trained them to pre-tick or pre-mark ballot papers. That is why when we heard about it, we went and rounded up the whole station and took all the polling officials to Police"*.

The only logical conclusion to be drawn from that is that Kiggundu thought the rogue EC officials had been trained to rig elections by some *"overzealous politicians"* whom he later described as the EC's *"adversaries".* But to fully appreciate the gravity of Kiggundu's revelations, I think it's important to bear one thing in mind.

The *Weekly Observer* story was essentially about a particular *Internal Security Organisation* [ISO] intelligence operative who the paper said had been planted at the EC by Museveni's regime to complement the work of the regime's election rigging taskforce code named *"Working Group Four".*

Interestingly, to this day, I have no knowledge of anyone from the regime's election rigging *"Working Group Four"* ever coming out to dispute the gist of the *Weekly Observer* story. If you think that is already telling, then brace yourself for more from Kiggundu; the Chairman of Uganda's beleaguered *Electoral Commission*.

While responding to further interrogation from the *Weekly Observer* Journalist, Kiggundu said, *"...there are so many things and sooner or later, I may write a book. I don't want to tell you the grim of the facts I will put in that book, but someday, I will write a book on what takes place in some of these electoral malpractices. There are lots of things that are done that sometimes make you weep".*

It's a mouth watering prospect isn't it? But before Kiggundu's book even goes into print, it is clear to me that quietly, Kiggundu appears to be furious with the regime's election rigging antics. In fact, I think he was literally itching for the time to come when he would be free to spill the rotten beans about how elections are rigged in Museveni's despotic household called Uganda.

Charles Ochen Okwir

The Deconstruction of Civil Service Ethics

In November 1964, Alexander Pope, in his book *"The Role of the Civil Servant in Developing Countries"*, attempted to discuss the *Civil Service* heritage and traditions. In so doing, he uttered these words: *"...the frequent identification of the Civil Service with the machinery of government suggests that it is a manufactured tool which can be discarded and replaced by a new one ever so often"*.

He added that, *"...this concept obscures the organic nature of the Service"*. One of the most important things to understand, he said, was that as a *Service*, *"...it grew out of past history to serve past occasions, it exists to serve present needs, and it must develop to anticipate future requirements"*.

There are a number of important things that one can take out of Alexander's assertions. The first is that the nature of a country's *Civil Service* does to a great extent reflect that country's history. In the case of Uganda, the debilitating bondages of colonialism and Britain's strategic national interests cannot be divorced from the nature and character of the *Civil Service* as it stands today.

It is also clear that the *"Good Governance"* principles of a non-partisan *Civil Service* never really took root in colonial Uganda. And the reason for that was that the *Civil Service* itself was for all intents and purposes a *"political party"*. After all, it was part of the government and it played a decisive role in implementing government policies and programmes.

Finally, it's now abundantly clear that the prohibition of *Civil Servants* from joining and actively participating in political party activities was in reality a means of stopping them from joining opposition parties. After all, by default, all political parties in colonial Uganda were effectively in opposition because their primary objective was to wrestle power from the British colonialists.

As I have said before in this book, I must say here again that it may indeed have been for those very reasons that the British saw it fit to ensure that the Ugandan *Civil Service* never took after the image and well established practices and ethics of their own *Civil Service* back in the United Kingdom.

So the post-independence Ugandan politicians who came in 1962 merely started from where the British had left. They then completed the job of concentrating power in the hands of a few privileged officials and relatives who towed the *"correct line"*. That was of course a practice that the British themselves couldn't have tolerated in their own country; even as early as 1962.

In Museveni's Uganda on the other hand, appointment to the *Civil Service* was strictly conditioned upon one's prior attendance and completion of a politicisation programme at the regime's ideological institute in Kyankwanzi. In later years, even NRM politicians who had lost their constituency seats were re-assured of re-deployment into the *Civil Service*.

Let me give you a related example. Yes, granted: Brig. Noble Mayombo [RIP] hadn't lost his parliamentary seat in an election like the others I alluded to. He merely stood down as army MP. But his appointment as *Permanent Secretary* in the *Ministry of Defence* still raised strong suspicions of typical modern despot foul play.

For a start, the *Permanent Secretary* is the *Chief Accounting Officer* in any Ministry. Secondly, in terms of proportion, the *Ministry of Defence* under Museveni's regime enjoyed the biggest budget allocation compared to all the other Ministries. In fact, the amount of money allocated to the *Ministry of Defence* is sometimes equivalent to the net total allocated to three or even four Ministries.

Now picture this: In Mayombo alone, Museveni had an ultra loyal political ideologue as the *Chief Accounting Officer* in the *"richest"* Ministry in the land; a land held hostage [by the throat] by an outstandingly corrupt gang of so-called liberators. What to expect in such circumstances is really not worthy of debate in a modern despot's country. Museveni could now requisition any amount of money he wanted from his loyal servant Mayombo and get it. What that money is then used for is really none of Mayombo's business.

In fact, Mayombo's loyalty to Museveni was almost legendary. As Museveni's *Aide de Camp*, Mayombo felt no qualms at all about polishing Museveni's shoes in front of television cameras. It was therefore sad that the same regime that he served so diligently was in the end suspected to have had a hand in his *"untimely"* death. At the time of his death, the grapevine had it that Mayombo was in no doubt as to who was responsible for his inevitable demise. The finger of blame was pointing straight towards the only person in the land who felt most threatened by Mayombo's much hyped intellect, wealth, and above all, political ambitions.

Post-Script Development

It's becoming a trend isn't it? Several weeks after I considered my submissions on the *Civil Service* closed, I was forced to revisit it by a screaming headline which read: *"NRM Plans to Place Cadres in Civil Service Jobs"*. The claim had its source in a paper presented to NRM legislators and cabinet Ministers by a one David Mafabi. Mafabi was a Lecturer at the regime's ideological school in Kyankwanzi where the ruling "dignitaries" had gathered for a retreat.

One of the key proposals in Mafabi's paper on *"Party/Organisation Building and Discipline"* was, and I quote, for Museveni's NRM-O party *"...to place party loyalists in key government Ministries and the entire Civil Service"*. Not only that. It was alleged that Mafabi also proposed that

NRM cadres be planted in all regional administration and local authorities. That these cadres should be made to serve as NRM-O party *Commissars*; *Regional* or *Provincial Governors*; and as *Resident District Commissioners* [RDCs]! Besides the *Civil Service*, the paper said, *NGOs, Labour Unions,* and *Civic Organisations* must also be targeted for infiltration.

There is simply no other way of looking at this plan other than that it bore all the hallmarks of a modern despot's wickedness. Wicked because if successful, it wouldhave transformed the *"Mafabi Plan"* into a pre-meditated criminal project whose effect would have fatally wounded the country's barely breathing *Civil Service* ethics, rules, and regulations!

I also thought the *"Mafabi Plan"* was cowardly. Cowardly because it demonstrated in no uncertain terms that Museveni's political strategists knew that to survive, they needed to preserve all positions of influence in the *Civil Service* for themselves; just like it's done in all regimes led by modern despots.

In fact, this sad *"Mafabi Plan"* story has just reminded me of something important that had skipped my mind. It is the suggestion by Alexander Pope [in his 1964 book that we talked about earlier] that the *Civil Service* should be viewed as *"...a manufactured tool which can be discarded and replaced by a new one ever so often"*.

I think Pope and I will respectfully part ways on this one. Instability in the *Civil Service* is in my view a recipe for disaster. For a start, it hinders evolutionary development within the *Civil Service* as an institution of State. In fact, in the end, it may even cause a total collapse of the elusive culture of institutionalism; the very one that is crucial to the proper functioning of any genuine democracy.

And just to re-emphasise my belief in what I just said, I will tell you something else. The most important lesson that I took from former British Prime Minister Margaret Thatcher's book *The Downing Street Years* was what she said about the British *Civil Service*. Thatcher said that one of the things that she was most proud to have found and left behind was the fact that in Britain, *"...political leaders come and go with minimum dislocation to the Civil Service".*

That for me is the best explanation for Britain's political stability over the years. Without it, or with the *"Mafabi Plan"* for that matter, you are likely to see nepotism, cronyism, and sectarianism getting entrenched. These horrible ills could in turn lead to serious political conflicts inspired by an uncontrollable urge by marginalised groups to revenge for injustices suffered.

In fact, as I write these lines from a tiny third floor *"Bed-Seater"* in a noisy Nairobi slum, some exiled Ugandans who are living in these conditions are struggling to contain their urge to visit revenge on Museveni and his cronies. These people are like the angry ghosts of a violent volcano that is about to erupt. Just hear this: Out of nowhere, this tall greying-fifty-something chap who had been sitting quietly next to me suddenly broke his silence said: *"...Museveni will pay very heavily one day".*

I laughed; quite loudly in fact. I thought his outburst had been caused by the usual social and financial hardships that most refugees face on a daily basis. But no, I was wrong. Something much deeper than that had provoked this guy's emotional outburst.

With his warrior eyes frozen in the direction of a rough dusty road littered with *"Jua Kali"* metal fabricators, he said *"...Charles, I have just seen my daughter walking past us. She is almost a grown up woman, but she has never set foot in Uganda; not even for minute. Can you imagine that"?*

Now that was something! Anyone with a conscience would have been deeply touched by that. In fact, it immediately changed my mood into one of remorse. But remorse for what, I hear you ask? Now here is the strange bit. I actually felt as though I was Museveni at that point. And because of that, I felt like apologising to this poor old fellow. Strange isn't it; very strange indeed!

Anyway back to Margaret Thatcher's pride in Britain's *Civil Service* ethics. In any country ruled by a modern despot, the sort of professionalism that ensures Britain's political stability can never be tolerated. Any *Civil Servant* whose loyalty to the regime is deemed "suspect" will be undermined, frustrated, and finally sacked. It is completely irrelevant to the modern despot that such *Civil Servants* could actually be men and women of impeccable integrity. In his eyes, that is the real problem with such people; their integrity!

Local Government & Political Mobilisation

In a book called *"Party and Locality in Northern Uganda"* [1945-1962], Cherry Gertzel, a Professor of Political Science at the University of Zambia, established that as early as the 1950's, District institutions had already assumed prominence as potent and in fact efficacious avenues for political mobilisation.

In Professor Gertzel's own words, *"...during these years, the creation of representative local government institutions, enjoying a good deal of patronage and responsible for the allocation of considerable resources in the way of local services, emphasised the district as a significant level at which to seek political power".*

But modern despots are too dishonest to publicly admit that. Their preference is to feed the people they rule over with the bogus excuse that new Districts are created as a means of *"...taking services closer to the people".* In their fantasy world, therefore, progress in public service delivery can only be measured by the number of new Districts created. What a whole load of rubbish!

As Gertzel pointed out, what these modern despots think is a clever new political trick is actually nothing new. It has all been tried and recorded as political deceit by history. In the case of Uganda, the senseless creation of new Districts actually means that the impecunious Ugandan taxpayer would end up shouldering the burden of a *"public service"* expenditure budget that had absolutely nothing to do with *"public service"* delivery.

On the contrary, I think it had everything to do with Museveni's political patronage strategy. After all, we all know that political patronage is a policy that modern despots thrive on. The inherent legitimacy deficit that they suffer from simply can't allow them to dump it. For the evidence, I invite you to consider what Museveni is reported to have said in May 2007 while campaigning for his party candidate in the Kamuli District *Local Council 5* [LC5] bi-election.

At a place called Budiope, Museveni promised the electorate there that he would finally grant their Township District status. But in perfect conformity with his patronage policy, Museveni also made it clear that he was only granting their little Eastern Uganda village District status on the implied understanding that they would return the favour by voting for the NRM-O party candidate.

Guess what happened next? The credulous, uncritical, and largely peasant electorate of Budiope bought the scam wholeheartedly. In fact, I think I now know what one famous Monk meant when he said years ago that, *"...the undiscerning mind, like the roots of a tree, absorbs all including what will kill it"*.

In the minds of Budiope's peasant electorate, the prospect of a brand new District of their own meant *Local Government* jobs for their children; it meant that medical services would finally come nearer; it meant local infrastructure development; and it meant the possibility of winning lucrative tenders from the new District. The only thing the people of Budiope didn't know was that it was all a big fat mirage.

And it must be viewed as a *mirage*! The reason I say that is because a strong body of evidence has now emerged which demonstrates beyond reasonable doubt that all the money that is spent on the creation of new Districts actually gets the inhabitants of the new patronage Districts nowhere.

Unemployment is still endemic. Abject poverty is still the order of the day. Millions a year still die needlessly from preventable or easily treatable diseases. Roads in the capital city Kampala, let alone rural Budiope, are like the blood drenched craters left behind by Al Qaeda's powerful bombs.

The other thing that Professor Gertzel found was that the infusion of factional politics into *Local Government* institutions actually affects their effectiveness. To prove his point, Gertzel made reference to a major political stalemate that had just unfolded in the Teso region over appointments to the District Council.

The British colonial administration at the time, exactly like today's modern despots, had used the law to further its strategic objectives. As always, laws that are conceived with ulterior motives often create their own problems that its architects are unable to foresee; largely because the pursuit of mischief will have blinded them.

The District Councils [District Administration] Ordinance of 1955 was one such law. It was recklessly permissive. Through it, every *District Council* enjoyed an unfettered discretion to determine how much of the *1955 Ordinance* to adopt. If that is not a death wish, then I don't know what is.

In fact, as a direct result of that, some Districts immediately introduced direct elections while others didn't. Others had an official majority while others had an unofficial majority. Busoga, Toro, and Bukedi for example, totally refused to adopt the *1955 Ordinance* and chose to remain under the *1949 African Local Government Regulations*.

The net result of that reckless *"choice of law"* freedom was that until the onset of independence, [in 1962] *District Councils* in Uganda never developed in the same way or followed the same rules. In fact even today, the corrosive legacy of those weak colonial laws is there for all to. Good governance practices have never taken root in Uganda. And, by giving *District Councils* unfettered discretion to decide how much of the *District Councils Ordinance* they could adopt, a clear message was sent out to the people of Uganda that full democracy and all its trappings was in fact an *optional* affair.

Is it any wonder, therefore, that in Uganda today, incumbent politicians seem to find great difficulty adhering to laws that purport to govern democratic processes? Just like Busoga, Toro and Bukedi Districts had done in colonial times, contemporary Ugandan politicians also feel that they can wilfully opt out of the ambit of laws that govern political contests and get away with it.

Going back to the Kamuli District LC5 bi-election where Museveni promised to turn the little Budiope Township into a District, the NRM-O party candidate of course *"won"* with a highly questionable majority of just under 2000 votes.

Indeed, the *Uganda Joint Christian Council* [UJCC], a non-partisan umbrella body of Christian Churches in Uganda that observed the Kamuli bi-elections, released a report into those elections and declared that the May 10th 2007 Kamuli LC5 bi-elections were, and I quote, "*...not free and fair*".

Rev. Canon Grace Kaiso, the *Executive Director* of UJCC, offered some instructive advice to Uganda's Legislature and by extension, to the country as a whole. In Canon Kaiso's view, electoral laws must be amended to restrain the President from making political offers during election campaigns.

Why, the man of God asked, *"...should the President for example give out gifts like new districts, electricity and roads during election time? Such things shouldn't occur during campaign time. It can influence voting patterns and thereby give undue advantage to the ruling party's candidates"*.

In another call that I am sure will remind you of the criticisms I threw at Museveni's partisan Police Force, the UJCC also called for a comprehensive review of the electoral laws in order *"...to restrain the police from harassing the opposition with impunity"*.

In particular, the UJCC added, *"...the law should be clear on whether party members coming from other districts to boost their party candidate have to seek accreditation from the Electoral Commission so that police doesn't brutalise people again on flimsy grounds. All should be done to ensure that what happened in Kamuli doesn't happen again"*.

UJCC's mention of the law as an accomplice to despotic political oppression was of particular interest to me; not least because it's something that I have condemned repeatedly in this book. But it's not just me. I recall Prof. Apollo Nsibambi warning *Constituent Assembly Delegates* of the dangers of what he called *"Legislative Tyranny"*. What UJCC and I are moaning about here today is the ultimate manifestation of what Nsibambi called *Legislative Tyranny* several years back.

But as they say, *"a week is [indeed] a long time in politics"*. The very man who warned against *Legislative Tyranny* is today [as I write] serving in a tyrants government as Prime Minister; leader of all despotic *"Government Business"* no less! It's a sad irony. Would he acknowledge today that he once warned against the *use of law as a tool of political oppression?* I would pay a few coins just to be allowed to put that question to him.

But the Kamuli bi-election did not only expose a modern despot's propensity to fraudulently hoodwink gullible peasants into voting for his interests. Something deeper and scary came out clearly too. For all his grandstanding bravado as a democrat, the modern despot actually loathes the rules that govern genuine democratic contests.

Just hear this: The Kamuli LC5 contest was over. Museveni's NRM candidate had *"won"*. It was now time to celebrate the *"victory"*. Well, not quite! Perhaps still nursing the wounds that FDC's female candidate Salaamu Musumba had inflicted on his massive ego, Museveni warned [during the Kamuli *"victory"* celebrations] that, *"...there is this opposition man, Baswale Kezaala, he was campaigning for Forum for Democratic Change's Salaamu and we cannot tolerate that"*.

Museveni's choice of language here was as explicit as it gets. You can clearly see that he was angry that some people even had the audacity to campaign for the opposition candidate. He is then reported to have ended with what in my view was effectively a threat to all who will in future dare challenge his NRM-O party. He said, *"...he [Jinja Mayor Baswale Kezaala] will see us. After all, the majority of the councillors he is working with belong to the NRM. You will hear soon of the revenge we are to unleash on Kezaala"*.

And guess what! Museveni is a modern despot who never forgets; and definitely never forgives! He constantly scans the political horizon for opportunities to visit his revenge. And, if this next development is not a tragic coincidence, then you simply have to give it to the man. The *Daily Monitor* newspaper of January 9th 2009 told the world that the same Jinja Mayor Kezaala had been charged with *"abuse of office"* and remanded in Luzira prison.

The paper revealed that "...*plain-clothed men holding Police identity cards picked Mr Kezaala from Jinja and brought him to the Inspector General of Government's [IGG's] office for interrogation*". Mayor Kezaala himself of course protested his innocence and maintained that "...*the IGG is being used to witch-hunt him*". And who can blame him?

After all, on 12th January 2009, just two days after he had been remanded in prison, news broke that on the day Kezaala was charged and remanded, he had been arraigned before court after 5:00pm [unusual to say the very least] and then "...*whisked away in a car with government plates that indicate that it belongs to the President's Office*". Isn't that the *"smoking gun"* that we have been looking for? As always, you will be the Judges of that.

I think the overwhelming evidence clearly suggests that deep down, Museveni still believes in the no-party individual merit *Movement* system of governance that he dreamt up from the jungles of Luwero. Problem is: I am not even sure it was Museveni who dreamt up the *Movement* system of governance. The whole thing, including the name *"Movement"* in fact, sounds suspiciously similar to the one Fidel Castro and Che Guevara conceived in the *Sierra Maestra* forest of Cuba in the 1950s.

The Truth From The Woods

The *National Forest Authority* [NFA] is the country's lead institution charged with the management of Uganda's forests. On paper, it is supposed to be steered by experts in the field. The assumption is that, if left to their own devices, these experts can come up with great forest management strategies. The hope is that the great strategies would then deliver a policy that will lead to sustainable exploitation of the nation's forest resource. Like most of the institutions that we have looked at so far, the rules that govern the NFA's operations are also admirable.

However, as soon as you inject a modern despot's politics and management style into the picture, the admiration evaporates instantly. A despot's political interference fatally undermines professional autonomy in any institution of State; leaving them severely crippled!

For the benefit of the uninformed, Uganda is home to a large forest reserve called *Mabira*. Situated along the Kampala-Jinja highway, Mabira forest is one of the worlds' leading bio-diversity sites. It is rich in fauna and flora. In fact, historians will probably tell you that it pre-dates the Republic of Uganda as a nation-state. That simple fact means that in the eyes of some, *Mabira* forest may even be considered a sacred national asset. It simply can't get any more significant than that. But a modern despot doesn't give a hoot about things like that. He is sacrilegious by nature. That sacrilegious propensity manifested itself in the regime's proposal to give away parts of *Mabira* forest to a sugar producing company. It was inevitable that such a proposal would attract immediate protests; not least from the NFA itself. In fact, the protests culminated in the resignation of a few NFA board members including its *Executive Director* Mr. Olav Bjella.

The controversy surrounding the giveaway of *Mabira* attracted instant media interest. With that, in no time, all the leading English newspapers had their pages packed with opinions and letters of protest from conservationists, environmentalists, politicians, and many other ordinary but fiercely patriotic Ugandans.

But something else happened too; something rather unusual in fact! This time round, even the regime's *"Yes Men"* like Ofwono Opondo and the *Presidential Adviser on the Media* John Nagenda joined in the fray of protests. I think this bi-partisan union of protests should demonstrate to absolutely anyone that the regime's proposal to give away parts of *Mabira* forest was simply unacceptable; even for Museveni's own *"Yes Men"*. Strange perhaps; I don't think so!

What this tells us is that actually, their sycophancy notwithstanding, some of these *"Yes Men"* men can still be rehabilitated if the cause is right. Their conscience only retracts into its shell like a tortoise when their greed and selfishness takes the better of them. On this occasion however, the *"Yes Men"* knew that the continued health and survival of *Mabira* forest has a direct ecological impact on their own survival. Drought, crop failure, and hunger would be brought that much closer.

So for once, both the trend and strength of public opinion was unmistakable. Surely, a response from the regime was inevitable. Sure enough, it hastily put together and published a *Cabinet Paper* in a desperate attempt to address the mounting public outrage. The regime's Minister of *Water and Environment* Maria Mutagamba claimed that although the *National Forestry Authority* had evicted encroachers from *Mabira* forest in the 1990s, the *Authority* had not carried out enrichment tree planting. According to her, this meant that the area of *Mabira* forest that SCOUL wanted for sugarcane growing was now occupied by tree species like Paper Mulberry which have no economic value. Mr Nsita, a senior member of the *Inter-Ministerial Committee* that visited *Mabira* central forest reserve in October 2006, came out immediately and dismissed the contents of the *Cabinet Paper* on *Mabira* forest.

In his rebuttal of Minister Mutagamba's baseless claims, Mr Nsita, a former *Director for Field Operations* at the NFA who had resigned in protest, said: *"...I am surprised that even a minister can lie to the nation. After evicting encroachers from the forest, we carried out enrichment planting. We even took them {the Ministers} to the areas where we planted Musizi and Terminalia tree species especially in parts which were badly affected"*.

So there you have it! They both can't be right. One of them was definitely lying. Was it the regime's Minister Maria

Mutagamba, the armchair politician, or was it Mr. Nsita, the former *Director of Field Operations* at the NFA? Whose testimony would you consider to be more credible? Oooooh! That's a "tough" one isn't it? Decisions, decisions, decisions! Not to worry. What happened thereafter should give you a priceless clue as to who the majority of Ugandans believed. The intellectual protests in the newspaper pages quickly metamorphosed into massive street protests in the capital city Kampala. The regime, clearly on the wrong side of public opinion, unleashed its rag-tag stick wielding *"Kiboko Squad"* militia to whip the protesters off the streets.

But to their utter amazement, the more passionate protesters stood their ground; having decided to take the regime's punishment with the dignity that we have seen in righteous men since the beginning of time. That was how far the dissenting public was prepared to go; even though they knew deep down that they could easily have fallen victim to the regime's trigger-happy Merchants of Death.

In spite of all that touching determination from the *Mabira* protesters, one man maintained his defiance. He said no amount of protests would *"intimidate"* or stop him from giving away parts of *Mabira* forest to SCOUL. Read my lips and keep your ears firmly on the ground: I think that is the authentic voice of vested interest through the ages. And yes, you guessed right! That man was Gen. Yoweri Tibuhaburwa Kaguta Museveni, a man whose second name, I am told, literally means the *"one who never listens"*. How fitting! Like a true modern despot, Museveni has been quick to seize every opportunity to boast about his record of attracting direct foreign investment to Uganda.

On this occasion however, not even the international investors who were attending the annual *Presidential Investors Round Table Meeting* in Kampala could convince him to change his mind.

His response to those crucial stakeholder concerns was consistent with his earlier stand on the matter. In his view, the *National Forestry Authority* was not in a position to handle the problem. This was a problem that would be best handled by politicians who *"know how to deal with people best"*, Museveni insisted.

I think the only reasonable conclusion to be drawn from Museveni's reaction is that perhaps, in his despotic mind, the NFA's role should be limited to dealing with trees and animals that threaten the lives of other trees and animals. The flip side of that ignorance coin is of course that the NFA should not concern itself with the unsustainable activities of human beings; activities that actually threaten the very existence of everything in those forests.

Extraordinary reasoning! Extraordinary because it tells us that perhaps in Museveni's mind, the management of the country's forest resources, and the management of human encroachment in those forests, should somehow be seen to be mutually exclusive of each other. I just can't get my head around that. It defies logic. And that may be exactly what modern despots intend to achieve. That way, the population will be left struggling to make sense of things as underhand political deals are being cut or fulfilled. In fact, the rumour-mill at the time had a perfect conspiracy theory to explain the regime's determination to give away parts of *Mabira* forest to SCOUL. According to some conspiracy theorists, the regime's determination was driven by a secret *"contractual"* obligation to pay back SCOUL for the *"support"* it had extended to Museveni's ruling NRM party during the 2006 general elections. Unproven allegations of course; but very interesting nonetheless!

But let me say this: Peter Thorneycroft once said, that *"...when people are called upon to lead great nations, they must look into the hearts and minds of the people whom they seek to govern"*.

Put differently, I think Thorneycroft was saying that if a political leader cannot respect the deepest instincts of the people he leads, then he has no business being in politics in the first place. But the key word to note here is lead. Modern despots don't lead, they rule! That is why they are incapable of having respect for the deepest instincts of the people they rule.

And in this *Mabira* forest case, the evidence was clear: The manner in which Museveni handled the massive outpour of opposition to the proposal to de-gazette and give away parts of *Mabira* forest really offended those deep instincts. The offence was so deep that even the Emperor's *"Yes Men"* joined the voices opposing the Emperor.

The Ultimate Betrayal of British Instincts

Across the seas, Tony Blair, the then Prime Minister of Britain, had also betrayed the deepest instincts of the British people when he decided to commit British troops to fight in Iraq. Over one million Britons took to the streets in freezing temperatures to protest against what they thought was a totally unjustified decision to invade Iraq.

And it didn't help matters in the least when the infamous *"Iraq Dossier"* Blair used to convince British parliamentarians to support the invasion turned out to be dodgy. When its credibility as an intelligence document finally collapsed, the hawkish *"Bush Doctrine"* of *"Pre-emptive Self Defence"* took over.

Then, when the weapons of mass destruction that Saddam Hussein allegedly had escaped the probing eyes of UN Weapons Inspectors, *"Regime Change"* became the official justification. That immediately made the *"Bush-Blair"* invasion of Iraq without an enabling UN Resolution controversial.

This British comparison was however only intended to bring us to this point where I argue that when modern despots stubbornly ignore the deepest instincts of the people they rule, then the implications can be grave for their careers and legacies. And the situation is made worse if it becomes apparent to the governed that their leaders, or rulers for that matter, have been less than honest to them.

If your integrity as a leader collapses, so does public trust in you. It is as simple as that. In the case of Uganda, there is absolutely no doubt that both the controversial amendment of Article 105[2] of the constitution of Uganda and the *Mabira* forest scandal caused a tragic collapse of trust and confidence in Museveni as a ruler.

In Britain, Tony Blair did not fare any better either. As the British themselves like to say after their promiscuous night adventures, it was now *"the morning after the night before"* for Tony Blair. This is the time when, to your utter disgust, payback is demanded; sometimes with menaces. If you have ever had to deal with a nasty hangover then you will know exactly what I am talking about.

In Blair's case, the *"night before"* was the illegal invasion of Iraq. The ultimate definition of his legacy was now out of his hands and into the hands of the British people. So how would he deal with this crisis that was threatening to cause serious harm to his legacy? Well, this is what he did.

While announcing his decision to step down from the leadership of the *Labour Party*, Blair left no doubt in the minds of his audience that he was now pleading for a fair judgement of his legacy. And he was now pleading with the very people whose deepest instincts he had betrayed with his capricious decision to send British troops to Iraq. They would now have the last laugh; and there was absolutely nothing that he or his image consultants could do about it. The jury had already delivered its verdict. And the miserable personal approval ratings he was now getting in opinion polls bore great testament to that. The trend was downwards and there was no stopping it.

All the once powerful leader could do was plead, plead, and plead again for some sort of understanding. One particular line from Blair's final speech captured the hopelessness that he now felt most beautifully. With his once powerful voice almost failing him, and looking every bit petrified, very humbly, Tony Blair said, *"...there is a judgment to be made on my Premiership. And in the end that is, for you, the people to make"*.
Call me what you like, but I was ecstatic to see *The Great* Tony Blair that I once admired finally come down to earth. For a man who was once said to be *"obsessed with his legacy"*, you have to wonder whether his legacy featured as prominently on his mind [then] as it does now that he is no longer Prime Minister. On the evidence, I will have to say that is debatable. And I think Blair's pain and dilemma here should serve as a great lesson for all modern despots and those who aspire to succeed them.

With a clear sense of helplessness oozing through his voice, the embattled Ex-Prime Minister said, *"...but I ask you to accept one thing. Hand on heart, I did what I thought was right. I may have been wrong. That's your call. But believe one thing if nothing else. I did what I thought was right for our country"*.

Finally, it had become clear to Tony Blair that the choices a leader makes while he is still in power in the end, define his legacy. He will carry that legacy for the rest of his life, to his grave, and perhaps even beyond! And, unfair though it might seem, whether he likes it or not, it is also a legacy that he will bequeath to his children and grandchildren alike. That is life in all its wonderful cruelty.

Yes; *wonderful cruelty*. I use that term very consciously because I think there is a great lesson to be learnt from it; and it is: If the all round betterment of the countries they lead is not exactly what they want to define their legacies, then perhaps the fact that their loved ones will forever carry the burden of their failures should be a cause for some serious introspection for despots. And there is a powerful precedent to emphasise this point; perhaps as powerful as they get.

One of Idi Amin's sons whose *"Revisionist"* website is dedicated to re-writing his father's legacy once told the BBC that his father, a devoted Moslem, believed that there was no need for him to go before a court of law to clear his name. That his father thought that was a matter for God; or most appropriately, Allah! But most importantly, Amin's son said, his father often told them that he did not educate them for nothing. That he did it with the expectation that in the end, it would fall upon them to defend his legacy.
You simply couldn't have failed to detect the pain and agony in Amin Jnr's voice as he fought in vain to defend his father's legacy. It was a legacy that he never shaped but now had to defend out love for his despotic late father! This is the unfortunate situation that children born to despotic fathers will have to live with.

For Tony Blair, when all the good things that he did for Britain are finally listed on a white piece of paper, the word *Iraq*, boldly written in the bright red colour of all the innocent blood shade in Iraq, will be tearing mercilessly through the dark cloud hanging over his legacy. In fact, it might even super-impose itself and overshadow every good thing that he ever did for Britain. On the other hand, for Uganda's Yoweri Museveni, the words *"Sacrilege in the Pearl of Africa"* will be doing the same [if not worse] to his legacy.

But let me make one thing clear here before I wrap up and wonder off into the distance. I believe that human beings, even the worst criminals in the world, are still much better than the worst things they ever did. What that means is that while a man's record of grotesque conduct can never be changed, the man himself can be rehabilitated and redeemed.

Charles Ochen Okwir

With bags of inspiration from the excellent work done by the *Mo Ibrahim Foundation*, I set off on a voyage in search of nothing but the shortfalls of modern despots like Uganda's Yoweri Museveni. The hope was, and still is, that present and future world leaders will learn some valuable lessons from the traumatic Ugandan experiences that we have gone through here.

And I dare say, what better way to set that process of reform rolling than to give you a random selection of the *Governance Lessons* from Museveni's egregious record of political governance. Indeed, as Mohammed Ibrahim [of the *Mo Foundation*] himself once put it, "...*Nothing; simply nothing is more important to Africa than good governance*". Sir, with great humility, I concur entirely.

Chapter Seven

Governance Lessons from the Museveni Years

Lesson 1
One of the most important civic duties for any democracy loving citizen anywhere in the world is to totally reject the notion that somehow, as a people, you should expect anything and everything except the highest possible standards of democracy and political accountability from your leaders. That is you right, not a privilege.

Lesson 2
It should also follow from the above that any attempt by a leader to cite political precedents from a previous period of bad governance as a benchmark from which his own shortfalls should be judged must treated with the contempt it deserves.

Lesson 3
Any leader who is always quick to pass the blame for mistakes in his administration to others must be viewed with utmost suspicion. That is the clearest indication that such a leader is dishonest and therefore incapable of taking political responsibility for his mistakes.

Lesson 4
Politics ought to be taken as a very serious affair. It determines a man's only quality of life on this planet. Therefore any leader who perpetuates the erroneous and trivial description of it as a "game" probably doesn't quite appreciate the real significance of politics and should be seriously challenged by all citizens.

Lesson 5
Those who aspire to lead must always appreciate that a State is not an "instrument". It does not function in the interest of one particular class within society but for all. Failure to appreciate that and avoid it breeds resentment from marginalized groups, inspires revenge, and causes political instability.

Lesson 6
Clear parameters of jurisdiction between institutions of State must be laid down as clearly as possible. This will eliminate unnecessary conflicts and struggles for supremacy between those institutions.

Lesson 7
It should also follow from lesson No. 6 that, without prejudice to the complementary functions of "brotherhood" between the three arms of the State, the independence of the Judiciary, and that of the Legislature, must be jealously guarded. The fact that the Judiciary and the Legislature depend entirely on the goodwill of the Executive for their budgetary needs should be urgently reviewed with a view to giving those institutions total financial independence from the Executive. Anything short of that would mean that the tripartite contest would be over before it even starts and the independence of the Judiciary and the Legislature would forever remain symbolic.

Lesson 8
Jurisprudence must reflect the aspirations of the people in any given jurisdiction. If that is accepted, then former colonies must expunge from their statute books any laws that served and continue to serve the interests of the former colonial powers and their indigenous proxies.

Lesson 9
Leaders should always resist the temptation to use the law as a tool with which to oppress their political opponents. The moral of this dictum is simple. Any sitting government should always strive to make laws that would allow it to not only exist, but freely operate if the roles were to be reversed and it finds itself as the opposition party of the day facing the party that it had previously oppressed.

Lesson 10
Leaders must always resist the temptation to make promises that they have no intention of keeping; even if such promises enhance their chances of acquiring or hanging onto power. "Crime is smarter than the criminal". Sooner or later, your lies will be laid bare to your chagrin and embarrassment.

Lesson 11
For a vibrant democracy to be established, the government of the day must do everything practicable to enable every political party to get its messages across the country. The importance of this cannot be over emphasised because some of the best policies for a country may actually come from the opposition parties. In any case, it is the very essence of democracy.

Lesson 12
If a government truly wants to entrench democracy, then it should make sure that there is no affront to freedom of expression. Freedom to speak one's mind is not only a vital aspect of individual liberty but it is also at the helm of the common quest for the truth. Truth defines the vitality of society. Besides, freedom of expression can emphatically discourage the State and its coercive apparatus from assuming total custodianship of the public mind.

Lesson 13
Any attempt to legally conscript citizens to belong to the ruling party must be resisted at all costs. That will stop the establishment of a One Party state system; a system that represents everything that democracy does not.

Lesson 14
All citizens and civil society organisations must constantly look out for and resist any attempts by the ruling party to use State structures and resources to further its own partisan interests.

Lesson 15
In the protection of human rights, particular heed must be paid to the way the State interprets and applies legal limitations to the enjoyment of human rights. Available evidence shows that most human rights abuses [especially by State security agencies] are often justified by an erroneous reference to such legal limitations.

Lesson 16
As a way of reinforcing the scrupulous observance of human rights, all State security agencies, and the army in particular, must be decisively divorced from any form of participation in national politics except as voters. The police force should only be allowed to police elections if its independence from the whims of the incumbent leader can be demonstrated.

Lesson 17
To borrow from the framers of the American Constitution, all those charged with the maintenance of law and order within a given jurisdiction should always bear in mind that, "order cannot be secured merely through fear of punishment for its infraction; that it is hazardous to discourage thought, hope and imagination; that fear breeds repression; that repression breeds hate; that hate menaces stable government; that the path of safety lies in the opportunity to discuss freely supposed grievances and proposed remedies".

Lesson 18
If true democracy is to reign supreme in any country, then there must be a strong case for untying all those in the armed services from the shackles and chains of command that demand total and unquestioning loyalty to their superiors during elections. The untying must especially happen if their Commander-in-Chief is himself a candidate in the same election. In other words, the men and women in the armed services must at such times be accorded the minimum dignity to obey their conscience so that they too, in their absolute discretion, like the rest of the civilian population,

voluntarily choose the leader that they deem fit to lead their country.

Lesson 19
To enhance proposal No. 18 above, there must be an equally strong case for stripping any incumbent offering himself for re-election of all the powers of State vested in him for the entire duration of the election campaigns.

Lesson 20
The Judiciary must constantly lookout for any attempts by the ruling party to apply the laws of the land selectively to ensure that it retains an upper hand. Failure to do this will affect confidence in the entire justice system and perhaps even force aggrieved parties to take the law into their own hands with disastrous consequences for national stability.

Lesson 21
To reinforce public confidence in the criminal justice system, and to deny the Executive undue influence over the Directorate of Public Prosecutions, it is strongly recommended that the President be stripped of the powers to appoint the Director of Public Prosecutions and all other senior officials within the Directorate who exercise powers to sanction criminal prosecutions on behalf of the Director.

Lesson 22
In doing the above, the approach and objective must be genuinely patriotic. Long term national interests must decisively replace the selfish interests of power hungry politicians.

Lesson 23
National leaders should always remember that in the conduct of the noble affairs of State, they must pursue the truth. This provides the basis for public confidence and trust in them; a fact that actually gives them the courage to serve the country with dignity.

Lesson 24
A government should be compassionate and generous to every citizen. This forms the fabric that holds society intact. So it must be the duty of the political leadership to work tireless towards letting its people not only know, but feel that they count for more and more.

Lesson 25
Political leaders should always remember that the choices they make while in office will in the end define their legacy. A legacy that they will carry for the rest of their lives and bequeath to their children and grandchildren alike!

Lesson 26
The Civil Service should never be viewed as"...a manufactured tool which can be discarded and replaced by a new one every so often". To view it as such hinders the evolutionary development of the Civil Service as an institution. It may even prove to be a key recipe for political instability.

Lesson 27
Corruption in all its forms must be rejected and ruthlessly fought. It is beyond debate now that there can be no such thing as democracy if votes can be "bought".

Lesson 28
A good leader should be able to recognise his political zenith and leave power while he is still loved and admired. The reason being that everything you become too attached to will in the end hurt you; just as it happens when any intense love affair collapses.

Lesson 29
When you suppress peaceful political dissent, you only succeed in forcing the dissenters into more desperate means of expressing their dissent. In the worst case scenario, that expression of dissent might even take the form of "a radical

people's revolution" to uproot the oppressive establishment in its entirety.

Lesson 30
When ordinary men and women pick the courage to resort to desperate and even unconstitutional means to assert their rights, then that should be the clearest indication to any incumbent leader that some people consider their right to dissent to be inherent and not granted by the State; that when injustice becomes law, then resistance becomes a patriotic duty.

Lesson 31
To those overzealous "blue eyed boys" who serve modern despots with great zeal, remember that the modern despot is not stupid. In his eyes, you are no more than a useful idiot. The service of a despot is hazardous business. You stand duly warned!